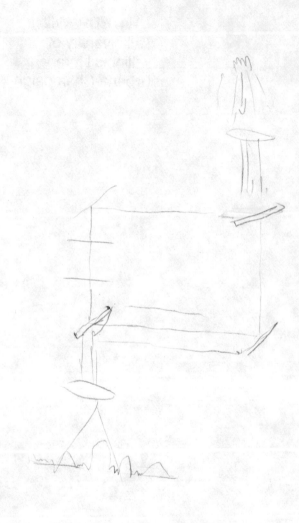

POPULISM
The Critical Issues

POPULISM
The Critical Issues

Edited by

SHELDON HACKNEY
Princeton University

LITTLE, BROWN AND COMPANY   BOSTON

CONTENTS

v

THE TEMPER OF POPULISM

INTRODUCTION

In current usage, "populist" has become a protean term whose connotations cover at times demagogic appeals to irrational popular prejudices and at other times a noble regard for the uncorrupted wisdom of the common man. Such a wide spectrum of meaning is not surprising, for in recent years this agrarian protest movement of the 1890s, whose name has been promiscuously appropriated for various popular urges, has been the subject of contradictory interpretations.

The participants in this frequently heated debate about where Populism belongs in American political history can be sorted into three general categories. The classical and still dominant view is most notably presented by John D. Hicks in *The Populist Revolt* (Minneapolis: University of Minnesota Press, 1931) and by C. Vann Woodward in *Origins of the New South, 1877–1913* (Baton Rouge: Louisiana State University Press, 1951). Other influential historians in this tradition include Solon Buck, *The Agrarian Crusade* (New Haven: Yale University Press, 1920); Theodore Saloutos, *Farmer Movements in the South, 1865–1933* (Berkeley: University of California Press, 1960); Robert Durden, *The Climax of Populism* (Lexington: University of Kentucky Press, 1965); and Walter Nugent, *The Tolerant Populists* (Chicago: The University of Chicago Press, 1963). Populism, according to this view, though at times parochial and ineffectual, was interest-group politics in the great reform tradition of Jacksonianism, Progressivism, and the New Deal.

While not totally denying Populism's constructive and rational components, a second category of scholars points to larger than normal doses of racism, anti-Semitism, jingoism, nativism, and xenophobia among the Populists. Victor Ferkiss, a political scientist, even noticed some similarities between American Populism and European Fascism and pointed these out initially in "Ezra Pound and American Fascism," *Journal of Politics,* XVII (May, 1955), pp. 173–197.

The most concerted attempt to reveal the authoritarian blemishes on the fair face of democracy, however, came almost tangentially in the essays by Daniel Bell, Peter Viereck, Talcott Parsons, Seymour Martin Lipset, and Richard Hofstadter contained in Daniel Bell (ed.), *The New American Right* (New York: Criterion Books, 1955). Reacting to their times as concerned scholars, all of whom were social scientists except Hofstadter, they sought an explanation for the repressive and almost hysterical aspects of the anticommunist movement in the post–World War II period and discovered it in the similar aspects of earlier popular movements. Not only did the Populists fail to understand the real causes of their plight, runs the indictment drafted by Richard Hofstadter in *The Age of Reform* (New York: Alfred A. Knopf, 1955), but they were haunted by nonexisting conspiracies and were given to scapegoating rather than to rational analysis. These anomalies suggest that Populism was responding to something more than the narrow economic interests of its constituency. Because its constituency drew heavily from the normally apolitical and uninvolved stratum of the population and because of its unmistakable antielitist appeal, Populism might best be thought of as a mass movement with unarticulated goals and desires having to do with perpetuating and celebrating a threatened way of life.

Recognizing Populism as a mass movement, a large collective effort outside the existing institutional structure and originating in the felt needs of the normally uninfluential portions of the population, the third category of commentators differs from the second by either denying or reinterpreting Populism's retrograde tendencies and by stressing Populist aspirations to transform the American social system. The most outspoken and unambiguous statement of this view is found in *The Populist Response to Industrial America: Midwestern Populist Thought* (Cambridge: Harvard University Press, 1962) by Norman Pollack, who maintains that the Populist critique of industrial America included rejecting laissez-faire capitalism, social Darwinism, and the success ethic. Other counter-revisionists, such as Michael Rogin in *The Intellectuals and McCarthy* (Cambridge: The M.I.T. Press, 1967), qualify Populist radicalism much more stringently, but they share the view that Populism can not be completely understood as a reform movement with specific and limited political objectives.

Each of these perspectives is incomplete. For those who defend Populism, such as Woodward and Walter T. K. Nugent, to view it as the last defensive stand of the yeoman farmer and at the same time as a forward-looking pressure group is at least paradoxical. On the other hand, if Pollack is correct in treating the Populists as proto-revolutionaries and crypto-Marxists because they attacked the growing disparity of wealth in the Gilded Age and denounced the new capitalists, then how does one explain the great gap between the Populist critique and their narrowly pragmatic program, which called for monetary inflation and other specific, nonstructural reforms? Any ideal society incorporating the values revealed in the Populist rhetoric as reconstructed by Pollack could never be created by the Populist program.

Populism's critics of the Hofstadter or of the Victor Ferkiss variety have an even more serious problem. The analysts of modern voting behavior have concluded that, even taking into account such factors as education and income, farmers have a very low level of political involvement and show a parochial disinterest in national affairs and even in farm organizations. Their political participation is sporadic and highly volatile. More important, their political behavior responds overwhelmingly to economic rather than to other pressures, and they react to changes in their own economic situation rather than to the situation of farmers in general. If this pattern results from psychological remoteness, as it apparently does, then it must have been even stronger in the last third of the nineteenth century than it is today. The farmer's habitually low level of involvement, low level of awareness, and low level of party identification underlie both the frequency and the short duration of third-party movements in American history. This apathy should also warn the historian that there may be little congruence between the program proposed by the movement's leaders and the felt needs of the supporters. Rather than developing an ideologically coherent program, the leaders may have settled for assembling a set of unrelated proposals backed by discontented special interest groups. Farmer preoccupation with economic issues both challenges the critics of Populism (Hofstadter and Ferkiss) who stress the noneconomic facets of the Populist mentality and underlines the interpretive consensus that places economic discontent in some fashion at the core of Populist motivation.

At first glance it may be a little difficult to locate the source of the farmer's discontent. Gross statistics indicate that in many ways the farmer was better off in 1900 than he had been in 1870. Farmland under cultivation doubled during this period, as did the absolute value of farm products, while farm output was increasing at twice the rate of farm population. Despite the secular decline in farm prices about which the farmers were so bitter, a decline that brought the wholesale index of farm products down from 112 in 1870 to 71 in 1890, per capita farm income actually increased during this period because of the greater drop in the prices that farmers paid for goods and services. There are two, mutually compatible, explanations for this phenomenon of protest amidst plenty.

In the first place, not every farmer could earn a living during twenty years or so of falling prices. Unlike oligopolistic businesses, which restrict production when prices fall, farmers generally react by producing more. The increased production adds to the deflationary pressures, of course, but for those who are able to increase their productivity, the tactic may be successful. In the late nineteenth century, increased productivity was achieved not so much by increasing the yield per acre as by bringing fresh lands under cultivation, frequently with the aid of fertilizers, and by using machinery to increase the number of acres that could be worked by a single man. Increasing production in response to overproduction was the self-perpetuating cycle that drew farmers westward to replace the wild, elemental scramble for windfall riches that was taking place in the mining towns and on the cattle trails with a more settled way of life.

Though movie fans may not be aware of it, the dull sod-busters with their barbed wire and shotguns enacted their own exciting and tragic drama. It is less romantic than that of the cowpokes and prospectors because the farmers' enemies could not be gunned down like claim jumpers or strung up like rustlers. The farmers' enemies were weather, climate, grasshoppers, and the impersonal forces of the marketplace. To be sure, the railroads were a more immanent villain, but a villain supported by a romantic legend of its own and by powerful interests.

It was the railroads, after all, that made possible and actually encouraged colonization in "the Garden of the West." In the 1870s, 190 million new acres were put under cultivation, mostly to the west of the Minnesota to Louisiana tier of states. By 1880, the frontier line was jutting irregular fingers into the semiarid plains. Kansas, Nebraska, the Dakotas, and Texas filled out at boomtime tempo. Between 1889 and 1893, the entire Indian territory of Oklahoma was settled in a wild melee led by the "Boomers" and "Sooners." Nine new states were added to the union between 1865 and 1890. The Director of the Census announced in 1890 that the "unsettled area had been so broken into by isolated bodies of settlement that there can hardly be said to be a frontier line." And east of the 95th meridian from North Dakota through Texas, settlement was sparse but continuous.

The agricultural pioneers on this last frontier had to adapt to new conditions in a treeless and waterless region. They did so with sod houses, windmills to pump water from deep wells, and new techniques of "dry farming." Most remarkable of all was the rapid mechanization of wheat farming, mechanization that made bonanza farms possible. Like modern businesses, bonanza farms put huge tracts of land under cultivation with central management, using the most advanced equipment possible, and specialized labor. The machinery involved in this agricultural revolution was largely invented before 1860, but it was after the Civil War that mass production, population growth, and open land lured the mammoth combines, steam tractors, and steel plows, seed planters and cultivators, mowers and harvesters across the increasing expanse of farmland. Various other farm machines replaced human labor and greatly increased individual productivity. Between 1860 and 1900, the annual value of American manufactures of agricultural implements rose from $21,000,000 to $101,000,000. In 1895, available machinery could reduce by one-half the time required to produce each unit of twenty-seven different crops. Mechanization was well on its way.

Not everyone in the wheat-growing belt of the West could afford a large, mechanized operation, however, and the less efficient operators were put in a profit squeeze by the long-term decline and the seemingly irrational fluctuation in prices. In retrospect, western farmers appear not to have been victimized by the railroads, machinery manufacturers, and mortgage companies upon whom they were so dependent. Railroad rates in the West were higher than in the East, but they were rapidly declining so that transportation costs absorbed a decreasing portion of the market price of wheat. In general, farm prices declined less rapidly than the prices of manufactured products, including machinery, though the market in machinery was certainly imperfect. While mortgage rates were higher than in the East, so were the risks, and the rates were lower than they had been earlier in the West. The average mortgage lasted about three and one-half years so that deflation did not have time to hurt the debtor severely, nor is there evidence that mortgage companies were eager to foreclose during hard times. Nevertheless, by 1890 in Kansas, Nebraska, North Dakota, and South Dakota, the western states experiencing the greatest incidence of Populism, there were more mortgages than families. Suffering farmers, as men frequently do in times of crisis, focused their discontent upon the most visible and most personal forces affecting their lives.

Southern farming sharply contrasts with the mechanized West. The value of farm equipment in the southern states in 1900 was one-half what it had been in 1860. The situation that was created by rampaging Yankees during the Civil War was perpetuated by the credit stringency existing after the war. In 1900, there was only one bank for every 58,130 southerners while there was one bank for every 16,000 Americans in the nation at large. Needing credit at the close of the war to pay for equipment, fertilizer, seed, land, and supplies to last until the first crop came in, southern farmers turned to the crop-lien system. Georgia passed in 1866 the first crop-lien law that established legal protection for the suppliers of tenant farmers and share croppers by giving the creditor a lien upon the crop that the debtor produced and by providing legal penalties for failure to carry out the contract. Because supply merchants themselves needed liquid assests to repay their creditors, farmers were required to produce cotton that, like gold, was durable and easily marketed. Advocates of diversified farming could make no headway against the system with mere exhortation. The boll weevil did more to change southern practices than all the agricultural reformers of the nineteenth century combined. Long-term credit was needed to break the pattern of dependency, and just at the time when the cost of credit was soaring because of the competing demands from the booming urban economy and because of the government's deflationary monetary policy.

As in the West, some southern farmers fared better than others under the prevailing conditions. William J. Cooper, Jr., in *The Conservative Regime: South Carolina, 1877–1890* (Baltimore: The Johns Hopkins Press, 1968), calculates that in South Carolina in 1880 the average farmer lost $6.00 per year on each acre of cotton. A few farmers, however, on ample amounts of good land, using sound techniques and superior equipment could still earn a profit. It was the underfinanced farmer, cultivating small parcels of marginal land who was chronically in trouble. By 1900 approximately one-third of the landholdings in the southern states were operated by tenants: 25 per cent of the white farmers and 75 per cent of black farmers tilled land that belonged to someone else. They became tenant farmers in thrall to the supply merchant because credit was available in no other form. Their existence and their increasing numbers provide a grim index to the dislocations in southern agriculture.

Though southern and western farmers differed in ways significant enough to produce stresses in the Populist movement, they shared the disadvantages of depending on a single commercial crop during disruptive changes to which small operators could not adjust. As rural sociologists have observed, farmers in one-crop economies are inherently more vulnerable to outside forces than other men and therefore are likely to feel less sure of their ability to cope with life and more anxious about their futures. In the late nineteenth century, railroads and steamships had just created a new world market at the same time as vast new tracts of land were being cultivated in Canada, Australia, the Ukraine, and South America. Farmers who raised those crops whose prices were determined on this world market were suddenly operating in a larger, more complex, and less predictable economic system over which they had even less control than before. In addition, a series of natural disasters cut into the crops in 1885, 1886, and 1887 precipitating a new wave of rural militancy.

Not only did farmers have these overt problems to overcome, but they had psychological problems also. Almost every scholar who has written about the Populists has mentioned that farmers in the late nineteenth century were acutely aware that as a group they were not as important as they had been earlier in the nation's history. In 1900 agriculture still provided 62 per cent of the value of American export trade, and thus continued to earn most of the nation's foreign exchange. But this dominance had reached its peak in 1880, when 84.3 per cent of domestic exports were agricultural, and had rapidly deteriorated in the following two decades. In 1890 for the first time the census showed that the majority of gainfully employed persons were working in nonagricultural pursuits. Between 1880 and 1890, the value of urban real estate dramatically surpassed the value of real property in farms. Though towns of 2,500 inhabitants or more did not contain most Americans until 1920, the population shift from rural to urban areas was clear in the last third of the nineteenth century. While farm population was increasing by one-half between 1860 and 1900, nonfarm population leaped by a multiple of four. This population trend was tellingly reflected in the decline of agriculture's share of total domestic product from 36 per cent in 1870 to 22 per cent in 1900 and in the decline of the farmer's share of national income and national wealth. As Napoleon B. Ashby, lecturer for the National Farmers' Alliance, noted in his book, *The Riddle of the Sphinx,* "The increase in wealth is apparent, but that is not the question. The question is, how is this gain in wealth to be distributed? Certainly it has not been among the farmers and laborers."

While farmers worked hard and remained poor they were aware of the seemingly fantastic increase in wealth elsewhere in society. At the time of the Civil War no more than 400 millionaires existed in the country, but in 1892 the New York *Tribune Monthly* listed 4,047 millionaires by name. "These men are not of the class who toil and spin," complained Ashby, "they simply gather into their vaults. These fortunes are not the result of slow accumulation, year after year, from one generation to another; most of them have been made in the thirty years since 1860." Ashby attacked the Goulds, Vanderbilts, and Huntingtons who preyed upon "the mighty rivers of commerce which the farmers have set flowing. . . ."

The cultural conflict between old rural ways and new city ways was heightened by the denigrating response from the spokesmen for the new ways. E. L. Godkin, editor of the *Nation,* attended one Populist meeting and reported that "the dominant tone of the assembly was discontent with existing conditions. A large part of this discontent was the vague dissatisfaction which is always felt by the incompetent and lazy and 'shiftless' when they contemplate those who have got on better in the world." The problem for the Populists was that this indictment seemed to be borne out by the gaudy success of the city and its rulers. "The Money Princes," Ashby wrote, "quite overtop the homespun farmers, and the roar and din of the traffic in a business street of any considerable city makes the farm seem mean and small."

As industrialization proceeded with quickening pace, contact between rural and urban cultures inevitably grew. The farmer was increasingly aware that, though his situation might be improving in absolute terms, he was less well off than the city folks with whom he compared himself. Thus it was not only actual deprivation but relative deprivation that fueled farm discontent. Farmers located the cause of their troubles in discriminatory railroad rates, in monopoly prices charged for farm machinery and fertilizer, in an oppressively high tariff, in unfair tax structures, in an urban-oriented and inflexible banking system, in a deflationary monetary policy based on a gold standard, in non-American corporations and railroads that held mammoth chunks of land, in political corruption, and in undemocratic political institutions. Together these various grievances indicated to Populists the chief culprits: unresponsive political leaders and parties. The solution was to organize and to protest. to gov't.

The first major thrust of rural protest after the Civil War was organized in the Patrons of Husbandry founded in 1867, whose members were known as Grangers because they were organized into local units called Granges. Undertaken initially as a social and educational order to counterbalance the drabness of rural life, the Grange soon focused upon cooperative buying and selling enterprises and upon the state regulation of railroad rates and of grain elevator fees. The Granger movement subsided into insignificance in the late 1870s after hitting its peak membership of over 1.5 million in 1875.

The second wave of rural protest was centered in the Farmers' Alliance movement consisting of both the National Farmers' Alliance and Industrial Union, known as the Southern Alliance, which began on the frontier in Lampedusa County, Texas in 1875, and the smaller Northwestern Farmers' Alliance, which was founded in Chicago in 1880. Expanding from 39,473 to 231,578 members between 1880 and 1885, the Farmers' Alliances experienced their greatest growth in the following five years, at the end of which they could claim 1,053,000 members. During this floodtide of organization in response to accentuated agricultural discontent, when Dr. C. W. McCune of Texas was leading the organizing drive, the Southern Alliance recruited eager landowners, tenants, and rural mechanics and also absorbed several smaller organizations. When the Southern and Northwestern Alliances failed in 1889 at St. Louis to reach an agreement on merger, the state Alliances of Kansas, North Dakota, and South Dakota withdrew from the Northwestern Alliance and joined the Southern Alliance. The Southern Alliance at the same time gained the endorsement of the Knights of Labor, an industrial union formed in 1869 but well past its peak membership of 700,000 by 1889 and rapidly declining. Though the two Alliances resembled each other in their extensive engagement in cooperative business ventures and in their educational and social functions, the diversified farmers represented by the Northwestern Alliance had different economic problems from the single-crop farmers of the Southern Alliance. The Northwestern Alliance objected to the Southern Alliance's policies of secrecy, centralized control, and separate organizations for blacks.

Even before the cooperative stores started by the various state Alliances in the late 1880s had begun to fail because of inadequate capitalization and poor management, the Southern Alliance in 1890 had entered politics by endorsing its favorite candidates within the Democratic party in the South. Alliancemen in the West set up third parties under various names and gained their most notable successes in Kansas, Nebraska, and South

Dakota. In the southern states in 1890, the Farmers' Alliance claimed that 4 governors, 44 congressmen, and 3 senators and the majority of legislators in eight states were elected as Democrats on pro-Alliance platforms.

Encouraged by these evidences of voter appeal and discouraged by the poor performances of the Alliance Democrats in Congress and in the state legislatures, the Alliance joined with representatives of dissident labor and other reform groups in 1892 to form the Peoples' party, or Populist party. Framed in urgent, conspiracy-haunted rhetoric, the Populist platform was a potpourri of contemporary reform ideas. The single most significant suggestion to be generated within the agrarian movement was the subtreasury scheme, a proposal for a federally financed commodity credit system that would have allowed a farmer to store his crop in a federal warehouse to await a favorable market price and meanwhile to borrow up to 80 per cent of the current market price. In addition to several proposals to democratize the political process and to support the struggles of organized labor, the platform aimed at the triumvirate of Populist concerns: land, transportation, and money.

The Populist party, judged in relation to the usual fate of third parties, enjoyed a brief but spectacular career. In 1892, when Grover Cleveland defeated Benjamin Harrison in the general election, James B. Weaver of Iowa, the Populist candidate, received 22 electoral votes and 1,027,329 popular votes: 8.5 per cent of the total. Half of the electoral votes came from the silver states of the far West — Idaho, Colorado, Nevada, and Oregon; the other half were from the more genuinely Populist states of the Middle Border — Kansas and North Dakota. In addition, Weaver polled more than one-third of the popular vote in South-Dakota, Nebraska, Wyoming, and Alabama. The Populists also elected 10 representatives, 5 senators, and 4 governors and were represented by 345 men in 19 of the 44 state legislatures. In terms of total popular votes, Populism reached its peak in 1894, even though in that year only 4 representatives and 4 senators were elected and the yield of the state offices also declined.

Of course, it was not evident in 1896 that Populism had already passed its peak, and the Populists entered that campaign year with high expectations. Attempting to broaden their base of popular support by emphasizing moderate reform, symbolized by their demand for the free coinage of silver, the Populists found themselves outmaneuvered in 1896 when the Democrats adopted a free-silver platform and then nominated William Jennings Bryan of Nebraska for President. The Populists had delayed their own convention until after the Democrats had met, on the assumption that the gold-standard conspiracy would control the Democrats and then the Populists could absorb the dissatisfied silver wing of the party and roll on to victory. Bryan's nomination by the Democrats consequently confronted the Populists with a serious dilemma: to stick in the "middle of the road" with their own candidates and thus ensure defeat for any reform candidate by splitting the silver vote or to attempt some fusion with the Democrats and risk the damage to party loyalties that such a policy might entail. The Populists chose the latter course. At their convention in St. Louis, they provided a sop to their middle-of-the-road faction by nominating Tom Watson, the Georgia Populist, for vice-president, but they endorsed Bryan as their nominee for president. Heated debate still rages over whether the leaders deliberately manipulated the convention to obtain the endorsement of Bryan knowing full well that Arthur Sewall, Bryan's Democratic running mate, would not step down to allow a formal fusion of the Populist and Democratic tickets. Opinions greatly differ about the consistency between fusion and Populist ideals and rhetoric, but there is general agreement that fusion was highly detrimental to the Populist party.

The strikingly sectional results of the election of 1896, in which Bryan was narrowly defeated by William McKinley and with which the Republican party began its three-decade reign as the majority party, indicates that the Populists had solved the first of their three basic strategic problems. They had managed to reactivate, for the Democrats at least, the old agrarian alliance between the West and the South that had been interrupted by the slavery controversy and the Civil War. They had not done so well with their second problem. Despite the support of the Knights of Labor and despite some important local coalitions, the Populists were not able to bridge the gap between the farmer and urban labor. The urban East was largely untouched by Populism, and Bryan lost the election because he ran so poorly in the eastern cities. The third task was the most difficult of all: to unite the white and black farmers of the South along lines of economic self-interest. How seriously the Populists worked at this task, with what motivations and results, is yet a matter on which historians disagree.

Election results can also help us understand who the Populists were, for it is immediately obvious that not all farmers became Populists. As the preceding discussion of the economic situation suggests, the smaller, more poorly financed farmers were hurt more than large, mechanized, efficiently run, and adequately capitalized operations. Historians generally agree that it was these less well-to-do farmers who comprised the rank and file of the Populist party, but beyond that generalization the evidence as yet is only suggestive. In Kansas, the more yeomanlike the wheat farmer the more likely he was to become a Populist; that is, Populists were drawn from those wheat farmers who bought and sold land less frequently, who carried fewer mortgages, who were not the overextended, entrepreneurial, modern, capitalistic operators that some historians have suggested provided the core of western Populism. Instead, they were solid family farmers trying to hang onto their own farms and make gradual improvements. This observation has been generally confirmed in Nebraska where Populism thrived among the less indebted and less commercial wheat farmers living between the frontier and the corn-hog economy to the East. Here, as elsewhere in the West, though the Populists appealed for support from all ethnic groups, they found Catholics much more resistant than groups with Protestant backgrounds. In Alabama, Populism evidently drew heavily from farmers who had just lost ownership of their land or who were living on the uneasy margin between ownership and tenancy. Throughout the South, except in Virginia, people generally associate Populism with poor land. Furthermore, Populism was not only popular in the newly settled states of the West, but it was popular within the South in the newly settled counties and in counties where new land was being brought under cultivation. This suggests that the most susceptible farmers were those who were most geographically mobile. Unfettered and unsupported by ties to local political organizations and to local elites, these shallowly entrenched husbandmen felt a greater need and a greater freedom to join the Populist movement. Everywhere, Populists in the rural precincts of a county set themselves apart from, and opposed to, town dwellers who earned their living by selling goods and services to farmers. Unlike the farmers who, at some time during the modernization of a society, decide that the town is the source of pleasures and benefits, Populists considered it still a liability and a threat.

Though the rural-urban division was an important aspect of Populism, the existence of potential friends in town and many enemies in the countryside suggests that this view is limited. The local divisions in the South and the West also reveal the inadequacy of viewing Populism simply as the reactivation of an old sectional alliance or as the revolt of the frontier against the East. If Populism is treated as economic-interest-group politics, as it is by many historians, then we are left to wonder about the opposition to Populism by those farmers with economic interests similar to those of Populists, and we would still need an explanation for the Populists' tactics and rhetoric very different from those used by other agricultural pressure groups. Nor is it sufficient to adopt the Marxist view that Populism was the defensive movement of a rural petty bourgeoisie. This interpretation may be accurate and reasonable, but it is also sterile. It does not lead to a more subtle understanding of what caused Populism, why it failed, why it employed the tactics and rhetoric it did, what people joined it, and what people opposed it.

Historians in the future may comprehend Populism more deeply by looking at it as social scientists might. Without making a complete or rigorous analysis, it might be possible to suggest here some of the fresh perspectives that would be uncovered by applying, for instance, the analytical framework set forth by Neil Smelser in his book, *Theory of Collective Behavior* (New York: The Free Press of Glencoe, 1963). He refers to Populism repeatedly as an example of the uninstitutionalized mobilization for action that he calls a "norm-oriented social movement." Norms are prescriptions for behavior. Frustration and anxiety giving rise to social movements occur when men can no longer achieve the ultimate goals and values upon which society rests by obeying the familiar norms. Norm-oriented social movements seek to change the old ways of doing things in order to relieve this stress. Various lower orders of collective behavior, such as scapegoating and mass hysteria, serve to vent the hostility generated by frustration. A value-oriented movement is of a higher order because it seeks to change the goals and ultimate values themselves.

The basic problem causing Populist anxiety was that after the Civil War impersonal changes in the economic system suddenly prevented farmers from achieving independence and the good life on a noncommercial farm. At least three broad alternatives were available to farmers who recognized that they were caught in this situation and who valued farming as a way of life. They might change their goal and adopt the values of achievement and accumulation that had always been present in American life and that had won a broad allegiance among the members of the urban and industrial society rapidly evolving in the late nineteenth century. This alternative posed serious problems. Successful commercial farming was inaccessible to most small farmers because they lacked capital and the requisite skills. In any case, the harsh demographic fact was that more people depended on the land than could earn a decent living under the prevailing economic conditions. Embracing the newly dominant materialist culture might also be accomplished by migrating into the city and finding employment, as millions of European immigrants were doing during this period. An unanswered, indeed unasked, question is why the surplus rural population did not flock to the city in greater numbers. It may be that, despite the rural poverty, a better standard of living was possible on the land than in the city. On the other hand, an explanation may be found in the deep psychological meaning that the land had for a people raised on it and the fears dredged up by the prospect of separation from it. Subsistence farming continued to offer a refuge to those who, for whatever reason, continued to believe in the agrarian creed.

A second alternative for the farmers, other than adopting the values present in other segments of society, might have been to attempt a radical transvaluation of the whole society, from bottom to top, substituting new values around which society could be organized. Such an attempt could have taken one or more of several forms: nationalism, religious revivalism, millenarianism, moral revitalization, secular or religious communal sects, political revolution, and undoubtedly others. In any form, these would have been value-oriented movements. They can arise, according to the Smelser theory, only when all other avenues of relief are perceived to be closed. Because the heterogeneity, political openness, and decentralization of the United States at least appear to be flexible, fundamental challenges to the existing order are infequent.

Discontented farmers chose a third route, a norm-oriented social movement that developed into the Populist party, through which they hoped to make the old values achievable by creating new rules, procedures, and norms. The crucial elements that mobilized people in the agrarian movement from the late 1860s onward was the early development of beliefs that explained the farmer's troubles. These explanations referred to the extraordinary power for harm wielded by monopolistic capitalists who preyed upon farmers: railroad owners, grain elevator operators, land monopolists, commodity futures dealers, mortgage companies, crop-lien merchants, bankers, and the producers of goods used on the farm. Populist rhetoric was based upon what might be called the "sleeping giant" motif: if the morally worthy parties will act together they will be omnipotent. The Populists divided the world into producers and nonproducers. The producers are "the people" and they are both good and all powerful, once awakened. Populist programs therefore called not only for measures that would neutralize the monopolistic capitalists, but they called for direct democracy and honest elections to give the people's voice full play.

Considering the agrarian crusade as a single movement from the Grangers through the Farmers' Alliance and Agricultural Wheel to Populism, it is evident that as one tactic for destroying or regulating the activities of the evil agents proved ineffective a new approach was quickly adopted. Improving life on the farm and promoting better farming techniques were quickly replaced by cooperative buying and selling operations designed to give farmers collectively a wallop in the marketplace that they would not have had individually. As these failed, the Alliances turned to boycotting monopolized products, which, though sometimes successful, were undramatic in the little improvement they brought. Alliancemen then began to lobby for favorable legislation; after that they turned to electioneering for friendly candidates; and finally they organized their own political party. The Populist party began with a broad reform program, which they eventually narrowed down to the single issue of free silver, and then decided to fuse with the national Democrats.

Rapid tactical shifting is characteristic of collective behavior and is a source for instability within the movement. Change breeds dissension. The adoption of a new tactic brings exhileration, but it also alienates many members who refuse to accept it. In the South particularly the successive decisions to go into politics and then to form a party in competition with the Democrats drove out of the movement many well-to-do farmers, country merchants, and members of the professional classes in country towns. By exaggerating the expected benefits of tactical shifts in order to mobilize support for them, the movement multiplies the fragmenting effect. Whether or not the tactic succeeds, the effect will be less than anticipated and discouragement will ensue.

The tactician therefore faces a dilemma. If the movement's demands are too radical, it risks appealing to no one but the misfits, consequently making no short-term gains and killing the movement through the psychology of failure. If the movement's demands are too bland, too congruent with the culture, the immediate response may be sympathetic and sizable, allowing short-term gains, but it will be difficult to generate either enthusiasm or long-term loyalty. The Populists actually grasped the second horn of this dilemma, and this helps to explain the decision for fusion and the rapidity with which the party subsequently dissolved.

Historians seldom ask why the urban public and the middle-class spokesman reacted so vehemently, characterizing Populists as either buffoons or dangerously radical anarchists, despite the Populists' choice of less than radical tactics. The answer is to be found in the curiously self-limiting dynamics of norm-oriented movements. Movements often counter the fragmenting from tactical changes and the depression from unfulfilled expectations by making the rhetoric more powerful. The stronger the rhetoric of redemption, the stronger the opposition; counter movements grow among those who feel threatened by the promised changes. Populists in particular felt a powerful urge toward making the qualitative jump from norm orientation to value orientation. As successive tactical plays failed over a long period of time, it looked more and more as if normative reform would not lead to redemption.

Populism was composed, after all, of just those elements of American society most susceptible to mobilization by a value-oriented movement. They considered themselves to be in semicolonial subservience to the industrial Northeast; they were disappointed by the inflexible political structures that prevented the major parties and government from acting in their behalf; and they came to feel that they constituted a despised and persecuted or forgotten group. In addition, Populists derived from that relatively nonmodern sector of American life that made little distinction between values and norms, the sector that interpreted breeches of behavioral codes as attacks on the whole way of life. No wonder that Populist rhetoric from time to time sounded wistfully radical. No wonder that Populists viewed with sympathy the utopian socialism of Edward Bellamy and the single-tax panacea of Henry George. The closer the Populists come to demanding that the basic values of society be reformed, the more adamant and the more extreme was the response to them.

The Smelser typology of movements, utilizing as it does the stress that gives rise to the movement and the solution the movement seeks, is not the only possible system. One could differentiate movements by the social origins of their members, whether they are seeking to conserve or to change social practices, whether they are seeking more freedom from external control or less, the way in which the members are organized, the level of violence involved in the movement's activities, the specific target group, and the relationship between the disaffected group and the power structure. The characteristic that is put under the microscope and the classification system that is used with regard to that characteristic will produce fruitful questions and hypotheses.

Populism was the political protest movement of a group that was being left behind by the forces associated with industrialization. It was launched just as rural America was becoming aware of the improving conditions under which other sectors of society lived. It is a fair hypothesis that when discontent stems from such double-edged, "progressive" deprivation the discontented are likely to be angrier and more violent than if their unhappiness depended on downward mobility or rising expectations alone. This hypothesis helps us to understand the violence that was such a part of Populist campaigns. That Populism was a voluntary association of people coming together for one purpose at one time, rather than a communal or some other "given" grouping, helps to explain why the violence was not more widespread and more organized and how the Populist party dissolved with such rapidity.

The mass character of Populism also significantly affected the movement. Even though the structure of Populism was more than an audience-manipulator relationship between leaders and followers, Populist policy-making was highly centralized. Scholars have repeatedly shown that in general Populist leaders came from social strata significantly below those that furnished the comparable Republican and Democratic leaders. There is also reason to infer that a large part of the following derived from normally politically inactive portions of the electorate. When such a mass movement is the vehicle of a group about to lose its position in the structure of power its goal is typically to retain the traditional rights that are being denied. Populists invoked the Jeffersonian tradition and the virtues of the early republic in their rhetoric, and in their tactics sought to purge the existing political elite and restore a preexisting condition.

One of the large questions concerning Populism arises because the preexisting condition was not restored. The Populist party faded and its constituency languished, yet many of the reforms appearing in the Populist platform were later realized, though not under Populist auspices. Whether they were realized because of Populism is impossible to say with certainty, just as it is impossible to determine how much the Populist critique of industrial capitalism added to the ideas and information that educated the

American public and made possible the strong current of reform running through twentieth-century American life. It could not have made a negligible contribution to that current, and Populism as a mythic source of a radical tradition has proved fruitful. Outside the intellectual realm one can be more specific but less confident. A question for which no definitive answer exists as yet has to do with the links between Populism and Progressivism. In Alabama there appears to have been very little continuity in either leadership or following between the Populist party and the Progressive faction of the Democratic party. Almost no leading Progressive in the Midwest had a Populist background. In Kansas, however, as Gene Clanton recently has shown in *Kansas Populism, Ideas and Men* (Lawrence: The University Press of Kansas, 1969), several Populist leaders remained active in reform causes after the turn of the century. Many expressed an admiration for Republican Insurgency or for Theodore Roosevelt's Progressivism, and countless men from all points of the political compass during the 1890s professed to see Populist principles being adopted by the major parties, as the Progressive movement gained strength in the early twentieth century. Even that irrepressible Populist baiter, William Allen White, looked back on the Populist era from the vantage point of 1906 and admitted that "this paper was wrong in those days and Judge Doster was right; but he was too early in the season and his views got frost bitten."

The longer-term residue is even more difficult to judge. The support for Senator Joseph McCarthy during his roughshod anticommunist crusade in the early 1950s did not derive from the same ethnic, economic, and geographic sectors of Wisconsin that supported Populism sixty years before. This does not solve the problem of the authoritarian strains in Populism detected by some historians, but it does point up the need for great care in tracing the heritage of Populism, a task that deserves scholarly attention as do the many other insufficiently resolved problems concerning Populism.

Scholarly reassessment of Populism will never end, but enough is known for one to make informed judgments about the Populist mentality. Was it authoritarian or democratic, provincial or penetrating, reactionary or radical, irrational or reasonable, retrogressive or progressive? More important, what can the history of Populism teach us about American society and about politics? How can dissent in such a society be mobilized most effectively? How does the dissenting group's position in society affect its success and its tactics? Does the need for cohesion within a protest movement come into conflict with its need to convert nonmembers? If the farmer-labor coalition attempted by Populism was an ill-fated venture, how can we explain the successful coalition of even more divergent interests within the major parties? What was Populism's contribution to the American political tradition? The following selections should aid in making judgments.

POPULISM
The Critical Issues

CONTEMPORARY VIEWS
OF POPULISM

The Omaha Platform
of the People's Party

Adopted at the first national convention of the People's party at Omaha, Nebraska, on July 4, 1892, the Omaha Platform became the touchstone of Populist orthodoxy. The platform incorporated the ideas set forth by the Farmers' Alliance in the St. Louis Demands of 1889 and the Ocala Demands of 1890 and added others. The eloquent Preamble is by Ignatius Donnelly of Minnesota, who was a prominent reformer in many causes throughout the last third of the nineteenth century. It captures the desperation experienced by Populists as they perceived all about them social dissolution, polarization of classes, and conspiracies to oppress the weak. One must make a great effort to put himself in the position of a farmer in 1892 in order to understand the resonance of this extreme rhetoric. Notice the clear call for expanded governmental powers. Is it consistent with all of the other demands? Notice also the determination to abolish poverty, a governmental commitment that was not recognized by statute until the Full Employment Act of 1946 and has since been more honored in pronouncements than in actions. Do you think the planks of the Platform and the Expressions of Sentiment are as radical as the tone of the Preamble?

Assembled upon the 116th anniversary of the Declaration of Independence, the People's Party of America, in their first national convention, invoking upon their action the blessing of Almighty God, put forth in the

From *The World Almanac*, II:14 (New York: Press Publishing Company; January, 1893), pp. 83–85.

name and on behalf of the people of this country, the following preamble
and declaration of principles:

PREAMBLE

The conditions which surround us best justify our co-operation; we
meet in the midst of a nation brought to the verge of moral, political, and
material ruin. Corruption dominates the ballot-box, the Legislatures, the
Congress, and touches even the ermine of the bench. The people are demoralized; most of the States have been compelled to isolate the voters at the
polling places to prevent universal intimidation and bribery. The newspapers are largely subsidized or muzzled, public opinion silenced, business
prostrated, homes covered with mortgages, labor impoverished, and the land
concentrating in the hands of capitalists. The urban workmen are denied
the right to organize for self-protection, imported pauperized labor beats
down their wages, a hireling standing army, unrecognized by our laws, is
established to shoot them down, and they are rapidly degenerating into
European conditions. The fruits of the toil of millions are boldly stolen to
build up colossal fortunes for a few, unprecedented in the history of mankind; and the possessors of those, in turn, despise the Republic and endanger liberty. From the same prolific womb of governmental injustice we breed
the two great classes — tramps and millionaires.

The national power to create money is appropriated to enrich bond-
holders; a vast public debt payable in legal tender currency has been funded
into gold-bearing bonds, thereby adding millions to the burdens of the
people.

Silver, which has been accepted as coin since the dawn of history,
has been demonetized to add to the purchasing power of gold by decreasing
the value of all forms of property as well as human labor, and the supply of
currency is purposely abridged to fatten usurers, bankrupt enterprise, and
enslave industry. A vast conspiracy against mankind has been organized on
two continents, and it is rapidly taking possession of the world. If not met
and overthrown at once it forebodes terrible social convulsions, the destruction of civilization, or the establishment of an absolute despotism.

We have witnessed for more than a quarter of a century the struggles
of the two great political parties for power and plunder, while grievous
wrongs have been inflicted upon the suffering people. We charge that the
controlling influences dominating both these parties have permitted the existing dreadful conditions to develop without serious effort to prevent or
restrain them. Neither do they now promise us any substantial reform.
They have agreed together to ignore, in the coming campaign, every issue
but one. They propose to drown the outcries of a plundered people with the

uproar of a sham battle over the tariff so that capitalists, corporations, national banks, rings, trusts, watered stock, the demonetization of silver and the oppressions of the usurers may all be lost sight of. They propose to sacrifice our homes, lives, and children on the altar of mammon; to destroy the multitude in order to secure corruption funds from the millionaires.

Assembled on the anniversary of the birthday of the nation, and filled with the spirit of the grand general and chief who established our independence, we seek to restore the government of the Republic to the hands of "the plain people," with which class it originated. We assert our purposes to be identical with the purposes of the National Constitution; to form a more perfect union and establish justice, insure domestic tranquillity, provide for the common defence, promote the general welfare, and secure the blessings of liberty for ourselves and our posterity.

We declare that this Republic can only endure as a free government while built upon the love of the whole people for each other and for the nation; that it cannot be pinned together by bayonets; that the civil war is over, and that every passion and resentment which grew out of it must die with it, and that we must be in fact, as we are in name, one united brotherhood of free men.

Our country finds itself confronted by conditions for which there is no precedent in the history of the world; our annual agricultural productions amount to billions of dollars in value, which must, within a few weeks or months, be exchanged for billions of dollars' worth of commodities consumed in their production; the existing currency supply is wholly inadequate to make this exchange; the results are falling prices, the formation of combines and rings, the impoverishment of the producing class. We pledge ourselves that if given power we will labor to correct these evils by wise and reasonable legislation, in accordance with the terms of our platform.

We believe that the power of government — in other words, of the people — should be expanded (as in the case of the postal service) as rapidly and as far as the good sense of an intelligent people and the teachings of experience shall justify, to the end that oppression, injustice, and poverty shall eventually cease in the land.

While our sympathies as a party of reform are naturally upon the side of every proposition which will tend to make men intelligent, virtuous, and temperate, we nevertheless regard these questions, important as they are, as secondary to the great issues now pressing for solution, and upon which not only our individual prosperity but the very existence of free institutions depend; and we ask all men to first help us to determine whether we are to have a republic to administer before we differ as to the conditions upon which it is to be administered, believing that the forces of reform this day organized will never cease to move forward until every wrong is remedied and equal rights and equal privileges securely established for all the men and women of this country.

PLATFORM

We declare, therefore —

FIRST. — That the union of the labor forces of the United States this day consummated shall be permanent and perpetual; may its spirit enter into all hearts for the salvation of the Republic and the uplifting of mankind.

SECOND. — Wealth belongs to him who creates it, and every dollar taken from industry without an equivalent is robbery. "If any will not work, neither shall he eat." The interests of rural and civic labor are the same; their enemies are identical.

THIRD. — We believe that the time has come when the railroad corporations will either own the people or the people must own the railroads, and should the government enter upon the work of owning and managing all railroads, we should favor an amendment to the Constitution by which all persons engaged in the government service shall be placed under a civil-service regulation of the most rigid character, so as to prevent the increase of the power of the national administration by the use of such additional government employés.

Finance. — We demand a national currency, safe, sound, and flexible, issued by the general government only, a full legal tender for all debts, public and private, and that without the use of banking corporations, a just, equitable, and efficient means of distribution direct to the people, at a tax not to exceed 2 per cent, per annum, to be provided as set forth in the subtreasury plan of the Farmers' Alliance, or a better system; also by payments in discharge of its obligations for public improvements.

1. We demand free and unlimited coinage of silver and gold at the present legal ratio of 16 to 1.

2. We demand that the amount of circulating medium be speedily increased to not less than $50 per capita.

3. We demand a graduated income tax.

4. We believe that the money of the country should be kept as much as possible in the hands of the people, and hence we demand that all State and national revenues shall be limited to the necessary expenses of the government, economically and honestly administered.

5. We demand that postal savings banks be established by the government for the safe deposit of the earnings of the people and to facilitate exchange.

Transportation. — Transportation being a means of exchange and a public necessity, the government should own and operate the railroads in the interest of the people. The telegraph, telephone, like the post-office system, being a necessity for the transmission of news, should be owned and operated by the government in the interest of the people.

Land. — The land, including all the natural sources of wealth, is the heritage of the people, and should not be monopolized for speculative purposes, and alien ownership of land should be prohibited. All land now held by railroads and other corporations in excess of their actual needs, and all lands now owned by aliens should be reclaimed by the government and held for actual settlers only.

EXPRESSION OF SENTIMENTS

Your Committee on Platform and Resolutions beg leave unanimously to report the following:

Whereas, Other questions have been presented for our consideration, we hereby submit the following, not as a part of the Platform of the People's Party, but as resolutions expressive of the sentiment of this Convention:

1. *Resolved,* That we demand a free ballot and a fair count in all elections, and pledge ourselves to secure it to every legal voter without Federal intervention, through the adoption by the States of the unperverted Australian or secret ballot system.

2. *Resolved,* That the revenue derived from a graduated income tax should be applied to the reduction of the burden of taxation now levied upon the domestic industries of this country.

3. *Resolved,* That we pledge our support to fair and liberal pensions to Ex-Union soldiers and sailors.

4. *Resolved,* That we condemn the fallacy of protecting American labor under the present system, which opens our ports to the pauper and criminal classes of the world and crowds out our wage-earners; and we denounce the present ineffective laws against contract labor, and demand the further restriction of undesirable emigration.

5. *Resolved,* That we cordially sympathize with the efforts of organized workingmen to shorten the hours of labor, and demand a rigid enforcement of the existing eight-hour law on Government work, and ask that a penalty clause be added to the said law.

6. *Resolved,* That we regard the maintenance of a large standing army of mercenaries, known as the Pinkerton system, as a menace to our liberties, and we demand its abolition; and we condemn the recent invasion of the Territory of Wyoming by the hired assassins of plutocracy, assisted by Federal officers.

7. *Resolved,* That we commend to the favorable consideration of the people and the reform press the legislative system known as the initiative and referendum.

8. *Resolved,* That we favor a constitutional provision limiting the office of President and Vice-President to one term, and providing for the election of Senators of the United States by a direct vote of the people.

9. *Resolved,* That we oppose any subsidy or national aid to any private corporation for any purpose.

10. *Resolved,* That this convention sympathizes with the Knights of Labor and their righteous contest with the tyrannical combine of clothing manufacturers of Rochester, and declare it to be the duty of all who hate tyranny and oppression to refuse to purchase the goods made by the said manufacturers, or to patronize any merchants who sell such goods.

What's the Matter with Kansas?

WILLIAM ALLEN WHITE

Published in the Emporia Gazette *on August 15, 1896, this editorial made William Allen White, then a young man, a political commentator of national stature, a position he occupied with distinction for the following four decades. Though White changed his attitude soon after the threat of Populism had passed, the hostility and disdain contained in his original editorial represent in an extreme form the genteel response to Populism.*

The confrontation between the genteel tradition and Populism is a good example of how nonrational conflict predominates when the life styles of the contestants are in sharp contrast. As Paul W. Glad has pointed out in his book, McKinley, Bryan, and the People *(Philadelphia: J. B. Lippincott Company, 1964), silver and gold in 1896 became symbols for competing urban and rural mythologies. White also understood that the Populists were challenging the natural elite's right to rule and to receive deference. His assumptions are instructive because they were typical. For White, growth measured prosperity, and growth depended upon white-collar initiative. Because the economy was a delicately related set of competing interests, the state risked unbalancing the system by inhibiting the businessman.*

These were the assumptions of most Progressives, for whom White was to become a conspicuous spokesman. They led to the conclusion that the general good was best served by stimulating economic growth and leaving economic power with the capitalists, while prohibiting the abuse of that power through legislation. More was at stake then is revealed in the persistently popular notion that the differences could be represented in the opposition between the "filter down" theory of prosperity and the "percolate up" theory. Like White, Populists understood that buyers and sellers were engaged in a mutually profitable relationship, or at least that the farmer and the consumer were thus happily related. Populists differed from White and his fellows by calling for the redistribution of wealth rather than for economic growth as the economic salvation of society and by challenging, or not understanding, the roles of various middlemen: grain elevators, railroads, factors, mortgage companies, banks, lien merchants, the futures market. To White, such middlemen were engaged in the necessary business of facilitating commerce. To the Populists, they were engaged in exploiting the famer by levying a toll upon the products of his labor. Notice how White transcribes this difference into the moral terms of the work and achievement ethic.

Today the Kansas Department of Agriculture sent out a statement which indicates that Kansas has gained less than two thousand people in the past year. There are about two hundred and twenty-five thousand families in this state, and there were ten thousand babies born in Kansas, and yet so many people have left the state that the natural increase is cut down to less than two thousand net.

This has been going on for eight years.

If there had been a high brick wall around the state eight years ago, and not a soul had been admitted or permitted to leave, Kansas would be a half million souls better off than she is today. And yet the nation has increased in population. In five years ten million people have been added to the national population, yet instead of gaining a share of this — say, half a milion — Kansas has apparently been a plague spot and, in the very garden of the world, has lost population by ten thousands every year.

Reprinted with permission of The Macmillan Company from *The Autobiography of William Allen White,* by William Allen White, 280–283. Copyright 1946 by The Macmillan Company.

Not only has she lost population, but she has lost money. Every moneyed man in the state who could get out without loss has gone. Every month in every community sees someone who has a little money pack up and leave the state. This has been going on for eight years. Money has been drained out all the time. In towns where ten years ago there were three or four or half a dozen money-lending concerns, stimulating industry by furnishing capital, there is now none, or one or two that are looking after the interests and principal already outstanding.

No one brings any money into Kansas any more. What community knows over one or two men who have moved in with more than $5,000 in the past three years? And what community cannot count half a score of men in that time who have left, taking all the money they could scrape together?

Yet the nation has grown rich; other states have increased in population and wealth — other neighboring states. Missouri has gained over two million, while Kansas has been losing half a million. Nebraska has gained in wealth and population while Kansas has gone downhill. Colorado has gained every way, while Kansas has lost every way since 1888.

What's the matter with Kansas?

There is no substantial city in the state. Every big town save one has lost in population. Yet Kansas City, Omaha, Lincoln, St. Louis, Denver, Colorado Springs, Sedalia, the cities of the Dakotas, St. Paul and Minneapolis and Des Moines — all cities and towns in the West — have steadily grown.

Take up the government blue book and you will see that Kansas is virtually off the map. Two or three little scrubby consular places in yellow-fever-stricken communities that do not aggregate ten thousand dollars a year is all the recognition that Kansas has. Nebraska draws about one hundred thousand dollars; little old North Dakota draws about fifty thousand dollars; Oklahoma doubles Kansas; Missouri leaves her a thousand miles behind; Colorado is almost seven times greater than Kansas — the whole west is ahead of Kansas.

Take it by any standard you please, Kansas is not in it.

Go east and you hear them laugh at Kansas; go west and they sneer at her; go south and they "cuss" her; go north and they have forgotten her. Go into any crowd of intelligent people gathered anywhere on the globe, and you will find the Kansas man on the defensive. The newspaper columns and magazines once devoted to praise of her, to boastful facts and startling figures concerning her resources, are now filled with cartoons, jibes and Pefferian speeches. Kansas just naturally isn't in it. She has traded places with Arkansas and Timbuctoo.

What's the matter with Kansas?

We all know; yet here we are at it again. We have an old mossback Jacksonian who snorts and howls because there is a bathtub in the State

House; we are running that old jay for Governor. We have another shabby, wild-eyed, rattlebrained fanatic who has said openly in a dozen speeches that "the rights of the user are paramount to the rights of the owner": we are running him for Chief Justice, so that capital will come tumbling over itself to get into the state. We have raked the old ash heap of failure in the state and found an old human hoop skirt who has failed as a businessman, who has failed as an editor, who has failed as a preacher, and we are going to run him for Congressman-at-Large. He will help the looks of the Kansas delegation at Washington. Then we have discovered a kid without a law practice and have decided to run him for Attorney General. Then, for fear some hint that the state had become respectable might percolate through the civilized portions of the nation, we have decided to send three or four harpies out lecturing, telling the people that Kansas is raising hell and letting the corn go to weed.

Oh, this is a state to be proud of! We are a people who can hold up our heads! What we need is not more money, but less capital, fewer white shirts and brains, fewer men with business judgment, and more of those fellows who boast that they are "just ordinary clodhoppers, but they know more in a minute about finance than John Sherman"; we need more men who are "posted," who can bellow about the crime of '73, who hate prosperity, and who think, because a man believes in national honor, he is a tool of Wall Street. We have had a few of them — some hundred fifty thousand — but we need more.

We need several thousand gibbering idiots to scream about the "Great Red Dragon" of Lombard Street. We don't need population, we don't need wealth, we don't need well-dressed men on the streets, we don't need cities on the fertile prairies; you bet we don't! What we are after is the money power. Because we have become poorer and ornerier and meaner than a spavined, distempered mule, we, the people of Kansas, propose to kick; we don't care to build up, we wish to tear down.

"There are two ideas of government," said our noble Bryan at Chicago. "There are those who believe that if you legislate to make the well-to-do prosperous, this prosperity will leak through on those below. The Democratic idea has been that if you legislate to make the masses prosperous their prosperity will find its way up and through every class and rest upon them."

That's the stuff! Give the prosperous man the dickens! Legislate the thriftless man into ease, whack the stuffing out of the creditors and tell the debtors who borrowed the money five years ago when money "per capita" was greater than it is now, that the contraction of currency gives him a right to repudiate.

Whoop it up for the ragged trousers; put the lazy, greasy fizzle, who can't pay his debts, on the altar, and bow down and worship him. Let the state ideal be high. What we need is not the respect of our fellow men, but the chance to get something for nothing.

Oh, yes, Kansas is a great state. Here are people fleeing from it by the score every day, capital going out of the state by the hundreds of dollars; and every industry but farming paralyzed, and that crippled, because its products have to go across the ocean before they can find a laboring man at work who can afford to buy them. Let's don't stop this year. Let's drive all the decent, self-respecting men out of the state. Let's keep the old clod-hoppers who know it all. Let's encourage the man who is "posted." He can talk, and what we need is not mill hands to eat our meat, nor factory hands to eat our wheat, nor cities to oppress the farmer by consuming his butter and eggs and chickens and produce. What Kansas needs is men who can talk, who have large leisure to argue the currency question while their wives wait at home for the nickel's worth of bluing.

What's the matter with Kansas?

Nothing under the shining sun. She is losing her wealth, population and standing. She has got her statesmen, and the money power is afraid of her. Kansas is all right. She has started in to raise hell, as Mrs. Lease advised, and she seems to have an overproduction. But that doesn't matter. Kansas never did believe in diversified crops. Kansas is all right. There is absolutely nothing wrong with Kansas. "Every prospect pleases and only man is vile."

FUSION

The Silver Panacea

C. VANN WOODWARD

*As the political maneuvering for the climactic campaign of 1896
began to accelerate, free silver increasingly became the issue
around which the electorate polarized. When the Republicans
refused to endorse free silver and nominated William McKinley
for president at their convention in St. Louis in June 1896, a
faction of silver Republicans led by Senator Henry M. Teller
bolted the party and began to cast about for a way to unite all
the silver forces behind a single candidate. Meanwhile, the silver
Democrats had been enormously successful in their organized
efforts to repudiate Grover Cleveland's Democratic administration and to seize control of the national party in the name of
silver. Their drive culminated with the nomination of William
Jennings Bryan by the Democrats at their Chicago convention in
early July. C. Vann Woodward, Sterling Professor of History at
Yale University, describes the ensuing dilemma faced by the Populists. He considers Populist willingness to "come down to silver"
a desertion of fundamental reform principles in favor of short-
sighted opportunism, and he blames the Populist leaders for
manipulating the convention and causing the ruinous endorsement of William Jennings Bryan for president on a Populist
ticket with Tom Watson of Georgia.*

*Coalition politics and the exigencies of compromise have al-
ways posed difficulties for American reformers, particularly for
minor parties that rest their claim partly on the charge that the
major parties are ethically bankrupt. Disillusionment and dis-
affection inevitably result when hypocrisy appears in a movement
that has generated the fervor of a crusade. Good tactics are consequently those that produce enough evidence of progress to keep*

the membership hopeful and growing, yet do not abandon the basic purposes that gave rise to the organization initially. The question here is whether the free coinage of silver was a legitimate goal for the Populists and, if it was not, whether a coalition based on the silver issue could have been expected to lead to further reform. One should also be alert to the possibility that the personal ambition of certain leaders somewhat affected the final decision. Leaders are usually much more interested in power for its own sake than are the rank and file. The decision made by the movement when faced with the trade-offs between short-term success and long-term health may also reveal its unannounced preference for reformation or transformation.

Now that the Democratic party was ripe for internal revolution, the problem and the temptation of fusion were more than ever before acute and pressing for Populist leaders. Fusion with one party or the other had, as a matter of fact, been a problem of the third party from the beginning. After all, every Populist recruit had to be won from one or the other of the old parties. In the South the fusion problem presented itself first with regard to the Republican party. After the death of Colonel L. L. Polk, the Populist party of North Carolina had effected a fusion with the Republican under the leadership of Marion Butler, an astute young politician who won a seat in the Senate at the age of thirty-three. Seeking to extend his Populist-Republican fusion throughout the South, Butler attempted in private conference to persuade Watson (as well as other Southern Populist leaders) to adopt the same policy. Watson flatly refused to countenance the plan, contending that it would destroy the integrity of his party.[1]* No accusation called forth such angry denial from the Georgia Populist as the suggestion that he was coöperating with the Republicans.

In the West the temptation from the founding of the third party had been fusion with the Democrats, the minority party there as the Republicans were in the South. From the beginning there had been a certain amount of coalition between the two parties, and in some states outright fusion. As the election year approached it became plain that if prominent Populist leaders of the West, such as Weaver and Taubeneck, had their way, fusion would go the whole way and become complete. The capitulation to the free silver panacea was merely another way of advocating fusion.[2]

On what basis could fusion between Democrats and Populists take place in the South? Henry Demarest Lloyd once observed that "The line between the old Democracy and Populism in the South is largely a line of bloody graves." As hyperbole goes, this strikes near the truth. For six years, during the whole life of Populism, the Demorcatic party had been recognized as the enemy against whose stubborn, and often treacherous, opposition every gain had to be won. In the bitter struggles of those six years Democrats had slandered, cursed, ostracized, defrauded, and killed Populists, and Populists had fought back with the same weapons. How could enemies be transformed into allies by what Populists suspected was a mere verbal change of heart?

Toward fusion of any kind Tom Watson adopted the policy then known as "the-middle-of-the-road."[3] Far from designating a conservative course, this term had come to signify those radical Populists who refused to compromise any principle in order to cooperate with either of the old parties. The "mid-road" Populists constituted the strictly anti-fusion rank and file of the party. In answer to a Louisiana Populist who wrote asking his advice on fusion with the silver-Democrats of that state, Watson wrote:

> In our judgment Populists should keep in the middle of the road, should make no coalition with either old party, and should avoid fusion as they would the devil. To meet Democrats or Republicans, acting in their individual capacities, in a free-for-all mass meeting, where a principle upon which we all agree can be discussed, and where no man need be bound by any action which he disapproves, is *one* thing; to make a barter and a trade as Populists with the official managers of either of the old parties to swap a certain number of votes for a stipulated price in Democratic partronage or Republican spoils, is quite *another* thing. . . .
>
> This may be an honest transaction; lots of good men in Kansas, Nebraska, North Carolina and elsewhere have gone into it. . . . It seems to agree very well with the fellows who squat near the flesh pots. But our observation has been that the People's Party never grows a single vote after that flesh pot feast begins . . . but wilts and dwindles away.
>
> We therefore advise our friend to meet and talk with all men — but fuse with no enemy, compromise no principle, surrender no vital conviction.[4]

He continued to warn against the blandishments of the Democratic advocates of fusion. " 'I am willing,' " he quoted Editor Howell of the *Constitution* as saying immediately before the Democratic National Convention of 1896, " 'to advocate every principle of the Populist Platform, if it is necessary, in order to keep the people inside the Democratic party.' " This, according to Watson, was a perfect illustration of the old party's motto: "Anything to keep the offices." It had promised the whole Alliance platform, the sub-treasury excepted, in 1890, and it would not scruple to promise the entire Populist platform, virtually the same, in 1896.[5]

It was this uncompromising rejection of fusion in the face of repeated defeats, when fusion would have won high office, that earned Watson the name of "as extreme a mid-road Populist as ever breathed or wrote." It also earned him the devotion of Southern Populists from Virginia to Texas, as well as the Western rank and file who had resisted silver and fusion. The radical Southern Populist, to whom fusion was anathema and silver a "mere drop in the bucket," found his clearest expression in the voice of Tom Watson, and in Watson he placed his faith. From the Middle West, the Lower South, and the Far West Watson received messages commending his stand against fusion.[6]

Upon the maneuvers of Western leaders toward fusion and silver, on the other hand, radical Populist of all sections looked with suspicion and misgivings, not to say hostility. From the West came Senator Peffer's denunciation of the policy of the National Committee of his own party as "treacherous"; [7] from the South came a North Carolina editor's judgment that it was an attempt to "deliver the entire People's party into the lap of Wall Street Democracy at one time." [8] Writing in the Middle West, though speaking for an intelligent element that was nonsectional, Lloyd lamented the curious paradox "that the new party, the Reform party, the People's party, should be more boss-ridden, ring-ruled, gang-gangrened, than the two old parties of monopoly. The party that makes itself the special champion of the Referendum and Initiative tricked out of its very life and soul by a permanent National Chairman — something no other party has!" [9]

Positions of Populist party leadership had passed from the South to the West by the middle 'nineties, largely because Westerners had been more successful in securing national office. It was a Western policy that was adopted as the strategy for 1896. The anti-fusionist South wished to hold the national convention in February, and step boldly forward with its nominees without regard to what the old party conventions did later. Western leaders succeeded in postponing the convention, however, until both old parties had held theirs. The Western argument assumed that the conventions of both opposing parties would be dominated by their reactionary wings and that the People's party would profit by gathering bolting silverites from both sides.[10]

As time approached for the conventions the fallacy of the Western theory grew more apparent. In June the Republican platform presented an outright stand against silver, a position that pointed more conclusively than ever to a victory for the silver-insurgents at the Democratic convention. Such an eventuality would put an entirely different complexion upon the naïve Western strategy of gathering in bolters. A complete revision of tactics was required without delay. H. E. Taubeneck, national chairman, thrashed about wildly for a new scheme, and at last settled upon the desperate plan of attempting to induce the Democrats to nominate Henry M. Teller, a silver Republican who had bolted the national convention. Teller had never been a Populist and was interested only in silver; yet Taubeneck and his cohorts were prepared to deliver their party to his cause if the Democrats would join them in his nomination.[11] Lloyd thought that Taubeneck had been "flimflammed" by the politicians at Washington, who had persuaded him that free silver was the supreme issue. If the party management had been in capable hands, he thought, instead of in the hands of " 'Glaubenichts' like Taubeneck, the full Omaha platform would easily have been made the issue that would have held us together for a brilliant campaign, but now that cannot be done."

The Chicago convention did go over to silver, as expected, but instead of Teller, it nominated William Jennings Bryan of Nebraska, a man dear to the hearts of Western Populists with whom he had flirted for years.[12] The platform was likewise richly baited for Populists. Besides the expected demand for free silver, it contained denunciation of Cleveland's bond-selling policy and his action in the Pullman strike; it condemned the Supreme Court's decision against income tax legislation; it favored stricter federal control of railroads. It now became the plain duty of Populists and all sincere reformers, the Democrats loudly proclaimed, to rally behind Bryan's cause, to renounce all "selfish" adherence to party in favor of "principle."

This appeal carried weight with the West. General Weaver had been at work for months promoting Bryan's nomination, and now set out for the Populist convention to make the chief nominating speech for him. "I care not for party names," said Watson's friend and former colleague, Jerry Simpson; "it is the substance we are after, and we have it in William J. Bryan." Ex-Governor "Bloody-Bridles" Waite of Colorado capitulated, and even Senator Peffer thought that the West was going for Bryan, no matter what happened. Ignatius Donnelly remained to speak for the more inarticulate mass of anti-fusionist, mid-road Populists of the West.[13]

For the South, Watson voiced the practically unanimous sentiment that to go back to the Democratic party now would be to "return as the hog did to its wallow." He knew his enemies too well to be taken in by them again. "The Democratic party," he wrote, "realizing that it had lost the respect, the confidence and the patience of the people, determined to anticipate the triumph of Populism by a public confession of political guilt, an earnest assertion of change of heart, a devout acceptance of Populist principles, and a modest demand that the People's party should vacate its quarters and surrender its political possessions. A very staggering piece of political impudence was this."[14] With his blessings the Georgia delegation to the

National Convention was sent off with strict instructions "to insist upon the original Ocala declaration" and fight fusion.[15] The head of the delegation wired headquarters at St. Louis: "Tell the boys I am coming — in the middle of the road." [16]

Delegates from virtually all Southern states grimly chose the same route to St. Louis. It proved to be the road to their Waterloo and the Waterloo of Populism.

Declining to comment upon the possibility of his receiving the nomination, and offering no explanation for his failure to attend the Convention, Tom Watson remained quietly at home.

The fourteen hundred delegates who gathered at Convention Hall in St. Louis on July 22 presented a striking contrast to those who had nominated Mark Hanna's friend in that same hall a month before. City journalists, spotting salable copy, described their rustic manners and quaint doings. A group was found sitting with shoes off. Some took no regular sleeping quarters and fared upon nickel meals at lunch counters. A part of one important delegation was found actually suffering for want of food, as the sessions dragged out longer than planned. An interview with an "eminent physician of Washington" was printed in mock solemnity listing insanity symptoms among the delegates. They were poor men, the majority of them, terribly in earnest, and therefore, one gathers, rather ridiculous.[17]

A sympathetic observer found anxiety written in the face of everyone, no matter to what faction he belonged. Anxiety in the mass of delegates lest they be sold out — and there were both rumors and signs that they would be. Anxiety in the faces of busily caucusing and whispering managers lest the coveted fruits of fusion, finally within their grasp, be snatched from them by the radical middle-of-the-road Southerners. The radicals themselves, distrusting fusion and half measures as they did, feared at the same time lest their radicalism split the force of opposition to their real enemy — Eastern Capitalism. This might be the last opportunity for a union of reform forces. Edward Bellamy thought that the real issue of 1896 — that "between men and money" — was in the back of all minds. "It was in the air that there must be a union," wrote Lloyd. "It was a psychological moment of *rapprochement* against an appalling danger which for thirty years now had been seen rising in the sky. If the radicals made a mistake, it was a patriotic mistake." [18]

The radical mid-roaders were the most distraught and unorganized group of all. Chiefly Southern in membership, they were led by the huge, militant Texas delegation, the largest one present. Their most conspicuous figure was James H. "Cyclone" Davis, a gaunt giant with a bellowing voice. The radicals declared they would not be "swallowed" by the new Democracy, and they were out to nominate a straight Populist ticket. While probably the largest faction present, they were terribly handicapped by want of leadership and a candidate. Their chaotic state was made plain when at their caucus only a day before the Convention opened they were unable to agree upon a candidate. Debs, Donnelly, "Cyclone" Davis, Van Dervoort of Nebraska, and Mimms of Tennessee were all discussed but passed over.[19]

Despite confusion, the mid-roaders were still intent on not being sold out to the Democrats. Said one delegate at the caucus: "They may sell us out here at St. Louis, but before high heaven they can never deliver the goods. I was originally a Democrat. We West Virginia Populists left the Democrats never to return." Another echoed his anxiety: "While we have been shouting the other fellows, with a perfect organization, have been gathering in the stragglers. It makes no difference how many men we may have, if we are not organized we will be swallowed." [20]

The fusionists were not only well organized; they knew exactly what they wanted. Their object was the endorsement of Bryan and Sewall and the fusion of the two parties into one. General Weaver, in charge of the Bryan headquarters, was industriously working toward this end. Three days before the Convention opened Senator James K. Jones, chairman of the Democratic National Committee, arrived at St. Louis to remain throughout, closeted with Bryan Populists or buzzing in and out of committee room, hotel lobby, and Convention hall. Some 1,000 Missouri Democrats were said to be aiding the plot to steal the Convention. An additional advantage for the West lay in the rule of awarding delegates on a basis of Populist successes in the past three elections. This scheme put a premium upon the fusion victories of Western states, and accordingly penalized the South, which had resisted fusion.[21]

Following the first day's session, at which they showed a strength that shook the confidence of the Bryanites, the mid-road radicals of twenty-one states finally agreed, without especial enthusiasm for their choice, to support S. F. Norton of Illinois for President, and Frank Burkett of Mississippi for Vice-President. Their forces greatly rallied, they planned a mighty demonstration for the evening session that would sweep the Convention to the left. That night they found the hall in complete darkness, with no lights obtainable. A futile attempt to hold the demonstration anyway only succeeded in producing scenes "at once weird and picturesque" — the gaunt figure of "Cyclone" Davis gesticulating under the flickering light of a candle he held aloft; Mrs. Lease yelling from the platform; the mob of delegates in the darkness crying out accusations of "ugly work" against the fusionists. Twenty-five minutes after the attempt was abandoned, the lights were burning brightly in the hall. It was not the last time the charge of foul play was made at this Convention, nor the last occasion for the charge.[22]

The next day the radicals won the first fall in what was considered a test of the anti-Bryan strength. The vote was upon the seating of a contesting mid-road delegation of Eugene V. Debs supporters backed by Clarence Darrow. The margin was narrow, 665 to 642, but the mid-roaders were jubilant. Their hopes were speedily dashed, however, by the election of Senator William V. Allen of Nebraska, an out-and-out fusionist, as permanent chairman of the Convention by a vote of 758 to 564.[23]

With the nomination of Bryan now seemingly assured, the threat of a bolt by the mid-roaders that would split the party in half became more menacing than ever. "Texas is here to hold a Populist convention," exclaimed a delegate, "and we're going to do it before we go home. If some of the delegates nominate Bryan, they, being unpopulistic, will be the bolters." If the naming of Bryan promised a bolt, then the nomination of his running-mate, Arthur Sewall, portended a veritable rebellion. Yet Chairman Allen and his Democratic friends were plotting that as well.

Whatever case the fusionists might make for the Populist leanings of Bryan, they were hard put to it to discover like tendencies in Sewall of Maine. There could hardly have been produced in one figure a more comprehensive challenge to orthodox Populist doctrine. Not only was he the president of one national bank and the director of others, but also a railroad director, as well as the president of one trust and part owner of another. On top of this he was an Easterner, a man of wealth, and he enjoyed an evil name among workers for his labor policies. Scarcely a plank of the Populist platform was left unfouled. No Populist could countenance the nomination of such a man without a ludicrous confession of his party's bankruptcy. Yet the manipulators in control of the Convention demanded Sewall's nomination.

It was obvious that the hope for any compromise between radical mid-roaders and extreme fusionists lay in the nominee for Vice-President. Foreseeing this possibility early in the Convention, a group of Southern delegates led by Senator Marion Butler, who had served as temporary chairman of the Convention, agreed upon a plan of compromise that would embrace accepting Bryan for Presidential nominee, but substituting a radical Southern Populist for Sewall as his running mate.[24] As part of the plan members of the Georgia delegation were prevailed upon to obtain the consent of Tom Watson for allowing his name to be used.

Watson had instructed his friends before the Convention not to allow the use of his name. During the course of the Convention, he issued the following statement to the press:

> I am opposed to the nomination of Bryan and Sewall or either of them separately.

> The Populist party has good material within its own ranks. I would refuse. I would refuse a nomination.
>
> I say this now, as I do not expect it; and it is my present belief that I shall not change my mind.[25]

The messages he received from the Convention described the chaotic state of affairs and inquired whether he would accept a nomination for the Vice-Presidency on a ticket with Bryan as a means of harmonizing all factions and preventing a split in the party. He was given to understand that an agreement had been reached with the Democratic managers to withdraw Sewall from their ticket. He was told nothing of the caucus of mid-roaders and their candidates, and did not learn of them until after the Convention. Under these conditions he "reluctantly" wired his consent. "Yes, if it will harmonize all factions," was his reply. Later he said that had he known all the circumstances he would never have consented, and the mid-road candidates "would have received my hearty support . . ." [26]

Tom Watson's name was a magical one among the disaffected and intransigent radical Populists. It warmed the imagination. He had been the first in the South to cut the old ties and step forward boldly as a Populist. In Congress he had won the admiration of the Western representatives, who elected him their leader in the House and followed him enthusiastically. He had burned his bridges behind him, steadfastly resisted the temptation of fusion, and suffered much for his principles. He was the hero of thousands of Southern Populists who had followed his periodic battles over the past four years against Democratic fraud and violence. The *People's Party Paper* was nationally known and frequently quoted, and its editor stood in the popular mind as the very incarnation of middle-of-the-road Populism, thorough-going, fearless, and uncompromising. He had been mentioned as a possible nominee from time to time since 1892.[27]

Rapid headway was being made at St. Louis with the scheme of compromise. The mid-roaders grasped at the suggestion of resorting to the unusual procedure of nominating the Vice-President before the President. They might at least dispose of Sewall. The report that the Democratic managers had promised that their candidate would withdraw in favor of a Populist nominee if Bryan were nominated for the Presidency was well circulated. Delegates voted with that report in mind. The decision to nominate the Vice-President first was made by a vote of 738 to 637.[28]

Jubilant because of their victory over the determined opposition of fusionists, the radicals expressed their feelings in a flood of nomination oratory. Congressman M. W. Howard of Alabama, "a man of enormous stature, tall and swarthy, with raven black hair that falls to his shoulders," the author of *The American Plutocracy*,[29] nominated Watson. His nominee, said Howard, was "a man who has suffered in the cause; a man who has sacrificed his money and his time for its good; a man who has borne the cross and should wear the crown." All speeches in second to Watson's nomination, of which there were many, stressed his unshakable loyalty to principle. A Negro delegate from Georgia expressed gratitude for his courageous defense of Negro political rights. Ignatius Donnelly, representing the compromise idea, said that he was "willing to swallow Democracy gilded with the genius of a Bryan" but he could not "stomach plutocracy in the body of Sewall." He hoped Watson's nomination would be made unanimous. A cautious Texan asked whether Watson, if nominated, would remain on the ticket till the election. "Yes, sir!" came an immediate answer. "Until hell freezes over!" The reply so completely, so accurately, summed up the popular conception of Tom Watson's character, and so well expressed the mid-roaders' feeling in calling upon him in this emergency, that it brought the Convention to its feet in a spontaneous demonstration. On the first ballot he received 539¾ votes against 257 for Sewall, his closest and only serious opponent. It was an impressive proof that Watson's policy was the real will of the Convention. The lights of the hall were again being tampered with, flickering out. Votes were frantically changed to give him a majority, and a motion was passed suspending the rules and nominating Watson unanimously. In pitch darkness the Watson Populists wildly and blindly celebrated their triumph.[30]

The midnight darkness of that hall was symbolic of the conditions in which that whole lamentable Convention groped. The delegates read in the morning papers a telegram from Bryan asking Senator Jones to withdraw his name from consideration if Sewall were not nominated. Chairman Allen had refused to give this information to the Convention. The delegates also read a letter from Senator Jones, which "underwent a remarkable change after it was given to the newspapers," denying that he had made any commitment as to the withdrawal of Sewall. The air was again thick with cries of "treachery." "Gagged, clique-ridden, and machine ruled," pronounced delegate Lloyd. What had been anxiety was rapidly souring to disgust.[31]

Relentlessly the steam-roller tactics were continued by the managers, still determined to nominate Bryan. Three times, while the roll call of the states was in progress, Chairman Allen denied point blank when the question was put to him from the floor the existence of a further message from Bryan asking that he not be nominated, despite the fact that he was perfectly aware of the message.[32] Twice during the roll call the Texas delegation hurriedly withdrew to caucus on the proposal of bolting. Once when Bryan stampeders attempted to wrest their banner from them a dozen Texans reached for their guns — and then looked sheepish. Once when the Convention seemed wavering Henry Demarest Lloyd, with a carefully prepared speech in hand designed to rally the delegates back to their principles, stood hesitating while he was urged to speak. He turned to Clarence Darrow, who advised against it. Other men of courage and intelligence "stood spellbound, fearing to break the union." While they "waited for a protest, a halt," the machine rolled on. Bryan was nominated. Lloyd burst in upon his host late that night "in feverish excitement" and exploded with the exclamation that the party was "buried, hopelessly sold out." [33]

The St. Louis Convention

ROBERT DURDEN

Robert Durden, professor of history at Duke University, questions some details essential to the Woodward version of the Populist convention of 1896. According to Woodward, the delegates at the convention would not have favored fusion had they not been denied essential information about Bryan's position by leaders who were committed to a merger of all the silver forces behind Bryan's candidacy. Upon what does the difference between the accounts of Woodward and Durden hinge? Who is correct? Durden suggests that fusion was in keeping with Populist principles and purposes. According to him, the majority of Populists embraced fusion as "the first step and symbol of overdue reform." Norman Pollack, in The Populist Response to Industrial America *(Cambridge: Harvard University Press, 1962), vigorously endorses the view of a contemporary radical participant, Henry Demarest Lloyd, that fusion was the attempt to consolidate radicalism "until ready for a more decisive advance." Recognized radicals at the convention did not oppose fusion, according to Pollack, and many radicals who had once objected to it became converts. There was so much confusion and vacillation among Populists regarding fusion that it is difficult to imagine how it could have been the result of a rigged convention. Pollack, along with his Populist radical exemplars, admits that fusion turned out to be a disaster, but he does not confront the charge that thoroughgoing radicals would not have found much to prefer in Bryan as opposed to McKinley or that they should have known better than to try to build a radical force through coalition politics. Was fusion the wisest tactic to achieve reform and to preserve the People's party, or were these two goals mutually exclusive?*

Several prominent western Populists announced shortly after Bryan's nomination that they favored Populist endorsement of the Democratic national ticket. Butler, Taubeneck, and some of the Silver Republican leaders, however, still favored Senator Teller as the candidate for the Populists and for the National Silver party, whose convention was also to begin in St. Louis on July 22. Butler's newspaper continued to attack the Democratic party on the state and national levels, though the Tarheel Populist leader carefully refrained from attacking Bryan himself.

As Butler saw the situation on the eve of the Populist convention and described his views to Senator Stewart, there were two courses open to the Populists. They could endorse Bryan under certain conditions or they could name their own candidates, with the understanding that after the election the presidential electors would use every honorable effort to combine the votes of all electors who favored silver and opposed the rule of the national banks. Butler added that he preferred the latter course, which would certainly simplify matters for the southern Populists, and believed that it was not only necessary but the most promising plan for good results. But he did not favor publicity for either of the plans until the Populist convention had actually begun.[1]*

Teller was not available for the Populist-National Silver nomination for the simple reason that he supported the Democratic ticket and insisted that all the silver forces should do the same. After writing his Republican friends as well as Butler, Taubeneck, and other Populists to this effect, Teller informed Bryan: "I have written to all the Populist leaders that I know and some that I do not urging them to nominate you and I made it impossible for my name to be used." [2]

Butler's own conversion to the idea of accepting Bryan was facilitated by the advice he received from Senator Stewart, who had attended the Democratic convention. The Nevadan informed Butler that the Democrats who controlled the Chicago convention "were as emphatically Populists in their sentiments and actions as yourself" and that the "platform is radical

From Robert Durden, *The Climax of Populism: The Election of 1896* (Lexington, Ky.: University of Kentucky Press, 1965), 23–44. Reprinted by permission.
* [See pp. 148–150 for notes to this article. — Ed.]

enough for you or me." Since Bryan was "more of a Populist than a Democrat," Stewart continued, the western Populists were emphatically for him.
Any attempt to run an opposing candidate would not only fail but destroy
the party. Stewart insisted: "There is no use fighting the movement now. We
must join with it or be destroyed. There was nothing left of the Democratic
party at Chicago but the name." [3]

Since the Populist response even to the name "Democrat" differed
greatly according to sectional circumstances, confusion and anxiety mounted
as the Populists began to converge on St. Louis. Reporters found that some
delegates, too poor to pay railway fares, had walked long distances to reach
the convention. Some were forced to sleep in the parks in order to afford the
"nickel-lunch." Heat gripped the city. Eastern newsmen, like their publishers and editors, were apt to be intolerant of the desperate farmers. The
correspondent for the New York *Times* wrote: "The crazy people who fancy
that some one is always sneaking paris green into their chowder or needles
into their hash are not more suspicious than this body of 1,400 more or less
'touched' would-be rulers of the country." [4]

Marion Butler refused interviews and kept quiet as he had said he
would, but few other Populist leaders chose that course. Captain Reuben F.
Kolb, prominent leader of the Alabama delegation, declared strongly for
Bryan: "I am willing to make the fight on one plank, so long as it is monetary reform. That is the paramount issue. I'm a middle-of-the-road Populist,
but I've got sense enough to walk around a mud hole." From Texas, where
anti-Bryan and midroad sentiment was strongest, a delegate asserted that a
straight Populist ticket would be named because "Texas is going to run this
convention and dictate the nominations." Although Tom Watson had
chosen not to attend the convention, he had dispatched the Georgia delegation with instructions to stand by the full Populist platform and fight fusion
with the Democrats.[5]

At the other extreme from Watson and the Texans, most western
Populists were loud in their praises for the Democratic candidates and platform. Representative Jerry Simpson of Kansas told the large and generally
approving Kansas delegation that the "issue is paramount, and men dare
not play politics at such a time as this. If this Convention should refuse to
indorse Bryan the Populist party would not contain a corporal's guard in
November." [6]

Out of this babel a plan emerged. The party not only made nominations but was also largely held together. Leadership, bold and imaginative as
the difficult situation required, played a key role. The fundamental fact was
that most Populists wanted free silver as the first step and symbol of overdue
reforms. Most Populists wanted also to maintain their party organization
intact for the national purpose of keeping the Democrats "honest" and out

of the hands of Cleveland men and for various local purposes that differed according to geography and circumstance. Henry D. Lloyd's widely accepted charge that the Populist leaders at St. Louis "tricked and bulldozed and betrayed" as they carried out a program to destroy Populism is not only untrue but also ignores the dilemma that faced the party.[7]

No one can say with assurance who first suggested that the Populists should nominate Bryan, reject the Democrats' vice-presidential nominee, Arthur Sewall of Maine, and put up their own candidate for the vice-presidency. Senator Marion Butler, however, carefully considered the plan and its complications before arriving in St. Louis, and he early and energetically identified himself with this method of saving both the Populist party and the unity of the silver forces. As unprecedented and fraught with difficulty as the plan was, it alone seemed to meet the complexities of the party situation that the executive committeemen faced when they gathered in St. Louis on Sunday evening, July 19. And this was the plan that was ultimately accepted by the great majority both of the leaders and of the ordinary delegates who filled the hotel lobbies with noisy, often angry debate.[8]

Butler arrived with the reputation of being a midroader who opposed fusion with the Democrats. He was and continued to be a moderate one in the sense that he, Taubeneck, Senator William A. Peffer of Kansas and others in the majority agreed that the national organization of the Populist party should be preserved. It should neither be destroyed by a bolt of the extreme fusionists from the West, who favored endorsement of both Bryan and Sewall, or by the extreme midroaders of the deep South, who insisted on a straight Populist ticket, nor should the party be eliminated by being absorbed in the Democracy. This sentiment the executive committee established at its first meeting.[9]

Senator James K. Jones of Arkansas, the Democratic national chairman, and Governor William J. Stone, Democrat of Missouri, met with the Populist leaders and insisted on full endorsement of the Democratic ticket or nothing. Bryan's spokesmen emphatically rejected, as did the western Populists, the idea that Butler and others presented of an independent Populist ticket with Populist candidates, to be followed by fusion with the other silver groups on the electoral ticket according to the proportionate strength of the various parties in each state. One alleged spokesman for Bryan, Matt Ward of Omaha, Nebraska, declared flatly that, "This talk about dividing electors will not be allowed; it can't go. I have Mr. Bryan's ultimatum in my pocket, and will deliver it to the Populists at the proper time." [10]

Butler had discovered, even before arriving in St. Louis, that while it was both difficult and impolitic to attack Bryan himself, the same was not true of the Democratic vice-presidential nominee. Arthur Sewall was a well-to-do ship-builder who had, at one time or other, been connected with a national bank and with railway and other corporations. He also believed in free silver and was nominated because he was from Maine and would furnish a sectional balance for a ticket headed by a Nebraskan. Any hope that his eastern "respectability" would help hold irate Cleveland Democrats in the party proved futile.

The most enthusiastic Democrat knew that Bryan had about the same chance in New England as McKinley had in the deep South. Both the extremist minority of midroad Populists, who were ready to split the party rather than accept Bryan, and the more moderate leaders, who searched for a way to save the party and the silver cause, announced that Sewall could never be accepted by the Populists.[11]

Capitalizing on this anti-Sewall feeling, Butler conferred again with Senator Jones on Monday, July 20, and proposed, according to apparently reliable press accounts, that the Populists endorse Bryan if the Democrats would drop Sewall and accept the Populist nominee for vice president. When Jones refused to listen to this proposal, Butler reportedly became angry and assailed the Democrats for "wanting the earth." Butler's later statement to newsmen revealed little other than his hope for a way out: "Some seem to think that there is a danger of a split, but there will be none. The different elements will put their heads together and agree on a plan of action." [12]

Just as Jones rebuffed Butler, Weaver and other spokesmen for the complete Bryan-Sewall ticket rejected the same proposition when James H. ("Cyclone") Davis of Texas and Ignatius Donnelly of Minnesota presented it on behalf of the Populist executive committee. Any attempt to displace Sewall, according to Jones and his allies, would lead to irreconcilable complications and place both parties in a ridiculous attitude. "The committee," Jones declared, "must be as loyal to the vice presidential nominee as to the presidential candidate." [13]

In spite of Jones's refusal to talk about a sacrifice of Sewall, a key group of Populist leaders, including Marion Butler, had decided by Tuesday, July 21, the day before the convention opened, that the exigencies of the situation called for the nomination of Bryan and a southern Populist on a Populist ticket backed by a Populist platform. But this program would have to be fought for in open convention, where a slight misstep might see minorities on either extreme ganging up to thwart what seemed to be the complicated preference of the majority.

When the Populist national committee met on July 21, the executive committee, which had met earlier, recommended and secured Marion Butler's nomination as the temporary chairman and keynote speaker of the convention. Although "Cyclone" Davis of Texas and General Weaver of Kansas had been frequently mentioned by their respective factions for the temporary chairmanship, opposition to Butler scarcely materialized either in the meeting of the national committee or in the convention itself.[14]

The convention that finally opened on Wednesday, July 22, consisted of almost 1,400 hot, confused, and tense delegates. Palmetto fans agitated the stagnant air. The audibility of the speakers on the platform was so poor that a big-voiced delegate from Wisconsin had to be used as a "repeater." A few women and Negro delegates were scattered about the hall. Each state was allowed one delegate for every senator and representative it had in Congress and additional delegates in proportion to the Populist vote cast in the state. This plan of representation meant that New York had only forty-four delegates, based mostly on population, while Texas and North Carolina each had around a hundred votes, and Kansas, with the largest western delegation, had eighty-two. One analysis of the convention by sections showed that the South had about six hundred delegates, or nearly half; the East, one hundred and fifty; the North (including Ohio and to the Missouri river but not including Missouri and the Dakotas), two hundred and forty; and the West (beyond the Missouri), three hundred and fifty-six.[15]

With extremists on both sides waiting for their openings to yell in uninhibited Populist style, Butler successfully walked an oratorical tightrope in his keynote address. He suggested that the Democrats, from a mixture of alarm and conscience, had committed "petty and grand larceny by stealing the People's party platform almost in its entirety." What then should the Populists do? They should insist upon putting issues above partisanship, as they had traditionally demanded, and help settle the financial question so that other fundamental matters could be dealt with next.

But the separate People's party was still absolutely necessary. Without it, "the next Democratic National Convention would repudiate the platform it recently adopted at Chicago, and Mr. Bryan would stand no more chance four years hence of being nominated by that party than Thomas Jefferson would if he were alive." Without alluding directly to the plan for a southern vice-presidential nominee, Butler concluded with a plea for unity, which, under the circumstances, was hardly mere rhetoric. A party that had raised up a great principle and split the two old parties, he argued, "is not going to be foolish enough to allow itself to split on methods and detail. We will stand together." [16]

After the keynote address the convention adjourned until evening to give the commitee on permanent organization time to prepare its report. Since there had been no floor fight about Butler's election, all hands prepared for battle about the election of the permanent chairman of the convention. The extreme midroaders filled the air with their threats of bolting if the leaders tried to force the nomination of Bryan. The election of the permanent chairman, as all declared at the time, would be the first test of the power of the various factions.

When the delegates reassembled at 8 P.M. they found the convention hall in darkness. A few candles at the press table cast a weird light as the band played bravely and some of the restless delegates tried to sing. Some of the extreme midroaders concluded that the darkness had resulted from a trick of the Bryan men. Someone yelled, "Its a scheme of the Bryan men" and if "they" nominate Bryan "we'll split this convention." "You're a disgrace to the party," came back from the dark depths of the hall. One delegate from Texas, a congressional candidate, declared, "There has been some ugly work, and the culprits had better beware." [17]

After the aisles began to choke with pushing and shouting delegates, Davis of Texas finally got the attention of the crowd: "As his tall form and broad, sweeping sombrero came within the narrow ring of light from the tallow dip, the delegates immediately recognized him, and there were shouts of 'shut up,' 'keep quiet,' 'Listen to Cyclone.'" He yelled that the "electric wires were 'disaffected'" but would be repaired soon. Nevertheless, at 8:45 P.M. Butler, probably fearing greater chaos in the darkness, announced that the accident in the lighting would prevent the committees from reporting that night and declared the convention recessed until the following morning.[18]

This episode is important both because it illustrates the mood of certain elements of the convention and because it has been cited by various historians as a mysterious development that Butler and other "manipulators" may really have been responsible for, a part of the "conspiracy" for Bryan at St. Louis. The simple truth was that the heat in St. Louis, which had reached a point that inspired editorial comment, exploded about 6 P.M. in a rain and electrical storm that knocked down some power lines.[19]

Regardless of the lights, those delegates who would proceed with passionate disregard of the danger of splitting the party were in a minority. Certainly the voting on the permanent chairmanship proved that the next day (Thursday, July 23). The majority report of the committee on permanent organization recommended Senator William Allen of Nebraska, a fervent supporter of Bryan who was also believed by most observers to favor Sewall. The minority report named James E. Campion, an obscure extreme midroader from Maine. Allen was chosen, 758 to 564.

Thus a majority of the convention agreed on a Bryan man for permanent chairman. An even larger majority later accepted the report of the committee on the platform as made by General Weaver and rejected proposals backed by some of the extremists led by Coxey of Ohio. The platform recognized the financial question as the "great and pressing issue" before the country, and Populists invited the "cooperation of all organizations and citizens" who agreed on "this vital question."

In addition to the important cluster of demands dealing with finance, the Populists joined the new Democracy in calling for an income tax, an end to the misuse of the injunction in labor disputes, and other reforms. The Populists still included several of their usual demands which the Democrats had not espoused, such as government ownership of the railroads and telegraph, reclamation by the Federal government of lands granted to the railroads and other corporations in "excess of their actual needs"; direct legislation through the initiative and referendum; the election of the president, vice president, and senators by a "direct vote of the people"; and jobs on public works for the unemployed in times of industrial depression. The platform, in short, represented the majority's desire to express the independence of the Populists as well as to invite cooperation with other reform forces on the paramount issue.[20]

The undecided, crucial question remained: would the extreme midroaders bolt, as they constantly threatened, after the majority named Bryan as the Populist candidate? The extreme fusionists, who insisted that the Populists had to accept Sewall as well as Bryan, were counting on either a stampede to Sewall in the enthusiastic aftermath of Bryan's nomination or an adjournment after that nomination to give them time to woo a majority to Sewall. If the Southern extremists bolted, moreover, the task of selling Sewall to the delegates remaining in the convention would become that much easier.[21]

In order to prevent any possibility of Sewall's being nominated, the minority report of the committee on rules and procedures called for a reversal of the usual order of nominations and the naming of the vice-presidential candidate first. Texans, Georgians, and others rallied to this idea, not only because they were anti-Sewall but also because they hoped that somehow the presidential nomination might be miraculously saved for a Populist too. The next round of voting began.

North Carolina, which had divided its ninety-five votes equally in the Allen-Campion contest for the permanent chairmanship, was a key state in the tense fight about the order of business. When the roll call reached it, Congressman Harry Skinner mounted a chair and shouted: "North Carolina stands with Nebraska. When we came here this morning we were for the minority report, but since then we have had assurances from Kansas, Nebraska, and other . . . States that, if we would permit the regular order to prevail the cause of Populism in the South should be recognized by the nomination of a Southern candidate for Vice-President. North Carolina therefore casts 85 votes for the majority report and 10 for the minority."

As the roll call neared the end, rumors began to circulate that the Bryanites had narrowly won with the majority report for the traditional order of nominations. Southern midroaders rushed to beg the North Carolina delegation to change its vote. Skinner hurriedly consulted with Butler, rushed back to his delegation, and again mounted the chair: "Mr. Chairman, North Carolina cast its vote to nominate a President first, after pledges from Kansas and other States that afterwards a [southern] Populist should be nominated for Vice-President. Are you sincere? I demand to know as I am empowered to change the vote of North Carolina."

Bedlam descended upon the convention. Cries of "yes, yes" and "no" filled the air. Thomas Patterson, head of the Colorado delegation and a leading supporter for the Bryan-Sewall ticket, yelled that it was "disgraceful that in a convention like this any such deals should be mentioned." He vowed that "Colorado had no part in it."

Skinner, probably exhausting the patience of many with his further remarks about a southern man's deserving the vice-presidential nomination, concluded by casting all of North Carolina's ninety-five votes for the minority report. With the convention again in churning commotion and Marion Butler on the platform cheering "as long as his voice held out," Allen finally restored order to announce that the minority report had carried by 785 votes to 615. A Populist vice-presidential candidate would be named first.[22]

The midroaders, both the extreme and moderate ones cooperating, had won their first clear victory. They celebrated accordingly, the extremists temporarily ignoring the limited nature of their victory. The anti-Bryan midroaders hurt their own cause through lack of organization and noisy immoderation in general. One sympathetic observer remarked that the large Texas delegation was composed of some of the "best men on the American continent" but was handicapped, nevertheless, by such "wild fools as a man named Wilkins from California, and a high cheeked and peak headed yahoo from Missouri, and two or three other similar characters. These cranks put the many good men of the mid-road faction to disadvantage."[23]

Despite these handicaps, the midroaders came into their own at about sixteen minutes before 1 A.M. (the appropriateness of the "sixteen to one" amused them) on Saturday, July 25, when one of their best-loved spokesmen, Tom Watson of Georgia, received the Populist nomination for the vice presidency. When the nominating speeches were made Friday night, Watson was not the candidate of the extreme midroaders; they preferred Frank Burkitt of Mississippi. But Watson's name had been mentioned among the delegates and in the newspapers in connection with the compromise plan that Marion Butler had advocated. Colorado, Kansas, and other western states stood by Sewall. When the first ballot showed that Watson had a large lead, but not a majority, with Sewall running second, Texas changed from Burkitt to Watson; Tennessee switched from her favorite son, A. L. Mimms, to Watson; as North Carolina prepared to change her vote from Harry Skinner to Watson, the chair announced that the Georgian had won the nomination.[24]

Just why Tom Watson, with his long record of strong opposition to fusion of any kind, had consented to play a vital role in a plan designed to bring about quasi-fusion of the Populists and Democrats is a puzzle that may never be solved. Perhaps the best answer is the one that he himself gave shortly after the convention. "I will accept the nomination," he explained, "in the interest of harmony and to prevent disruption of the Populist party, which seemed imminent." Watson added that under the circumstances he fully endorsed the convention's action; furthermore, when he and Bryan had been in the House of Representatives they had "voted together on every measure." Watson subsequently explained that he had been sincere in saying earlier that he would not accept either place on the straight Populist ticket that he had advocated. He added: "I stayed away from the Convention partly to avoid prominence, and the Georgia delegation had positive instructions not to allow the use of my name. . . . When I said I would not accept I did not dream that such a crisis could possibly come upon our party." [25]

In thinking that his candidacy was necessary to "harmonize the factions and save the party" Watson was partly correct. He was hardly the only southern Populist who could have served the purpose, but he was well qualified, aside from an erratic streak that was destined to cause much difficulty in the campaign. Where the real trouble came was in the later assertion by Watson and some of his followers that unnamed Democratic "lobbyists" and Senator Jones had promised that if the Populists would nominate Bryan the Democrats would manage to get Sewall off their ticket.[26]

If any of the Georgia delegates in St. Louis telegraphed to Watson that Jones had promised Sewall's withdrawal, and memories rather than documents are the only sources for the story, they were apparently guilty of either unintelligent wishful thinking or distortion of the truth. As early as July 21 accounts had been published of Jones' refusal to discuss any such bargain with Marion Butler; and after a majority of the delegates had voted for Allen for the permanent chairmanship, it was obvious that a solid majority of the Populists at St. Louis intended to nominate Bryan for the presidency. After that vote on July 23, as before it, Jones and the leaders of the extreme fusionists among the Populists worked not to conciliate the extreme midroaders but to secure the Populist nomination of Sewall as well as of Bryan. Not until Butler and the moderate midroaders joined the Texas-led extremists in proceeding first with the nomination of the vice-presidential candidate did the extreme fusionists see their hopes of nominating Sewall too begin to slip away. With a Populist majority established for Bryan, why should any of the Democratic leaders at St. Louis talk about replacing Sewall with a southern Populist?

Aside from these developments at St. Louis, the Democrats were confident after the triumph of the reformers at Chicago that the Bryan-Sewall ticket would win in the South. Thus Bryan's running mate had been chosen not from the "safe" section but from New England, which was "safe" for the Republicans. In all of the southern midroaders' fulminations against Sewall there ran a deep, sectional resentment that the South had again been bypassed in the selection of candidates for the highest national offices. Southern Populists, for all their brave, and to a large degree successful, efforts to transcend the old sectionalism, were still Southerners who carried their own share of what Professor C. Vann Woodward has called "the burden of Southern history."

That Senator Jones or any other responsible Democrat at St. Louis agreed to try to eliminate Sewall from the race is altogether improbable. What is much more likely is that Marion Butler at St. Louis said, and correctly, that he had done, was doing, and would do everything in his ability to bring about Sewall's withdrawal. Even a political novice might be expected to know that Butler's power concerning a nomination already made by a national Democratic convention was limited. Moreover, his primary purpose was not to eliminate Sewall, as desirable as that might be from his viewpoint and that of other Populists, but to save the national organization of the People's party. This was the purpose which had finally inspired so many outstanding Populists from all sections of the country to cooperate with Butler in the unprecedented program of action undertaken at St. Louis.

The early morning nomination of Watson brought the Populists to the last, and in many ways most delicate, phase of their convention, the nomination of the presidential candidate. It was delicate because the extreme fusionists had argued all along that the nomination of Bryan without Sewall was impossible and that Bryan would not, indeed could not, accept any such nomination. Could the Populists nominate him even if he asked that they not do so?

Many delegates were impatient for the answer to that question as the celebration following Watson's nomination began to die down in the hall. Some had come to the evening session with their luggage in tow. But the time was about 1 A.M. (Saturday, July 25), the end of a long day's exciting developments. Weaver's motion for adjournment was declared by the chair to be carried amid confusion and shouts of "no." [27]

The telegraph, even before the newspapers, kept Bryan in Lincoln fully informed of developments in the Populist convention. Jones had advised him, however, to ignore all embarrassing questions and let his well known record speak for itself.[28] But when the Populists voted to nominate their vice-presidential candidate first, and Sewall's chances faded accordingly, the Democratic national chairman telegraphed Bryan the news, asked him what should be done if Sewall were not nominated by the Populists, and advised him that in such event he (Jones) favored declining a nomination by the Populists.

Bryan responded, before or about the time that the Populists were making their speeches naming the various vice-presidential nominees, that he agreed with Jones and wished his name withdrawn from consideration if Sewall were not nominated also. These telegrams were in the hands of Thomas Patterson of Colorado that evening. The St. Louis newspapers as well as every other daily paper of any size in the nation carried either the texts or the substance of the telegrams on Saturday, July 25, 1896.[29]

In other words, every Populist who attended the last crucial session of the convention on that Saturday had read in the morning newspapers or had otherwise heard that Bryan did not wish to be nominated by the Populists unless Sewall was also. Yet the overwhelming majority of the Populists went ahead and nominated the Nebraskan as their own candidate for the presidency of the United States.

They were not tricked into this action. They did it because they had to do it for the survival of the national People's party and for an excellent fighting chance to win the reforms they and many others desired. The Populist leaders were gambling, for they did not know what Bryan would do; but, being politicians, they knew that candidates never go out of their way to reject votes. In his speech nominating Bryan, General Weaver first established clearly that he too had been won over to the program of Butler and the other moderate midroaders. Then Weaver went straight to the embarrassing news from Nebraska: "You have all read the papers this morning; you have all read the manly dispatch from . . . Bryan. No man could have done less and be a man. . . . But . . . this question has reached a point where neither Mr. Bryan nor his personal friends have any right whatever to say what the action of this convention shall be. This is a greater question than the personality of its candidates." [30]

General Field of Virginia, the vice-presidential candidate of the Populists' "blue-gray" team of 1892, seconded Bryan's nomination and moved that it be made unanimous. Although Allen was at first inclined to rule the motion in order, angry cries from the extreme midroaders led to a hasty huddle of the leaders on the platform and the decision to proceed with the roll call of states. Six more hours of oratory and nominations followed.

The extremists rallied behind S. F. Norton of Illinois, editor of a

Populist newspaper and author of one of the numerous books dealing with the money question. The balloting resulted in 1,042 votes for Bryan, 340 for Norton. After the traditional parade of the state banners and noisy celebration, which Josephus Daniels found about as enthusiastic as the scene he had witnessed when the Democrats named Bryan at Chicago, the exhausted Populists prepared to leave St. Louis.[31]

Henry D. Lloyd commented, soon after the convention, that if the "radicals" at St. Louis had only tried they might have carried the day against the "stultification" represented by Bryan and silver and carried it for "a 'stalwart' ticket" on a platform demanding "public ownership of all monopolies." Such an interpretation was obviously quite misleading about the temper and the composition of the convention. Lloyd, moreover, had a telegram in his pocket from Debs saying, "Please do not permit the use of my name for nomination." And Clarence Darrow, among others, advised Lloyd not to make the "radical" speech that he had all ready for delivery to convention.[32]

Such a struggle as the Populists had waged at St. Louis left serious divisions in the party. Yet the important fact was that the great majority of the party and its leaders had held together thus far for Bryan and national reforms. The campaign ahead posed difficult problems for the Populists as well as for Bryan. Tom Watson, as subsequent events would reveal, had allowed himself to be sadly miscast in the political drama. But under the leadership of Marion Butler, whom the Populist national committee elected as national chairman of the party at the conclusion of the convention, the bulk of the Populists prepared to fight valiantly for Bryan and free silver.

RACE

The Negro in the Populist Movement

JACK ABRAMOWITZ

Historians have for some time recognized that many people at the turn of the century saw no inconsistency between racism and reform, but the extent to which this observation applies to Populism has been a matter of contention. Jack Abramowitz of Hofstra University, the first scholar to survey comprehensively race relations within the Populist movement, presents a carefully impartial picture but concludes that in the contemporary context the white Populists behaved well. He maintains that Populism promised to improve the situation of black Americans and to break down some of the hostility between the races. In evaluating this argument, one must keep in mind that during the 1890s race relations were in rapid flux, as C. Vann Woodward has demonstrated in The Strange Career of Jim Crow *(New York: Oxford University Press, 1955). Tensions were high; lynchings of blacks reached their historic peak during the decade and blacks were being forced out of occupations in which they had once held strong positions. Jim Crow statutes were beginning to appear on the books in increasing numbers and in one area of life after another. Legal barriers were erected between the races where before there had been some flexibility and some contact. Though white supremacy notions and practices were not lacking in the late nineteenth century, there had been relatively few clearly defined and firmly recognized roles for the two races. Whether or not blacks could hold jobs and vote, whether they would be served in restaurants and seated on trains and could use public accommodations depended on highly varying local custom or momentary caprice. The insecurities bred from this fluctuating discrimination and the rapidity of the resulting changes made the Populist appeal for political co-operation with blacks very hazardous. The Democrats sought to make it more hazardous by obfuscating the distinctions between civil rights and social equality, between interracial co-operation and Negro domination. The reader should be alert, however, to detect Democratic tactics other than appeals to white supremacy.*

The success of the Granger movement of the 1870's and early 1880's pointed the way for a new rising, and in the late 1880's the mushrooming Agricultural Wheels, societies, and various Alliances were united in three great organizations: the National Farmers' Alliance or Northern Alliance, the National Farmers' Alliance and Industrial Union or Southern Alliance, and the Colored Farmers' National Alliance and Cooperative Union or Colored Alliance.

Though these organizations were non-political, the threat of entering politics was clearly implicit. The impressive membership claims of the Alliances left little doubt they were a potent force in the nation's political life. By 1890 the Southern Alliance boasted of its alleged three million members and the Colored Alliance asserted it had 750,000 adult male members, 300,000 females, and 150,000 youths. Acting separately and jointly these Alliances stirred the South and carried the hope of an economic and social regeneration of the region.

The interest of Negroes in the Alliance movement and the rapid spread of the organization through the South soon made it imperative that the Southern Alliance win Negro farmers as allies in the common struggle for reform. Contrary to the general assumption that the Colored Alliance was a mere "appendage" of the Southern Alliance, there were serious differences between the two organizations, particularly over the issue of the Lodge Bill or Force Bill as it was known in the South. Despite these barriers a path to unity was laid out in 1890 and in December both Alliances met in convention in Ocala, Florida. At these meetings a program of joint, united action was mapped out, and "it was mutually and unanimously agreed to unite . . . upon the basis adopted December 5, 1890." [1*]

The virtual fusion of the two organizations made the Alliance a real force in Southern life, but it soon became evident that no major reforms

From Jack Abramowitz, "The Negro in the Populist Movement," *The Journal of Negro History*, XXXVIII (July, 1953), 257–289. Copyright © by The Association for the Study of Negro Life and History, Inc. Footnotes selectively omitted.
* [See pp. 150–151 for notes to this article. — Ed.]

would be effected unless it went into politics. This issue of political action was a source of conflict between Negro and white alliancemen and created serious problems. Most Southern Alliance leaders were strongly Democratic and desired to win that party to the Alliance program. The Colored Alliance was hostile to Southern Democracy and its platform of white supremacy. Negro alliancemen generally looked to the Republicans for political guidance though there was a growing conviction that the party was turning from the Negro and his problems. Within both Alliances there were also substantial forces that favored the creation of an independent third party. This latter movement made rapid headway after 1890 when it became clear that neither Democrats nor Republicans intended instituting a program of genuine agrarian reform.

Strenuous efforts were made by the Southern Alliance to "capture" the Democratic party with success in some areas, notably South Carolina.[2] The question of whether this actually constituted success remains a moot point, for it is not clear at this time whether they captured the Democrats or were themselves made captive by that party, a charge made by many Populists. Like the white alliancemen, the Colored Alliance first tried to influence a major party, in this case the Republicans. Early in September, 1890, the *Atlanta Constitution* cited the "curious fact" that Negro alliancemen in South Carolina were not entering politics, but less than two weeks later said, "the Afro-American Farmers' Alliance is following the footsteps of his white brother and is going into politics." The article went on to say that the Colored Alliance was exerting pressure on Republicans to name the president of the state Colored Alliance, W. A. Grant, for Congress in the First District.[3] In Georgia, too, the Colored Alliance entered politics through the Republican party and an Allianceman named Lectured Crawford was elected to the Assembly from McIntosh County in 1890 and 1892.

The fact that the Colored Alliance seemed to be directing its political energies to the task of reforming the Republicans and was creating some disunity within that party seems to have dulled the edge of Southern fears of the Negro in politics, and the *Atlanta Constitution* calmly headlined its story on the 1890 Ocala convention with the declaration, "Black and white will unite in stamping out sectionalism. The Colored Alliance in Ocala ready to join a third party which will lead to the welfare of the farmer." The article went on to report, "The important news today is the discovery of a third party of nearly 1,000,000 voters, organized, ready and waiting to follow the lead of the Farmers' Alliance, if it should see fit to strike out in the independent line of the people's party. This body is the Colored Farmers' Alliance which met here today."

The next day the paper elaborated further and asserted that the plan of the third party men was to capture "an allianceman here and there

in the south and raking in most of them in the west. With this added to the
750,000 colored voters who await them, they will have a party over 1,000,000
strong to start on." [4] The manner in which the paper greeted the stirrings
of the nascent third party was in direct contrast to its choleric wrath a few
months later and indicates the extent to which many leaders of Southern
life were ignorant of the explosive times in which they lived. Part of the rea-
soning behind this attitude of complacency is explained in an editorial
which observed, "it is true that the western farmers are free to form a third
party, but in an experiment of this kind they cannot take the southern farmers with them. . . . Here the whites are compelled to form themselves into a
compact body to resist the dangers of negro domination." [5]

Small wonder the editor viewed Populism in so detached a manner.
At the very least he saw it as a disruptive force in Mid-Western Republicanism, while at best it might develop into a force that would split the
Republicans in rural areas, remove Negro support of the party, and pave
the way for an era of Democratic political pluralities.

At the conclusion of the Ocala conventions of the Alliances in December, 1890, a call was issued for a conference to be held in Cincinnati on
February 20, 1891, to discuss the question of a third party. The conference
date was later shifted to May 19, 1891, and there were about 1,400 delegates
present representing, among others, the Northern Alliance, Southern Alliance, Colored Alliance, Knights of Labor, and the Union Labor party.
Nothing much was accomplished because of the hesitancy of the Southern
Alliance which wished first to explore all possible avenues of approach to.
the Democratic party. The Southern delegation was small and when some of
them tried to introduce segregation of Colored Alliancemen the convention
defeated them by overwhelming vote. They also failed to prevent the conference from establishing a tentative People's Party committee which was to
exist pending the formation of a permanent party organization for the 1892
elections. The inability of the Southerners to prevent establishment of this
temporary committee meant that a third party virtually was assured within
the next year.

The vote for a third party was supported by all the Negro delegates
except E. A. Richardson of the Georgia Colored Alliance. The reason for his
hesitancy is not clear but it may have stemmed from the opposition of the
Southern Alliance of his state to any third party. Richardson seems to have
been strongly influenced by Leonidas Livingston, Georgia Southern Alliance
leader, who was then fighting off the efforts of young Tom Watson to swing
the state Alliance behind the third party. The battle between Watson and
Livingston was a bitter one but was soon to be won by the Watson forces who

were to lead Georgia to the most unique experiment in race relations in the history of the South.

The Cincinnati conference had endeavored to guarantee the founding of a third party, but there were other forces working for the same end. In January, 1891, a conference of the Alliances and sympathetic groups had set up a Conference of Industrial Organizations in Washington, D.C., and this organization sent out a call for a convention in St. Louis on February 22, 1892, where all interested groups were to discuss the issue of a national third party. Though few in numbers the Negro delegation to this convention included some of the most active members of the Colored Alliance, notably J. L. Moore of Florida, W. A. Patillo of North Carolina, E. A. Richardson of Georgia, H. D. Cassdall of Missouri, L. D. Larned of Louisiana, W. H. Warwick of Virginia, E. C. Cabel of Kansas and Virginia, and L. D. Laurent of Louisiana.

Most of these men had a long and active career in politics and in Alliance work. Patillo had been a Republican candidate for Register of Deeds in Oxford County, North Carolina, in 1884. Soon after this he seems to have entered the Colored Alliance, and he was a delegate to the Ocala convention where his name appeared on the resolution of greeting sent to the Southern Alliance. L. D. Laurent had been active also for some time and had represented Louisiana at the Ocala meeting where he, too, signed the resolution greeting the Southern Alliance.

At the St. Louis convention the Negro delegation proved a spirited group and was active in the work of the assemblage. The resistance of white Southern delegates had again stymied the meeting preventing a clear cut stand on the third party issue, but this was overcome by the strategy of waiting until the convention adjourned and then reconvening as a mass meeting to discuss the third party issue. At the start of the meeting the name of William Warwick of the Virginia Colored Alliance was advanced for the post of assistant secretary and a white delegate from Georgia moved to make it unanimous, telling the convention, "We can stand that down in Georgia." Up rose an Alabama delegate to object and the motion was finally put to vote and "only one 'no' was heard in the whole House." [6]

This new found unity was soon disrupted and trouble arose when Negro delegates discovered that Superintendent Humphrey, the white leader of the Colored Alliance, was permitting some of the ballots of the Georgia Colored Alliance to be cast by white Georgians in favor of a third party. The Colored Alliancemen of Georgia reacted strongly against this improper act and are supposed to have withdrawn from the convention as a gesture of protest. It is probable they were partly influenced by the opposition of E. A. Richardson, their state president, to any third party moves. In any event, it is clear the withdrawal did not affect all the Negro delegates for the name of L. D. Laurent appeared on the call that was issued at the end of the convention for a People's Party founding convention at Omaha in July.

The St. Louis convention had set the stage for the formalities required to establish a national party, but the agrarian insurgents did not wait upon the niceties of political custom. As early as 1890 there were Alliance parties, People's parties, or Union Labor parties in nearly all Mid-Western and Southern states. It was increasingly evident that the independent political movement was moving into high gear.

The potentialities awaiting the Populist movement, should it seek to win the Negro vote and integrate the Negro in the party itself, were first discernible in Kansas where there was less tradition of anti-Negro sentiment to hinder this development. In their 1890 convention the Kansas Populists, then widely known as the Alliance party, named the Reverend Benjamin F. Foster, a Negro minister of Topeka, as candidate for state Auditor. The Populist state ticket was the result of a fusion of Union Laborites, Alliance-men, and Democrats, and it was generally believed that the nomination of a Negro for the post of auditor was designed to win Negroes away from the Republican party. "Fearless," the Topeka correspondent of the Negro paper *Indianapolis Freeman*, felt that the move might succeed in endangering the 82,000 Republican majority and went on to say that Reverend Foster was a man of high standing and no "dabbler" in politics.[7]

The nomination of Foster by the fusion group brought a demand by Negro Republicans that their party meet the challenge by naming the prominent Kansas Negro, John L. Waller, for auditor. This suggestion was rejected and caused much bad feeling. Meantime, the honor accorded Foster created such widespread interest that the *Indianapolis Freeman* carried a front page picture of him and also a biographical sketch that stated he had been born a slave in 1856, had attended Trinity School and Emerson Institute in Alabama and had studied at Fisk University and the Chicago Theological Seminary. At the time of the nomination he was minister of the Lincoln Street Congregational Church in Topeka. Though the *Freeman* was a strong supporter of the Republican party, it was most sympathetic in its treatment of Foster. It noted that whites were generally apathetic about voting for Negroes but admitted that "the Alliance voters are standing firm for Foster."[8] Undoubtedly the faith of the Negro voters in the intentions of the white Populists was considerably strengthened when Foster was selected as chairman of a rally at which Leonidas Polk, Southern Alliance president and ex-Confederate from North Carolina, was the main speaker. "As the former slave owner and the former slave shook hands warmly 'the enthusiasm knew no bounds.' " [9]

The results of this new approach were evident in the election returns which saw the Republican majority reduced to about 15,000 compared to the previous 82,000. Foster ran six thousand votes *ahead* of the ticket and received 112,000 votes. This impressive display of strength increased demands by Negro Republicans that their party plan to put a Negro on the ticket in 1892. These pleas again fell on deaf ears, but an effort was made to mollify Negro feelings by the appointment of John L. Waller to the Madagascar consulate, a move that pacified the Kansas political scene but added more turmoil to the national scene when Waller was imprisoned later by the French on charges of aiding a local revolutionary movement.

Strangely, the Populists did not follow up their advantage by nominating a Negro for state office in 1892; however, this may have been due to internal problems since they did have a Negro fusion candidate in Kansas City that year. Nor did the party give up efforts to enlist Negro support in the state. Foster continued to work with the party, "because its doctrines are in favor of the masses and against monopolies," and his work led the *Times-Observer* to predict that he would be nominated again. The same paper quoted Nick North, "the rustling Alliance Negro politician," as saying that the party had gained 1,500 votes in Wyandotte County, an area where Negroes lived in substantial numbers.[10]

The extent to which Negroes continued to function within the Kansas populist movement is not clear, but it is known that the Kansas delegation to the founding of the national People's Party in Omaha in 1892 included at least one Negro member, and the party made sufficient headway in Negro districts to occasion a comment from an anti-Populist Negro paper in November, 1892 that "it was reported that in some sections of the state there were breaks in the solid colored voters towards the People's party." This observation was partly substantiated in the complaint of another Negro Republican paper in Parsons, Kansas, that "the most sickening sight that we beheld last Tuesday was a few Negroes who claimed to be leaders of the colored people of this city, distributing People's party tickets."[11]

Though Kansas was one of the first to appeal directly for the Negro vote, other states were not long in following suit. Arkansas independents had pointed the way when the Union Labor party nominated a Negro, the Reverend I. P. Langley, for Congress from the 2nd District in 1890. In 1892 the state convention wrote into its platform the resolution of Negro delegate I. Glopsy, "That it is the object of the People's party to elevate the downtrodden irrespective of race or color." [12] In Louisiana the

People's party held its first convention in Alexandria on February 1, 1892, and there were twenty-four Negroes among the delegates. The leader of the Negro delegation, C. A. Roachborough, was nominated for State Treasurer but withdrew his name.

Texas, the founding state of both the Southern and the Colored Alliance, showed an early tendency toward Negro-white cooperation. A Populist state convention in Dallas on August 17, 1891, named two Negroes to the party's executive committee and Negroes remained on the committee until 1900.

The new party must have made strong efforts to win Negro members, for its 1892 convention heard a report from delegates from some of the southern counties "that the colored people .are coming into the new party in squads and companies. They have colored third party speakers and are organizing colored clubs." On the afternoon of the first day's session of the 1892 convention, seventy-one year old Henry Jennings, Negro state committeeman, reported that, "he had organized many people's party colored clubs in Texas and had branded them." He was followed later in the convention by Watson, a Negro delegate from Grayson County, who addressed the delegates with these words:

> I hope it is no embarrassment to you for a colored man to stand before you. I am an emancipated slave of this state. I was emancipated in 1865 and it is now useless to tell you my interest is yours and yours mine. You look over this large assembly and find very few of my people represented in this great movement. It is recognized that the Negro holds the balance of power, and the democrats and republicans are trying to hold him down. You should remember that those parties intend to keep the Negro out of this reform movement if they can, and when you bring up your old war-horses you are putting tools into democratic and republican hands to help them keep the Negro out of your movement.[13]

Mr. Watson's advice that Negroes be organized was heeded apparently, for a later issue of the Alliance paper carried a notice that the Colored National Alliance, a political arm of the Alliance movement of the First Congressional District, would meet in Conroe, Texas. The notice was signed by E. S. Eldridge and D. H. Stilven. The same issue announced that the Reverend Henry Jenkins, a Negro speaker, would address rallies for the People's party in fourteen counties between July 15 and August 14.

Texas Populism was only mildly successful in 1892, and its coalition with the dissident Democratic element known as the Jeffersonian Democrats won only eight seats in the legislature. In 1894 the coalition was more successful and captured twenty-two of the 128 seats. The degree to which the Texas third party actually attracted Negroes may never be known but the significance of the open appeal made for Negro votes cannot be overlooked.

Indicative of the effort to win Negro support was the summoning of Negroes for jury duty in Nacogdoches County by the Populist sheriff, an act that incurred the displeasure of some elements in the county. Such actions undoubtedly stimulated the early interest of Texas Negroes in the party. Mention has already been made of the presence of Negroes at the founding of the state party, and the files of the *Southern Mercury* give additional evidence of substantial Negro participation in the movement. In August, 1892, the paper published a one-column lead article by a Negro, P. K. Chase, titled, "The Colored Man and Politics," which declared, "The one and only advantageous political course of the Negro, under present existing affairs is to support the people's party." He then went on to say wishfully, "The people's party is not heard to say that 'this is a white man's government' but that this is a people's government." [14]

Mr. Chase was not accurate in his estimate of the views of Populist leaders on the race question, for evidence will be given later to show that certain party leaders were not unwilling to use the race issue in a futile effort to avoid the Democratic characterization of "Negro lover." The sincerity of the Populists on the race issue was not, however, the main obstacle to winning Negro adherents. A stronger impediment was the able and vigorous leadership given the Texas Republican party by a corps of Negroes, particularly Norris Wright Cuney. During the very period when the People's party was trying to win the Negro vote, Cuney was leading the fight against the "lily-white" Republican faction. It is conceivable that many Negroes who might otherwise have joined the People's party felt compelled to aid Cuney in his losing battle against those seeking to subvert the Republican party. Cuney was opposed to Populism, but he did favor a fusion ticket in 1896 and was able to beat off the opposition of the "lily-whites" on the issue. This was his last victory, for the opposition took over the party later that year and he died in 1898.

Though Cuney, the outstanding leader of Texas Negroes, remained outside the third party the Populists did make a notable conversion in John B. Rayner who served as spokesman for Negro Populists from 1894 to 1898. Rayner was born a slave in 1850 in North Carolina and had attended schools in that state after the Civil War. During the 1870's he was elected a sheriff's deputy, and in 1881 he moved to Texas where he served as a teacher and preacher. Though originally a Republican he left the party in the 1890's and joined the third party. At the 1894 state convention he was on the Committee on Platforms and Resolutions and in 1895 and 1896 he served on the executive committee of the Texas People's party. A fearless and capable agitator, he stumped the countryside for the party and "took his life in his hands when he went into certain counties of East Texas." His work was described as "organizing colored Populist clubs, himself, and directing the work of a corps of colored assistants. Up and down the state he roamed, to the uttermost limits of the negro empire, preaching always the doctrine of Populism, with special reference to the hope which it held for the colored man." [15]

In the 1896 campaign, Rayner as a member of the state committee, addressed meetings in seventeen counties. In addition, he wrote two lengthy articles, one titled "Political Imbroglio in Texas," and a later one on "Modern Political Methods." In the latter article he gave this advice to the Populists:

> We must manoeuver to get our recruits from the Negro race, and how to do this should tax our power of research and political ingenuity. Now, if you want the Negro to vote a straight people's party ticket you must put men on the precinct or county tickets whom he likes. Kind words and just treament go further with the Negro than money or promises.[16]

The party seemed to take this advice to heart and its 1896 platform, "We are in favor of equal justice and protection under the law to all citizens, without reference to race, color, or nationality." [17] At the national convention that year the Texans were staunch middle-roaders and opposed fusion with the Democrats, warning that such a move would lead to the ruin of the party. The state ticket bid openly for power when it fused with the Republicans who threw their support to the People's party candidate for Governor. In a hotly contested race marked by violence and fraud on the part of the Democrats, the fusion ticket lost but polled 238,000 votes to 298,000 for the Democrats. The defeat marked the virtual death of Populism in Texas. A small portion of the party joined the newly organized Socialists, most of the whites were absorbed by the Democrats, and a handful of the stalwarts remained with the Populists. Negro third party men had nowhere to turn since the Republican state organization was now firmly "lily-white." Rayner continued to work with the Populists and addressed meetings in nineteen counties in 1898. However, he seems to have dropped out of the party at about the turn of the century. His next appearance in Texas life was in 1905 when he turned to newspaper writing and Negro educational work. He eventually returned to the Republican party though he did work for the election of the former Populist Joseph Eagle when the latter was a successful Democratic candidate for Congress in 1912.

The appeal to the Negro and the appearance of Negroes in prominent posts in the third party resulted in a change of tone by Southern editors who had heretofore been prone to regard Populism as an essentially Western innovation. In Georgia the *Atlanta Constitution* had viewed the

third party complacently in early 1891, but the headway made by the Populists led to a startling change of attitude before the year ended. When
President Polk of the Southern Alliance appeared with General Weaver,
"Sockless" Jerry Simpson, and others at an Atlanta Alliance rally in July,
1891, the press bitterly attacked the third party moves. By August the Atlanta *Journal* was fulminating against the "trio of communists and south
haters" — Messrs. Lease, Simpson, and Weaver.[18]

As the 1892 election drew closer the Georgia press became nearly
hysterical in its efforts to turn back the new movement, the consequences of
which had been so completely overlooked the year before. When a long time
Democrat, Seaborn Wright, was offered the Populist nomination for Congress in the 7th District, the *Atlanta Constitution* warned editorially: "Don't
do it, Mr. Wright. For," concluded the editor, "to accept the nomination of
a party which is blatantly opposed to democracy, and which has for its purpose the division of the white vote will be to place himself outside the democratic organization. Don't do it, Mr. Wright. Don't!" [19]

The overwrought tones of the editor were justified for in that critical period of Georgia history it must have seemed to the old line political
bosses that their house was being blown apart by the Populist gale. The
Georgia Alliance had been captured for the third party by young Tom
Watson, and the threat of the new party was a grim reality. In their battle
against this insurgency the Democrats fired all their volleys and warned that
a Populist victory would bring Negro supremacy, race mongrelism, and the
destruction of the Saxon womanhood of wives and daughters.

The reason for such an unbridled appeal to race hate is not difficult
to ascertain. In a word, it was the strenuous and successful effort of the Watson forces to unite the Negro vote with that of the poor white. Typical of
Watson's approach was a speech he made to Negroes of his district during
the 1892 campaign:

> I want you colored citizens to draw near that you may hear what I
> have got to say for I have something to say to you especially. . . . It is a
> well known fact that when I ran for the legislature in 1882, the black
> people supported me almost to a man. . . . I was hounded down and
> abused because I stood up at the courthouse and thanked you for giving
> me your support. I said that I could see no reason why, because a man
> was colored, he should not have his say as to who was the representative
> from McDuffie county as well as the proudest white man. Now I want to
> say another thing to you and what I say to you I want to say in public
> in the blaze of day. I pledge you my word and honor that if you stand up
> for your rights and for your manhood, if you stand shoulder to shoulder
> with us in this fight, you shall have fair play and fair treatment as men
> and as citizens, irrespective of your color. (Great cheering) . . . My

friends, this campaign will decide whether or not your people and ours can daily meet in harmony, and work for law, and order, and morality, and wipe out the color line and put every man on his citizenship irrespective of color.

This daring and outspoken appeal for the Negro vote was reinforced by Watson's speeches to white audiences where he would "pledge the white listeners to defend the Negro's constitutional rights, making them hold up their hands and promise." These efforts to secure Negro-white unity were carried through to the lowest levels of the party and on one occasion, in Greene County, the local Populists placed five Negroes on the campaign committee, an act that brought much comment and criticism.[20]

The vigor with which the Georgia third party undertook to win the Negro vote may have cost them some white votes, but this did not deter them from their task. The 1892 campaign brought high hope of success. When General Weaver spoke at Waycross, Georgia, "300 people, many of them negroes, were gathered." [21] In the fiercely contested struggle for the 10th District Congressional seat, Watson's stirring appeals won him the support of Anton Graves, Negro secretary of the state Republican organization. Additional support came from a Negro who had once been an opponent of Watson's, a Republican named Anthony Wilson.

In 1882 Wilson had contested the election of a Democratic opponent to the Assembly from Camden County. He won the seat over the opposition of Tom Watson, then a fledgling Assemblyman. Despite this earlier dispute, Wilson came forward in 1892 to rally the Negro vote for Watson. He was a man of considerable influence in the Negro community and this was recognized by the hostile *Atlanta Constitution* which tried to smear him by asserting, "Anthony Wilson's presence on the stump with Watson, while it created a hurrah among the negroes at first, is proving a boomerang. The negroes have conceived the idea that he is speaking for a consideration." [22]

The courageous stand taken by Watson won him active support from many Negroes including the Reverend H. S. Doyle, a Negro preacher of outstanding ability and incredible courage. In the 1892 campaign he delivered sixty-three speeches in Watson's behalf despite many attempts on his life. On one occasion he was forced to flee to Watson's home for protection, and Watson sent out a call to his supporters to defend Doyle from threatened lynching. The response was such that "all that day and the next night farmers continued to assemble until 'fully two thousand' Populists crowded the village — arms stacked on Watson's veranda. The farmers remained on guard for two nights." [23]

The spectacle of masses of "wool hat boys" rallying to the defense of a Negro was truly suggestive of the revolution taking place in Georgia life, but the old line politicians knew how to save the day. Reckless and unfounded charges of "Negro domination" whipped doubting whites into line; outright fraud at the polls secured dubious majorities; and force and violence removed "notorious" Negroes to such an extent that it was estimated at least fifteen Negroes were killed by Democrats in the 1892 election. The result of such activity was the victory of the Democrats by a 70,000 vote majority in the October state elections and the defeat of Watson in the November polling.

Failure to win did not diminish the enthusiasm of the state Populists who now began to gear their work toward the 1894 elections. Once again they appealed to the Negro voter and this time it would seem they achieved considerable success. It is strange that the 1894 election in Georgia has not received fuller attention to date, for there is little question that the results demonstrated the outstanding success of Populist tactics. The *Atlanta Constitution* devoted nearly a full page in its October 4 and 5 issues to the results and in nearly every county carried by the Populists it was reported that the victory was the result of Negro votes. Even if one allows for the efforts of the dominant party to portray the third party as the "Negro party" is must be stated that the reports reflect a strong measure of Negro support for the party.

Reporters in Upson County declared that the rise in Populist votes was "due to the work the third party people have done among the negroes." In Butts County it was declared, "The Negroes voted solidly for the populist candidate." Pike County reported, "Three-fifths of the third party vote was negroes. For some reason not known the populists have been able to do much better with negroes than was counted on."

The next day the paper reported in its headline, "The Negroes Voted Solidly with the Third Party," and gloomily added that the Democratic victory had been achieved by the vastly reduced majority of thirty thousand. In an effort at explanation it asserted, "The chief populist gains are due to negro accessions." Typical of the comments from counties carried by the Populists were these:

> Ware County — "A great surprise to many persons was the solid support of populism by the negroes."
> Laurens County — "The negroes voted with the populists largely and secured a populist victory."
> Gwinnett County — "Negroes carried Gwinnett. They held the balance of power and voted with the Populists."
> Putnam County — "Perhaps three-fourths of the third party votes were cast by negroes." [24]

Despite the appreciable gain in Populist voting strength Watson failed to win the Congressional seat, but this time the frauds were so obvious that his opponent felt honor bound to resign and run again in a new election. Though Watson was again defeated in the special election, the menace of the Populist vote led the Democratic majority in the legislature to set up a new registration law in December, 1894, which established district committees on which the Democrats outvoted the Populists two to one. The committees regulated registration and ensured Democratic control of that important phase of the elective franchise, a vital factor in enabling them to "count out" the Negro vote.

In 1896 the Democrats did not have to repeat such crudities as awarding a candidate a majority of 13,780 in a district of 11,240 voters! With the registration machinery firmly in their hands and with the Populist party split over the fusion with the Bryant forces, the state machine rode roughshod over the third party. After 1896 the Populists were finished as a major force in the state and little remained of that remarkable time in Georgia history which has been best described in Woodward's assertion that "never before or since have the two races in the South come so close together politically." [25]

The vigor with which the third party men had undertaken to win the Negro vote did not mean People's party leaders were free from anti-Negro practices. With the Democrats raising the cry of "Negro lover" against them the Populists sought to deny the charge by establishing themselves as the "white man's party." This was especially true in the early days before the party leadership became fully wakened to the powerful weapon of Negro-white cooperation. In this early period the party leaders made Frederick Douglass their target for abuse. In July, 1892, the *Southern Mercury* quoted the Goldthwait *Advocate* in asking, "Do you forget how Cleveland invited Fred Douglass, the negro, and white wife to receptions in Washington? Negro social equality beats any force bill. . . . Go with the party that does place the negro where he belongs, giving him his rights under law, and nothing more." [26] On September 22, the paper continued its attack on Douglass by referring to him as "the notorious negro with a white wife" and denouncing the Democrats for staying with Cleveland after his cordiality to Douglass.

While the Populists adopted the program of fusion in many states, their outstanding success was achieved in North Carolina. Populism had an early start in that state because of the strong support of the Alliances and the gradual conversion to Populism of Leonidas Polk, editor and president of the Southern Alliance. Though a staunch Democrat all his life, Polk was becoming disillusioned with the chances of reform through that party. In fact, he was being boomed for the Populist nomination for President when his sudden death in 1892 removed what might well have been the greatest political threat to the Democratic "solid South."

The North Carolina People's party was founded in Raleigh on August 16, 1892, at a convention described by the unfriendly Wilmington *Star* as "about equally composed of Republican whites and negroes and disappointed Democrats." [27]

The relatively enlightened attitude of the party toward the Negro was a carry over of the friendly relations begun by the Alliances. In 1891 Polk's newspaper, the *Progressive Farmer,* had underscored Southern Alliance sympathy for the Negro by stating that when it requested more educational facilities in North Carolina "we want it understood that we embrace in this appeal to our General Assembly the negro children of the state." [28] The new party exhibited a similar spirit and the interest of Negroes in the movement was demonstrated when General Weaver spoke in Raleigh during the 1892 campaign. He "was escorted to Brookside Park by 300 white men and fifty negroes, all on horseback." [29] Though Negroes exhibited interest in the movement the Populists did not bid openly for their vote at first. Even so the newly formed party did very well in its debut in 1892, polling 47,000 votes of a total of 274,000 and electing eleven members of the state legislature.

By 1894 the Populists had come to recognize the value of fusion and after toying with the idea of joining the Democrats they set up a joint ticket with the state Republicans. In addition, they courted the vote of reform Democrats by endorsing the Democratic candidate for the state Supreme Court, Walter Clark. Though Clark remained a Democrat he was respected among all sections of the electorate and his views were very close to those of the Populists. The respectability gained by this endorsement plus the coalition effected with the Republicans enabled the fusionists to sweep the legislature.

During the period of fusion control significant reforms were enacted. In addition, hundreds of Negroes were appointed or elected to local offices and the size of the electorate expanded from 278,000 to a total of 330,000 as the restrictive laws of the Democratic regimes were cast aside and election rather than appointment of local officials was made general.

In 1896 the North Carolina Populists achieved the ultimate in political ambidexterity by endorsing Bryan, a Democrat, for President, running a Populist for Governor, and fusing with the Republicans for state offices. This bewildering condition was rivaled by the result of the election which found the Demorcats carrying the state for the Presidency, the Republicans winning the Governorship, and the fusionists triumphant in the state legislature. For the fourth time since the Civil War a Negro, George C. White, was elected from the state to serve in Congress.

The victory of the fusionists roused the Democrats to action to forestall any repetition of the maneuver in 1898. Furnifold M. Simmons, new

Democratic leader of the state, undertook a vigorous campaign aimed at splitting the alliance between Populist and Republicans. Sounding the tocsin of "white supremacy" he proceeded energetically to rally the Democratic party to the task of driving the Negro out of politics. In this battle no holds were barred and even a representative of genteel Southern womanhood might write, "It is time for the shotgun to play a part, and an active one, in the elections." Southern chivalry saw nothing shocking in the added assertion, "We applaud to the echo your determination that our old heroic river shall be choked with the bodies of our enemies white and black, but what the state shall be redeemed." [30]

The press was virtually unanimous in denouncing the fusionists and young Josephus Daniels converted his *News and Observer* into a veritable hate sheet, publishing reckless charges of "Negro domination" and inciting the white population against the Negroes. The much vaunted dislike for "outsiders" by the local population was overlooked and "Pitchfork Ben" Tillman came from South Carolina to give first-hand advice on how to bar the Negro from the polls. In his wake there rose a crop of organizations aping the tactics of the South Carolina Red Shirts.

The result of this activity coupled with the national debacle of Populism in 1896 brought on a split in the fusion ranks in the 1898 election and the Democrats rode to victory. Within forty-eight hours of their triumph the evil seed sown by Simmons, Daniels, Tillman, and their followers bore fruit in the Wilmington riot, a holocaust of death and destruction in which scores of Negroes were beaten and killed by a hate crazed mob. Their purpose accomplished, the Democratic leaders now piously professed shock but withal held to the belief that it was the fault of the "intolerable" conditions of Negro "domination." In far off Dayton, Ohio, a young Negro poet looked askance as the victory of hate and the carnage it had wrought and cried,

> Loud, from the South, Damascan cries
> Fall on our ears, unheeded still.
> No helping powers stir and rise.
> Hate's opiate numbs the nation's will.
> Slumbers the North (while Honor dies!)
> Soothed by the insidious breath of lies.[31]

While the North slept the Democrats pushed through a state constitutional amendment in 1899 that virtually disfranchised the Negro. If the amendment was adopted by methods highly suggestive of wholesale fraud, the means were overlooked in deference to the nobility of the ends served. North Carolina had again been "redeemed." This time the Negro was effectively barred from any future alliance with the poor white by a legislative requirement of a literacy test which acted to keep Negroes from the ballot box.

The collapse of Populism in 1896 put an end to a movement that had every chance of producing a truly emancipated South in which the Negro would have been accorded a respectable position which might in time have broken down hostility and suspicion between Negro and white.

With the smash-up of Populism and the loss of hope of reform through active and aggressive political activity, and with the right to vote suppressed by a vindictive band of demagogues, the direction of Negro leadership became confused. Out of this confusion were created the circumstances that made possible the rise of Booker T. Washington and his philosophy.

Southern Populists and the Negro

ROBERT SAUNDERS

Examining the same question as Abramowitz, Robert Saunders, of Christopher Newport College at the College of William and Mary, comes to conclusions similarly judicious but nonetheless fresh. Any attempt to assess black participation in Populism or the Populist effect on race relations runs head on into the problem of context. Were white Populists more prejudiced or less prejudiced than other whites, and what evidence can be adduced for and against the assumption of Populist liberalism on race? Many historians, including C. Vann Woodward in Origins of the New South *(Baton Rouge: Lousiana State University Press, 1951), have suggested that Populist chances of success suffered greatly because the Democrats were able to appeal to the racial antipathies of potential Populists. Populist attempts to purge themselves of racial equalitarianism make it clear that Populists thought they were being hurt by the Democratic appeal to white supremacy. If Robert Saunders is correct both in believing that there was very little difference between Populist and Democratic racial attitudes and political tactics and in assuming that there was no significant difference in the racial balance of the two parties, one would have to conclude that forces other than racism prevented the white masses from embracing Populism.*

At the opposite extreme, some historians, notably Herbert Shapiro in his essay, "The Populists and the Negro: A Reconsideration," in August Meier and Elliott Rudwick (eds.), The Making of Black America, II (New York: Atheneum, 1969), 27–36, have hinted that perhaps Populists would have fared better at the polls with a more forthrightly equalitarian racial policy. Shapiro rounds up the evidence and demonstrates that though some Populists genuinely sought to ally blacks and poor whites, and though Populist resistance to the vicious race baiting of the Democrats was courageous, Populists were not altogether innocent of racism and in general acted from political expediency. Rather than attacking racism outright, they argued that race was but a camouflage for the real economic issue in which poor blacks and poor whites had a common interest. Even their economic appeal slighted the tenant farmers in favor of small property owners, and most black farmers were tenants. Shapiro's argument that race was the Achilles heel of Populism rests on the assumption that blacks did not respond positively to Populism and would have done so had the Populists addressed themselves to the problems black men faced because they were black. Unfortunately, we have no extensive evidence about the unfettered response of blacks to the Populist appeal, and most black votes in the deep South were probably stolen by the Democrats in any case. The evidence we do have from voting returns in Alabama indicates that outside the Black Belt and urban centers there was no correlation, either positive or negative, between the size of the Populist vote and the percentage of blacks in the population. But this may not be a general pattern. Much more research is needed before historians can say anything with confidence about black attitudes toward Populism. If you were a black tenant farmer in the 1890s, would you have thought Populism worth supporting? How realistic would a Populist demand for racial equality have been in the 1890s?

Shortly after the Virginia gubernatorial election of 1893 John Mitchell, Jr., editor of the Negro newspaper, the Richmond *Planet,* asserted that in the campaign "the colored people were practically ignored by the

From Robert Saunders, "Southern Populists and the Negro, 1893–1895," *Journal of Negro History,* LIV (July, 1969), 240–261. Copyright © by The Association for the Study of Negro Life and History, Inc. Footnotes selectively omitted.

Populists" and that the Populist "platform must furnish strong inducements" or the Negro would stay at home.[1]* In assessing the situation Mitchell assumed that the Virginia Populists would continue to deal with the
Negro vote fundamentally as a separate entity independent of their party
machinery. With the unstated premise, however, that the Populists must
obtain Negro backing in order to be a credible challenge to the Democrats,
Mitchell cited two planes on which the Populists would have to appeal for
Negro support — in their platforms and in their campaigns.

A third level which Mitchell failed to mention, since it was contrary to his belief that the Negro would stay aloof from the People's party,
was Negro representation at Populist conventions. In 1892 the Populist had
relied heavily on token Negro participation at the top of the party machinery to attract the Negro vote. But only in Virginia did the Populists
make any serious plans to bring the Negro into the party on the local level.
In the summer of 1892 the state Populist party committee issued directives
to organize counties by precincts with at least one Negro as a member of
each precinct committee. Soon after the initial instruction, Charles Herbert
Pierson, chairman of the state committee and editor of the *Virginia Sun,*
urged the county chairmen not to cease their efforts until every precinct was
organized. Moreover, he reminded the chairman that each precinct committee "should have one or more colored citizens on it to look after the
colored vote." [2]

It is unlikely, however, that these plans were implemented on any
large scale. By fall, in fact, the Virginia Populists had shifted their strategy
to that of organizing separate Negro clubs. One W. L. Stevens of Orange
county in a letter to the *Virginia Sun* claimed that he had organized a
Negro club of thirty-six members. Stevens' advice to those who wished to
emulate his efforts was to select the most influential Negro in the community, convert him to Populism, and then go from there. In the same issue
Pierson urged Populists to help Negroes organize clubs. This brought Virginia in line with the practice in other Southern states in 1892.

The years 1893 through 1895 saw a continuation of this pattern. As
far as can be determined, in no state did the Populists attempt to resuscitate
the 1892 Virginia experiment of incorporating the Negro into the party
from the bottom up. Virginia Populists, in fact, not only abandoned the
effort to organize the Negro at the grass roots but apparently reduced the
influence of the Negro at state and local conventions in 1893–1894. There is
no evidence of Negro attendance at state Populist conventions or any of the
local conventions, except in the heavily black-populated southside after
1892.

* [See pp. 151–152 for notes to this article. — Ed.]

On the other hand, Georgia Populists increased Negro representation at their state conventions between 1892 and 1894 from two to twenty-four. Based on a similar proportion at the 1895 convention of about twenty-five Negro delegates out of a total of five hundred, the percentage breakdown for Negro representatives in 1894 and 1895 approximates only 5 per cent. An exception to this pattern was the 1894 convention nominating Tom Watson as a candidate for the United States House of Representatives in the tenth district of Georgia. According to the *Augusta Chronicle* as many blacks as whites were present, but other than in Richmond county the *Chronicle* failed to designate specifically who was a Negro. For Richmond county three of the ten delegates were Negroes. Assuming that this ratio held for the other counties in the district, one can estimate that about thirty per cent of the delegates were Negroes. If this estimation is substantially correct Watson's nominating convention represented a high point for Negro participation in the South. In other Southern states the number of Negroes present in any one convention ranged from a token delegation in Texas to a refusal to seat Negroes in Alabama and Mississippi.

On the periphery would best describe the role of the Negro at the various Populist conventions. Making speeches, seconding nominations, and occasional selection for party offices constituted the extent of Negro activity. The substance of power, of course, came only with the holding of office. The usual ploy to invest Negro office holding in the Populist party machinery with only the shadow of power was to make the Negro a delegate for the state-at-large rather than assigning him to a particular district. Undoubtedly this was done to avoid any one area of a state having to fend off Democratic attacks of "Negro domination," but it also served to deprive the Negro officeholder of a power base and thereby made his position meaningless. And even if the state-at-large technique had not been used the smaller number of Negroes selected for office made their importance inconsequential.

"Strong inducements" in the Populist platforms, according to John Mitchell, Jr., would bring out the Negro vote. In 1894 the planks in the Populist platforms that appealed directly to the Negro and that would possibly meet Mitchell's requirements boiled down to reforms in the election laws, the convict lease system, and the schools. Only Georgia Populists had planks pertaining to all these areas, and the intensity and scope of the proposals varied considerably from state to state. Moreover, in some states Populists ignored one or more of these issues. Mississippi Populists, for example, said nothing about election laws that disfranchised a large population of the Negro voters.

By 1894 several southern states had followed Mississippi's lead in restricting the Negro vote. While no state other than Mississippi had adopted a new constitution, a wide variety of laws in Virginia, Tennessee, and Alabama made meaningful Negro participation in the voting process difficult. Virginia Populists, in response to a grossly partisan voting act that put the election machinery firmly in the hands of the Democrats, strongly urged repeal of the law. In Tennessee the Populists deplored the disfranchisement of 50,000 voters through the requirement that poll tax receipts had to be shown to vote. After his 1892 defeat in Alabama, Reuben F. Kolb had called for election reform, but he loudly denounced the Sayre election law adopted in 1894 by Democrats to the grounds that it would simply perpetuate past chicanery.

Uncertainty as to how the Populists would implement election reform left them open to attack. The secret ballot as proposed in the Omaha platform, while by most standards an enlightened measure, had a double-edged character. It would help to eliminate many fraudulent election practices, but it would be also an insurmountable barrier to illiterates voting. Georgia Populists tried to get around this possibility in their secret ballot plan by providing aid to the unlettered. Undoubtedly Negroes remained suspicious of the secret ballot as a reform proposal.

In the final analysis the Populists never came to grips with the problem of election fraud. They harangued the Democrats for their misdeeds and called for general reforms on the state level, but they failed to formulate specific solutions to block Democratic manipulations of the elections. With Democrats in firm control of the Southern states the only possible alternative for the Populists was to turn to the federal government. Yet, the Populists shared with other Southern whites an abhorrence of outside interference in Southern elections. As a result, the Populists acquiesced in the perpetuation of the election frauds in the South that kept them out of power.

Amelioration of the convict lease system presented perhaps a less ambiguous and more attractive issue to Negroes than election reform. Populists in several state platforms condemned the brutal, almost medieval, method of exploiting labor. Tennessee Populists, however, blunted almost entirely their platform's appeal by opposing changes of the system in the legislature in 1892 and by criticizing Democratic issuance of $600,000 in bonds for building a state penitentiary. Elsewhere Democrats neutralized the charges to some extent by censuring the system themselves.

The importance and range of Populist pronouncements on education varied greatly. In Virginia the Populists simply criticized the diversion of funds from education without any suggestions as to how to improve the schools. In Georgia the followers of Tom Watson issued a call for the state to furnish text books. The most specific and far-reaching Populist platform on education was in Texas. Taking a stand that has ironic overtones for today, Texas Populists favored a six month school term for children six to eighteen years old with each race having separate trustees and control of their own schools. With Negro support, the Populists condemned the state legislature for repealing the law establishing separate Negro trustees. Apparently Negroes feared that white control would facilitate the decreasing of funds for Negro schools.

A unique issue raised by Texas Populists concerned state support for mental hospitals. The Populists demanded that Texas maintain "sufficient accommodation for all its insane without discrimination in color." [3] Probably such an arrangement would have upgraded Negro facilities. But the Populists made the provision general enough to avoid taking a firm stand on whether or not the hospitals should be segregated. This was done to placate some important individuals in the party, including Thomas Nugent, who advocated separate asylums for each race.

Frank Burkitt and Mississippi Populists supported Negro schools, but the motivation behind their support is difficult to discern. In the course of the 1895 gubernatorial campaign, Burkitt pledged to the Negroes that if they voted for him he would see that they received a fair share of the school funds. This pledge was in line with the Populist platform which called for free public schools for all regardless of "race, color or condition in life." Burkitt's acceptance speech for the nomination as governor casts doubts, however, upon his attachment to Negro schools. In this speech, the primary importance of Negro schools to Burkitt appears to have been a front line of defense against Democratic attacks on public schools in general. Burkitt accused the Democrats of planning first to destroy Negro schools and then white ones. For that reason he opposed shifting the financing of schools from the state to the county level.

Just how much the Populists reinforced their platform promises through campaigning is difficult to measure. Besides inflationary monetary proposals, the weight of the available evidence shows a concentration on election reform in Virginia, North Carolina, Georgia, and Alabama in 1893–1894. This was especially true in Alabama, where Kolb concerned himself with practically no other issue.

If Democratic reports were true, Georgia Populists sought vigorously in the 1894 campaign to contact Negroes and to obtain pledges of support. One source contended that the Populists made a house-to-house canvas for the Negro vote by "going to their homes and sitting up at night in convention on terms of equality with them, all for the sake of their votes. . . ." [4] Whether any other Southern Populists were as energetic and bold in attempting to reach the Negro vote is doubtful. It is perhaps significant that even in Georgia the Populists denied fusing with the Republicans and pointed out that they had not adopted a single plank of the Republican party.

On the issues of schools and the convict leave system, it appears unlikely that the Populists strengthened their appeal to Negroes significantly
in the campaigns. A passing condemnation of the convict lease system usually comprised the extent of Populist oratory on the subject. Concerning
schools, the Populists found it expedient to continue the 1892 attacks on
Cleveland for instituting racially mixed schools while he was governor of
New York. In an elaboration of the Populist position in mid-1894, Watson
argued that it was inappropriate to have teachers teaching students not of
their own race; he called for giving Negroes their fair share of schools, but
to themselves.

In seeking to gain the Negro vote, issues confronted the Populists
that were of more importance to the Negro than the issues recognized in the
Populist platforms. Arising spontaneously and bringing to light attitudes
not carefully hammered-out at political conventions, the non-platform issues
frequently went to the core of traditional black-white mores in the South.
In such areas as lynching and jury service, historians today credit the Populists with uniquely enlightened views for the time. It will be the purpose of
the next few pages to reexamine Populists' attitudes not only on lynching
and jury service but on a wide spectrum of issues ranging from equal protection before the laws to Negro rights on public transportation. Perhaps in
this way it can be determined whether in fact the Populists deserve their
present day reputation for racial liberalism.

It would be historically misleading to chastise the Populists for fail-
ing to adhere to mid-twentieth century racial standards. For this reason,
Populist efforts to draw a line between legal equality and social equality
should not be surprising. Not only would the advocacy of social equality
have been political suicide, it was also contrary to beliefs the Populists held
in common with other white Southerners. Likewise the Negro, in public at
least, disavowed any intentions to acquire that mystical status. Generally, in
conjunction with the non-social-equality proviso, Populists would state that
they favored legal equality for the Negro.

Obviously, blanket endorsements of legal impartiality for all men
are easier to proclaim than is the implementation of specific measures designed to reach that lofty goal. Consequently, it might be of value to examine the contention that Populists advocated Negro jury service. C. Vann
Woodward's generalization for Populist support of biracial juries rests on
Roscoe C. Martin's study of Texas Populism. Martin's evidence in turn re-
lies on a citation from the *Galveston Daily News*, October 19, 1894 of Negroes being called for jury service in Nacogdoches County, Texas. Martin,
however, failed to consult the *Dallas Morning News* which carried two
illuminating stories on the political situation in Nacogdoches County. In
the first article the *Morning News* reported that the Populists in 1892 had

captured control of the county, but in the coming election the Negro held the balance of power. The Populist sheriff, A. J. Spradley, in response to Negro pressure, summoned five Negroes along with whites to fill the jury. The chairman of the Democratic committee in the county stated the position of his party as being "utterly and unqualifiedly" opposed to jury duty for Negroes and called on his Populist counterpart to make his views known.[5]

A short time later the *Dallas Morning News* published a letter from Sheriff Spradley which puts the Populist position in a slightly different light. According to Spradley, the Democrats had informed the Negroes that the Democratic party had passed a law allowing Negroes on juries, but this had not been done in fact because the Negro had never requested it and because the Democrats in Nacogdoches had found out about the law when they were no longer in power. Nevertheless, the Democrats gave the Negroes the impression that if they were in power the Negro would be called to serve on juries. Therefore, to test the sincerity of the Democrats, Spradley called "five, educated, sober, well-qualified" Negroes for a jury panel of thirty-six; accordingly, the Democrats by their reaction had shown their true colors.[6]

The ambiguity of the Populist position can be further illustrated by what was essentially a shoe-on-the-other-foot situation as compared to the Nacogdoches episode. In the closing days of the 1894 election for the United States House of Representatives seat in the tenth district of Georgia between Tom Watson and James C. C. Black, Watson's *People's Party Paper* published a reprint with the headline "How Mr. Black begs for Negro Votes" of a circular distributed by the Black supporters to Negroes. According to the *People's Party Paper,* "Many a democrat who has heretofore held an exalted opinion [of] Mr. Black will read this circular with amazement and disgust."[7] Among the reasons for "amazement and disgust" was Black's contention that in the counties the Populists had controlled for two years not one Negro had served on a jury. On the other hand, Black asserted that in Richmond county where he lived Negroes were placed on juries. In answer to Black, the *People's Party Paper* retorted that "no such bid for votes has ever been made by the Populists, nor any of their candidates."[8]

Strictly speaking, Black had not promised to place Negroes on juries; he simply endorsed an existing practice in Richmond county by not being critical of Negroes on juries. Nevertheless, Watson interpreted Black's position as "promising to put the negroes in the jury boxes," and he continued to hammer away at Black's appeals to the Negro.[9]

In sum, the available evidence fails to show a discernible distinction between Populist and Democratic attitudes concerning Negro jury service.

If anything, James C. C. Black put forth a more positive stand than any Populist.

In the early 1890's, many Negroes accused of crimes were fortunate indeed if their case ever got to a jury. In five southern states alone, between 1889–1894, nearly 300 Negroes were lynched. Once again the Populists have been credited with uniquely liberal views on a question which the evidence fails to support. Prior to 1896 no Populist platform condemned lynching. Although general Populist indictments of lynching can easily be cited, the same can be done from Democratic sources. To speak out against a specific lynching, in the face of an inflamed public opinion, demanded much courage. In such cases the Populists failed utterly to exhibit any uniqueness of attitude in the early 1890's.

Oftentimes the rule "silence-equals-consent" speaks volumes for the Populists. At the height of the Virginia gubernatorial election of 1893, an accused Negro rapist was "hanged, Riddled with Bullets, and Afterwards Burned" by a Roanoke mob.[10] The victim was not obtained from the authorities without an effort, however. Altogether some eight people died from shots of the Roanoke militia. The resistance to the hanging so inflamed the lynch mob that the mayor felt disposed to flee the city. Neither at this time nor a few days later when a wave of revulsion swept through the state against the episode is there any record of Populists deploring the lynching. In fact, the only group on record in Virginia at this time with an anti-lynching stand is a number of what the Richmond *Dispatch* labeled "prominent" lawyers who took such a position in articles on the deficiencies of Virginia law.[11]

In a specific case in which the Populists are on record, their two-time nominee for governor in Texas, Thomas L. Nugent, refused to support fully strong anti-lynching measures proposed by the incumbent Democratic governor, James S. Hogg. In reaction to the brutal lynching of Henry Smith at Paris, Texas, in early 1893, Hogg condemned public lynchings. He argued that innocent men had been lynched in the past, and he suggested legislation designed to strike at the root causes for lynching. In contrast, Nugent's stand was quite mild. Nugent took a humane, non-agitated approach and deplored the argument that a barbarous crime justified such retribution; at the same time he refused to censure the people who lynched Smith on the grounds that they were so wrought up that they were not responsible for their actions. Nugent took a similar view toward Hogg's proposals to the legislature. They were "creditable to his humanity," Nugent asserted, although "extreme." [12]

Populists in Texas and elsewhere in the South echoed Nugent's approach — displeasure over mob violence with no concrete proposals to abolish or to ameliorate the practice. Jerome Kearby, a prominent Populist in Texas, denounced mob violence when commenting on the Hogg anti-lynching proposals, but he stated that if he were on the jury trying Smith lynchers he would not vote to convict them. To the *Southern Mercury* the solution of the lynching problem lay in prompt execution of the laws, which put the *Mercury* in line with Democratic newspapers such as the *Atlanta Constitution* and the Dallas *Morning News* which offered similar suggestions.

The most persistent and vocal critic of lynching in general was Tom Watson. Yet Watson, like other Southern Populists, failed to single out a particular lynching or to offer constructive methods to combat it. He took no stand on the Smith lynching for example.

An issue that had become almost a dead-letter in most Southern states by the time the Populist Party emerged was segregation on public transportation. Nearly all the Southern legislatures had adopted Jim Crow laws in the late 1880's or in 1890–91. The Populists apparently fully sympathized with the legislation. The Georgia Populists in 1894 nominated for Congress in the 11th district S. W. Johnson, a former member of the state legislature from Appling County in 1890–1891. Johnson had introduced a bill requiring railroads to provide separate but equal facilities for the races. The object of the law, according to Watson's *People's Party Paper,* was to "prevent race riots" and to protect Negroes from "insults, etc., by rough, card playing, drunkenness, etc., in cars provided for the colored people." On these grounds the *People's Party Paper* supported the proposal and stated that "no one can fail to see the propriety and necessity for such a law." [13] The motives of the *People's Party Paper* for this stand are not altogether clear, but they do not appear to stem entirely from racist precepts. True, the *People's Party Paper's* position precluded full integration on all classes of the railroad, yet the desire for change apparently sprang more from a dissatisfaction with the existing practices than a repugnance from contact with the Negro per se.

The clearest illustration of the Populist failure to accept the Negro as an intellectual, moral, or political equal is shown in the contempt and lack of appreciation for Negro leaders like Frederick Douglass and Booker T. Washington. Populists had long sniped at Cleveland's social invitations to Douglass in the 1880's. The attack of Josephus Daniels, however, on the Fusionist legislature in North Carolina early in 1895 for allegedly adjourning in respect to the death of Douglass, set the Populists off on a number of vituperative assaults against the deceased Negro leader. The major goal of the Populists was to neutralize the Democratic charges. But in choosing to retaliate in kind the Populists exhibited an utter lack of respect for Douglass and sowed the seeds of racial hatred.

Shortly before Daniels launched his bombardment against the North

Carolina legislature, Marion Butler, who would be one of the chief beneficiaries of the Fusionist triumph, had been the epitome of racial moderation. According to Butler, the Negro was "entitled to the dignities and honors of citizenship." [14] With the publishing of Daniels' stories and their strong impact, Butler shifted abruptly in late March, 1895. Butler outlined, in a frantic article entitled "Committed to Miscegenation" that took up almost the entire paper, the details of how Frederick Douglass and his white wife had been invited to social events at the White House during Cleveland's first administration. The obvious point of Butler's none-too-subtle argument was that in fact the Democrats rather than the Populists favored social equality, miscegenation, and all the other bugbears of Southern race relations.

Similarly the fanfare around Booker T. Washington's famous Atlanta Exposition speech in September 1895 elicited a disparaging tone of disrespect from Populist journals. The *People's Party Paper* after explaining that Republicans had opened with addresses declared "and then came a full-blooded negro professor [sic] Booker T. Washington, and *he* made an address: — and according to that worthy organ of truth, the *Atlanta Constitution,* the negro made the most notable speech of the day!" Despite the mocking description of Washington's role at Atlanta, Watson grasped the substance of Washington's speech as a defense of his 1892 position. According to Watson, Washington announced "the same opinions as to the Negro question which we were hounded down for uttering in 1892." [15]

The Populists had never been immune from using the racial issue for partisan purposes. In the presidential campaign of 1892 they stepped up Negro-related stories as the elections neared. After the 1892 elections the Populists resorted to a relatively innocuous chastisement of Cleveland for appointing a Negro diplomat to Bolivia, a white man's country according to the Populists. Watson argued that Cleveland favored social equality, which the Populists had always been against.

Early in 1895 the Populists intensified the attacks on Democrats for their alleged violations of Southern racial customs. The credit for the mud slinging on both sides belongs in large measure to Josephus Daniels for his demagogic stories on the North Carolina legislature. The Populists for their part not only attempted to turn the Frederick Douglass story against the Democrats, but they also took the initiative in publicizing lurid examples of other Democratic breaches of Southern race practices.

The Populists seized upon Virginia Governor Charles O'Ferrall's invitation to a delegation from the Massachusetts legislature that included a Negro. Despite denials by O'Ferrall of any knowledge of a Negro being a member of the group, Tom Watson ridiculed unmercifully the whole episode in the style of the old plantation darkey: O'Ferrall may have been unaware of the Negro, Watson conceded, but he certainly found it out when they "came prancing into the mansion." According to Watson, the Negro's name, Teamoh, was probably picked just after " 'mancipation." Watson, dripping with sarcasm, stated: "Teamoh was there in great shape. He drank with the proudest, ate with the most select, and wiped his distinguished lips with O'Ferrall's napkins just as if he had been at it all his life." [16] Shortly after this when Watson discovered that John Mitchell, Jr., a Richmond Negro, had likewise dined at the Virginia Governor's Mansion, he asserted: "Mitchell saw, ate and drank along with the Massachusetts delegation, the Governor and the Governor's wife, just as natural as if he was a human being, and Governor O'Ferrall hasn't found it out as yet." [17]

Similarly Marion Butler in North Carolina played up the O'Ferrall incident. Butler, like Watson, undoubtedly hoped to divert attention from Josephus Daniels' headlines on Frederick Douglass. After outlining the alleged invitation of two Negroes to the Virginia Capital, Butler concluded with a challenge to the Democrats that showed an acquaintance with John Milton's "Paradise Lost." Butler threw down the gauntlet as follows: "Oh! ye generation of serpents and hypocrites; you who for a pretense make such defamation! Come forth now. Belch out the 'miscegenation' condemnation of your souls. Dismaw the filth of your disapproval. Vomit the spleen of disgust over the land." [18]

Partisanship and the conflict of ideas with the Democrats did not always drive the Populists toward intellectual sterility and demagoguery. At times the Populists dared to question firmly held clichés which justified the Negro as a mud-sill in Southern society. One of the most overpowering of these myths, of course, was the innate inability of the Negro to exercise responsible political leadership as vividly illustrated during the rampant corruption of the Reconstruction era. Marion Butler, early in 1895 before the Frederick Douglass episode, pointed out the weakness in this Southern catechism. Butler reminded his readers that in the late 1860's the Republicans in North Carolina were not the only ones wrong; the Democrats were also involved.

Tom Watson's *People's Party Paper* published a much more detailed critique of standard Reconstruction views than Butler's. The *People's Party Paper* mockingly claimed that Governor R. B. Bullock had been removed from office twenty years ago "by a tax ridden, exasperated and indignant people." But the *People's Party Paper* wondered what the great charges and great burdens were. It pointed out that the tax rate and government expenditures were lower in 1870 than under the Democrats in 1893, that "contrary to the notions of the average Democrat" Bullock had left a surplus in the treasury, and that Bullock had never been tried for all the crimes he was accused of and in fact still lived in Georgia. The *People's Party Pa-*

per concluded that in reality "Bullock taxed the people only about enough to raise sufficient funds to run the government." [19]

On occasions, the rays of intellectual honesty were accompanied with political moderation. In several closely contested areas in the South the campaigns of 1893–94, the potentiality of the Negro vote as a balance of power induced both the Populists and the Democrats to treat the Negroes humanely and to hold out the possibility of significant political concessions. Rather than inaugurating an orgy of intimidation and violence, the Democrats either matched or went beyond the Populists in appealing to the Negro. On the other hand, the Populists deserve the credit for providing the stimuli that forced the Democrats to conduct racially moderate campaigns.

Georgia and Alabama are the best examples in the 1894 campaigns of the healthy impact of the vying for Negro votes on Southern politics. In Georgia, as pointed out previously, J. C. Black challenged the Populist monopolization of the Negro vote with an outspoken stand on Negro jury service. But Black expanded his appeal beyond this one issue. He pointed out to Negroes that he had voted for free silver to increase the money in circulation to benefit the "colored farmers and laborers," for free wool to make clothes cheaper, and for free bagging and ties with which Negroes wrapped and bound their cotton. Furthermore, Black contended that he had gotten jobs with the government for the Negro, and that Negro boys and girls in Richmond county were educated "at the expense of the whites for eight months each year not just two or three months," as in many Populist counties.[20]

On the organizational level, Black made some minor efforts to bring a few Negroes into the lower levels of the Democratic party machinery. A permanent Black Club including blacks and whites was formed in the third ward of Augusta. There is no indication that any of the Negroes were elected officers in the club, but a committee of five Negroes was appointed to organize a meeting for Negro voters. Whether the club persisted or whether the Negroes ever played a meaningful role in the club is not known. But Democratic willingness to grant the Negro even a modicum of power is noteworthy.

Watson's counterattack to the attempts of Black to secure at least a portion of the Negro vote presents a curious melange of political opportunism and intellectual realism. Watson sought, as shown above, to alienate whites through exaggerating Black's stand on Negro jury service. On other issues, however, he leveled a devastating critique of Black's recently found friendship for the Negro, and at the same time he argued that in fact the Populists were the true champions of the Negro rights. Watson ridiculed Black's appointment of Negroes to government offices on the grounds that only Negroes from Populist counties were appointed and that Black did not want "his colored friends to know that his appointees swept floors and cleaned spittoons." [21] Watson dared to deny, contrary to Black's assertion, that Negroes were educated at white expense, and he contended that Negroes paid their fair share of school funds. In addition, Watson asserted that no Negroes were on Democratic party committees in the state and that Black had been nominated at a convention without a single Negro present. He, in contrast, had been nominated at a convention where "colored delegates represented the colored race, and helped to choose the candidate they are asked to help elect." [22]

The massive amount of fraud in the 1894 Black-Watson election, which eventually led to a special election in late 1895, left in abeyance the effectiveness of either Black's or Watson's appeal to the Negro. But the unresolved nature of the election put considerable pressure on both candidates to continue the moderate racial approach of the past. Shortly before the 1895 special election, the *Augusta Chronicle* appealed once again to the Negro in Richmond county to support the Democratic cause. Without making any specific promises the *Chronicle* stated the Democrat's case.

> Mr. Black is your fellow citizen, your neighbor, your personal friend, the advocate of your public schools, . . . of equal and perfect justice to your race under the law. . . . He has never been known to do or say a harsh thing of the colored people.
>
> Contrast Richmond County and her people in their bearing toward the colored people and the attitude of Mr. Watson and his Populist counties. Here your race is respected on their civil right. The colored man becomes a teacher, a doctor, a lawyer, a juror, a respected and self-respecting citizen as fast as he develops the intelligence and merit to justify his recognition as such. He encounters less race prejudice in his legal and civil claims than perhaps anywhere in the State.[23]

The *Chronicle* concluded that it would be "ungrateful" of the Negro to vote for the enemies of Augusta, that Watson had never done anything for the Negro's "advancement," and that the Negro should follow Booker T. Washington's advice and support the best Southern whites.[24]

Alabama Democrats failed to equal the racial moderation of Georgia Democrats; but under the stress of a severe political challenge they also adopted a conciliatory tone toward the Negro. One factor in the failure of Alabama Democrats to match the moderate attempts of the Georgia Democrats was the checkered approach of the dissident elements in Alabama to the Negro. The straight-out Populists in Alabama, led by Joseph C. Manning, represented only one faction of the Kolb forces. While Manning favored a strong defense of Negro political rights, Reuben F. Kolb equivocated on a rapprochement with the Negro and from time to time let a strong strain of antipathy for the Negro erupt which made Negroes hesitant to support him. On the other hand, elements within the straight-out Populist ranks had reputations as repressors of Negro rights. Negroes accused Milford W. Howard, who was elected to Congress from the seventh district of Alabama in 1894 as a Populist, of leading mobs in the past to intimidate Negroes who desired to vote.

The most authoritative commitment the Democrats made to Negroes during the 1894 Kolb-Oates campaign for the governorship resulted from a letter published by seventeen Negro ministers in Birmingham. According to the ministers, the Negroes desired equal protection before the law, enforcement of equal and separate accommodations on railroads, equal punishment for criminals of both races, and the opportunity to work where their ability warranted. In reply to the ministers' publication, H. C. Tompkins, chairman of the state Democratic executive committee, contended that while he could not speak for the party as a whole he believed that the Negroes were entitled to those things for which they had asked. Despite the somewhat less than emphatic endorsement of their proposals, the ministers seized upon Tompkins' answer as sufficient to justify endorsing William C. Oates, the Democratic candidate for governor.

The Birmingham *News* endorsed the mild policy toward the Negro. It called for equal justice to blacks and whites and expressed a preference for Negroes to foreigners. The *News* and other Democrats also attacked Kolb for various alleged anti-Negro positions. One prominent Kolb supporter, according to the *News,* denounced Negro voting and favored "shooting every God damned one who goes to the polls to cast his ballot!" [25] For his part, Oates accused the Kolbites of simply desiring to use the Negro vote and warned the Negroes of deteriorating race relations if Kolb were elected. The Democrats also charged the Kolb supporters of firing a Negro teacher who favored Oates.

The failure of Texas Populists to ally formally with the Negro Republicans in the race for Governor decreased considerably the pressure on Democrats to make concessions to the Negro. Nevertheless, the Populists did not write off the Negro vote. They fused with Republicans for some offices in the state; they made use of a Negro speaker, J. B. Rayner; and they placed planks in their platform designed to attract Negro support. This policy accounts in large measure for the corresponding lack of race baiting by Democrats in 1894.

The Populists' efforts in Texas reaped some results. According to Democratic estimates, they polled 35% of the Republican vote in the 1894 elections. But the failure of the Populists to unite with the Republican Party doomed Nugent to defeat. Dallas is an excellent illustration of the impact of the Negro vote on Nugent's fortunes. The Populist candidates for the House of Representatives, Jerome Kearby, received the Negro vote; consequently, he carried Dallas city and county and came within a shade of capturing the district. On the other hand, without Nugent, Negro support, lost the city by 1400 votes, the county by 2300 votes, and the state by 80,0000 votes.

Despite the token representation in party machinery, the minimal concessions in party platforms, the ambiguity of appeals for Negro support, and the deep-seated white supremacy attitude, the tempering of views by both Populists and Democrats, in campaigns where the outcome was in doubt, marked a potentially significant development in Southern history. But the racially moderate atmosphere engendered in a hard fought campaign could survive only with honest elections. Fraudulent elections negated the Negro as a possible balance of power and removed the political necessity for whites to treat the Negro humanely. This was the tragedy of the South in the early 1890's. The whites made the Negro a political eunuch and then blamed him for the corrupt elections that they themselves had spawned. The Populists were unwitting accomplices in the process. In the end they took the easy path out by blaming the Negro for the election chicanery.

THE TEMPER OF POPULISM

The Folklore of Populism

RICHARD HOFSTADTER

Among the critics of Populism, none has been more influential than Richard Hofstadter, former Dewitt Clinton Professor of History at Columbia University. Exposing for analysis the dual image that farmers had of themselves, Hofstadter argues that Populism was an outgrowth of the "soft side" of agricultural existence, the side deriving satisfactions from the moral content of an agrarian myth. The coherence of that myth and its discontinuity with realities are dealt with in the stimulating selection printed here from The Age of Reform, *which was awarded the Pulitzer Prize for history in 1956. Norman Pollack in his essay, "Hofstadter on Populism: A Critique of* The Age of Reform," *in* The Journal of Southern History, XXVI *(November, 1960), 478–500, has criticized the adequacy of the sources consulted by Hofstadter and has questioned the inferences drawn by Hofstadter from those sources. Pollack charges that Hofstadter dismisses Populism as an irrational protest because Populism as a radical movement does not fit into the capitalist consensus that Hofstadter assumes. In assessing these charges the reader should heed Hofstadter's warning: "by 'Populism' I do not mean only the People's (or Populist) Party of the 1890s; for I consider the Populist Party to be merely a heightened expression, at a particular moment of time, of a kind of popular impulse that is endemic in American political culture."*

The most effective response to Hofstadter and such critics as Ferkiss has been that by C. Vann Woodward, "The Populist Heritage and the Intellectual," The Burden of Southern History *(rev. ed.; Baton Rouge: Louisiana State University Press, 1968). Woodward suggests that it would be more accurate to view the retro-*

grade aspects of Populism elucidated by Hofstadter as part of the nineteenth-century provincialism from which Populism sprang rather than as characteristics unique to Populism itself. Woodward also observes that many of the less rational strains in Populism had their counterparts among sophisticated city folk. The primacy of the money question, for instance, was a belief shared by many adherents to the gold standard, and anti-Semitism and nativism flourished in important circles of the eastern elite. Besides, Populists were much more often the victims than the perpetrators of illiberal acts, and Populism was not very strong in those areas of the Midwest that later spawned McCarthyism. Nor does Populism fit the prescription for "status politics." It was a hard times movement and was "obsessively concerned" with economic issues, so that Woodward thinks it is best seen as economic interest politics rather than class or status politics. It may be understandable, writes Woodward, that intellectuals in the 1950s should be suspicious of the masses, but that is no reason to swap one false stereotype for another. Intellectuals, Woodward thinks, should not alienate themselves from "the sources of revolt" even though there may be much to learn from such analyses as Hofstadter makes here.

The American farmer was unusual in the agricultural world in the sense that he was running a mechanized and commercialized agricultural unit of a size far greater than the small proprietary holdings common elsewhere, and yet he was running it as a family enterprise on the assumption that the family could supply not only the necessary capital and managerial talent but also most of the labor. This system, however applicable to the subsistence farm or the small yeoman's farm, was hardly adequate to the conditions of commercial agriculture.[1]* As a businessman, the farmer was appropriately hardheaded; he tried to act upon a cold and realistic strategy of self-interest. As the head of a family, however, the farmer felt that he was investing not only his capital but his hard work and that of his wife and children, that when he risked his farm he risked his home — that he was, in short, a single man running a personal enterprise in a world of impersonal forces. It was from this aspect of his situation — seen in the hazy glow of the agrarian myth — that his political leaders in the 1890's developed their rhetoric and some of their concepts of political action. The farmer's commercial

* [See pp. 153–155 for notes to this article. — Ed.]

position pointed to the usual strategies of the business world: combination, co-operation, pressure politics, lobbying, piecemeal activity directed toward specific goals. But the bathos of the agrarian rhetoric pointed in a different direction: broad political goals, ideological mass politics, third parties, the conquest of the "money power," the united action of all labor, rural and urban. When times were persistently bad, the farmer tended to reject his business role and its failures to withdraw into the role of the injured little yeoman. This made the differences between his situation and that of any other victim of exploitation seem unimportant to him. As a Southern journalist wrote of the situation in the cotton country: "The landowner was so poor and distressed that he forgot that he was a capitalist . . . so weary of hand and sick of spirit that he imagined himself in precisely the same plight as the hired man. . . ." [2]

The American farmer thus had a dual character, and one way of understanding our agrarian movements is to observe which aspect of the farmer's double personality is uppermost at a given time. It is my contention that both the Populist rhetoric and the modern liberal's indulgent view of the farmers' revolt have been derived from the "soft" side of the farmer's existence — that is, from agrarian "radicalism" and agrarian ideology — while most farm organizations since the decline of the Populists have been based primarily upon the "hard" side, upon agricultural improvement, business methods, and pressure politics. Populism itself had a hard side, especially in the early days of the Farmers' Alliance and the Populist Party, but this became less and less important as the depression of the nineties deepened and other issues were dropped in favor of the silver panacea. . . .

There is indeed much that is good and usable in our Populist past. While the Populist tradition had defects that have been too much neglected, it does not follow that the virtues claimed for it are all fictitious. Populism was the first modern political movement of practical importance in the United States to insist that the federal government has some responsibility for the common weal; indeed, it was the first such movement to attack seriously the problems created by industrialism. The complaints and demands and prophetic denunciations of the Populists stirred the latent liberalism in many Americans and startled many conservatives into a new flexibility. Most of the "radical" reforms in the Populist program proved in later years to be either harmless or useful. In at least one important area of American life a few Populist leaders in the South attempted something profoundly radical and humane — to build a popular movement that would cut across the old barriers of race — until persistent use of the Negro bogy distracted their following. To discuss the broad ideology of the Populist does them some injustice, for it was in their concrete programs that they added most constructively to our political life, and in their more general picture of the world that they were most credulous and vulnerable. Moreover, any account of the fallibility of Populist thinking that does not acknowledge the stress and suffering out of which that thinking emerged will be seriously remiss. But anyone who enlarges our portrait of the Populist tradition is likely to bring out some unseen blemishes. In the books that have been written about the Populist movement, only passing mention has been made of its significant provincialism; little has been said of its relations with nativism and nationalism; nothing has been said of its tincture of anti-Semitism.

The Populist impulse expressed itself in a set of notions that represent what I have called the "soft" side of agrarianism. These notions, which appeared with regularity in the political literature, must be examined if we are to re-create for ourselves the Populist spirit. To extract them from the full context of the polemical writings in which they appeared is undoubtedly to oversimplify them; even to name them in any language that comes readily to the historian of ideas is perhaps to suggest that they had a formality and coherence that in reality they clearly lacked. But since it is less feasible to have no labels than to have somewhat too facile ones, we may enumerate the dominant themes in Populist ideology as these: the idea of a golden age; the concept of natural harmonies; the dualistic version of social struggles; the conspiracy theory of history; and the doctrine of the primacy of money. The last of these I will touch upon in connection with the free-silver issue. Here I propose to analyze the others, and to show how they were nurtured by the traditions of the agrarian myth.

The utopia of the Populists was in the past, not the future. According to the agrarian myth, the health of the state was proportionate to the degree to which it was dominated by the agricultural class, and this assumption pointed to the superiority of an earlier age. The Populists looked backward with longing to the lost agrarian Eden, to the republican America of the early years of the nineteenth century in which there were few millionaires and, as they saw it, no beggars, when the laborer had excellent prospects and the farmer had abundance, when statesmen still responded to the mood of the people and there was no such thing as the money power.[3] What they meant — though they did not express themselves in such terms — was that they would like to restore the conditions prevailing before the development of industrialism and the commercialization of agriculture. It should not be surprising that they inherited the traditions of Jacksonian democracy, that they revived the old Jacksonian cry: "Equal Rights for All, Special Privileges for None," or that most of the slogans of 1896 echoed the battle cries of 1836.[4] General James B. Weaver, the Populist candidate for the presidency in 1892, was an old Democrat and Free-Soiler, born during the days of Jackson's battle with the United States Bank, who drifted into the

Greenback movement after a short spell as a Republican, and from there to Populism. His book, *A Call to Action,* published in 1892, drew up an indictment of the business corporation which reads like a Jacksonian polemic. Even in those hopeful early days of the People's Party, Weaver projected no grandiose plans for the future, but lamented the course of recent history, the growth of economic oppression, and the emergence of great contrasts of wealth and poverty, and called upon his readers to do "All in [their] power to arrest the alarming tendencies of our times." [5]

Nature, as the agrarian tradition had it, was beneficent. The United States was abundantly endowed with rich land and rich resources, and the "natural" consequence of such an endowment should be the prosperity of the people. If the people failed to enjoy prosperity, it must be because of a harsh and arbitrary intrusion of human greed and error. "Hard times, then," said one popular writer, "as well as the bankruptcies, enforced idleness, starvation, and the crime, misery, and moral degradation growing out of conditions like the present, being unnatural, not in accordance with, or the result of any natural law, must be attributed to that kind of unwise and pernicious legislation which history proves to have produced similar results in all ages of the world. It is the mission of the age to correct these errors in human legislation, to adopt and establish policies and systems, in accord with, rather than in opposition to divine law." [6] In assuming a lush natural order whose workings were being deranged by human laws, Populist writers were again drawing on the Jacksonian tradition, whose spokesmen also had pleaded for a proper obedience to "natural" laws as a prerequisite of social justice. [7]

Somewhat akin to the notion of the beneficence of nature was the idea of a natural harmony of interests among the productive classes. To the Populist mind there was no fundamental conflict between the farmer and the worker, between the toiling people and the small businessman. While there might be corrupt individuals in any group, the underlying interests of the productive majority were the same; predatory behavior existed only because it was initiated and underwritten by a small parasitic minority in the highest places of power. As opposed to the idea that society consists of a number of different and frequently clashing interests — the social pluralism expressed, for instance, by Madison in the *Federalist* — the Populists adhered, less formally to be sure, but quite persistently, to a kind of social dualism: although they knew perfectly well that society was composed of a number of classes, for all practical purposes only one simple division need be considered. There were two nations. "It is a struggle," said Sockless Jerry Simpson, "between the robbers and the robbed." [8] "There are but two sides in the conflict that is being waged in this country today," declared a Populist manifesto. "On the one side are the allied hosts of monopolies, the

money power, great trusts and railroad corporations, who seek the enactment of laws to benefit them and impoverish the people. On the other are
the farmers, laborers, merchants, and all other people who produce wealth
and bear the burdens of taxation. . . . Between these two there is no middle ground." [9] "On the one side," said Bryan in his famous speech against
the repeal of the Sherman Silver Purchase Act, "stand the corporate interests
of the United States, the moneyed interests, aggregated wealth and capital,
imperious, arrogant, compassionless. . . . On the other side stand an un-
numbered throng, those who gave to the Democratic party a name and for
whom it has assumed to speak." [10] The people versus the interests, the public versus the plutocrats, the toiling multitude versus the money power —
in various phrases this central antagonism was expressed. From this simple
social classification it seemed to follow that once the techniques of misleading the people were exposed, victory over the money power ought to be
easily accomplished, for in sheer numbers the people were overwhelming.
"There is no power on earth that can defeat us," said General Weaver during the optimistic days of the campaign of 1892. "It is a fight between labor
and capital, and labor is in the vast majority." [11]

The problems that faced the Populists assumed a delusive simplic-
ity: the victory over injustice, the solution for all social ills, was concentrated in the crusade against a single, relatively small but immensely strong
interest, the money power. "With the destruction of the money power,"
said Senator Peffer, "the death knell of gambling in grain and other commodities will be sounded; for the business of the worst men on earth will
have been broken up, and the mainstay of the gamblers removed. It will be
an easy matter, after the greater spoilsmen have been shorn of their power,
to clip the wings of the little ones. Once get rid of the men who hold the
country by the throat, the parasites can be easily removed." [12] Since the old
political parties were the primary means by which the people were kept
wandering in the wilderness, the People's Party advocates insisted, only a
new and independent political party could do this essential job.[13] As the
silver question became more prominent and the idea of a third party faded,
the need for a monolithic solution became transmuted into another form:
there was only one *issue* upon which the money power could really be
beaten and this was the money issue. "When we have restored the money
of the Constitution," said Bryan in his Cross of Gold speech, "all other
necessary reforms will be possible; but . . . until this is done there is no
other reform that can be accomplished."

While the conditions of victory were thus made to appear simple,
they did not always appear easy, and it would be misleading to imply that
the tone of Populistic thinking was uniformly optimistic. Often, indeed, a
deep-lying vein of anxiety showed through. The very sharpness of the

struggle, as the Populists experienced it, the alleged absence of compromise solutions and of intermediate groups in the body politic, the brutality and desperation that were imputed to the plutocracy — all these suggested that failure of the people to win the final contest peacefully could result only in total victory for the plutocrats and total extinction of democratic institutions, possibly after a period of bloodshed and anarchy. "We are nearing a serious crisis," declared Weaver. "If the present strained relations between wealth owners and wealth producers continue much longer they will ripen into frightful disaster. This universal discontent must be quickly interpreted and its causes removed." [14] "We meet," said the Populist platform of 1892, "in the midst of a nation brought to the verge of moral, political, and material ruin. Corruption dominates the ballot-box, the Legislatures, the Congress, and touches even the ermine of the bench. The people are demoralized. . . . The newspapers are largely subsidized or muzzled, public opinion silenced, business prostrated, homes covered with mortgages, labor impoverished, and the land concentrating in the hands of the capitalists. The urban workmen are denied the right to organize for self-protection, imported pauperized labor beats down their wages, a hireling standing army, unrecognized by our laws, is established to shoot them down, and they are rapidly degenerating into European conditions. The fruits of the toil of millions are boldly stolen to build up colossal fortunes for a few, unprecedented in the history of mankind; and the possessors of these, in turn, despise the Republic and endanger liberty." Such conditions foreboded "the destruction of civilization, or the establishment of an absolute despotism.". . .

HISTORY AS CONSPIRACY

Both sides of Donnelly's struggle, the Council of governing plutocrats and the Brotherhood of Destruction, are significantly portrayed as secret organizations — this despite the fact that the Brotherhood has millions of members. There was something about the Populist imagination that loved the secret plot and the conspiratorial meeting. There was in fact a widespread Populist idea that all American history since the Civil War could be understood as a sustained conspiracy of the international money power.

The pervasiveness of this way of looking at things may be attributed to the common feeling that farmers and workers were not simply oppressed but oppressed deliberately, consciously, continuously, and with wanton malice by "the interests." It would of course be misleading to imply that the Populists stand alone in thinking of the events of their time as the results of a conspiracy. This kind of thinking frequently occurs when political and social antagonisms are sharp. Certain audiences are especially susceptible to

it — particularly, I believe, those who have attained only a low level of education, whose access to information is poor,[15] and who are so completely
shut out from access to the centers of power that they feel themselves completely deprived of self-defense and subjected to unlimited manipulation by
those who wield power. There are, moreover, certain types of popular movements of dissent that offer special opportunities to agitators with paranoid
tendencies, who are able to make a vocational asset out of their psychic dis-
turbances.[16] Such persons have an opportunity to impose their own style
of thought upon the movements they lead. It would of course be misleading
to imply that there are no such things as conspiracies in history. Anything
that partakes of political strategy may need, for a time at least, an element
of secrecy, and is thus vulnerable to being dubbed conspiratorial. Corruption itself has the character of conspiracy. In this sense the Crédit Mobilier
was a conspiracy, as was the Teapot Dome affair. If we tend to be too con-
descending to the Populists at this point, it may be necessary to remind
ourselves that they had seen so much bribery and corruption, particularly
on the part of the railroads, that they had before them a convincing model
of the management of affairs through conspiratorial behavior. Indeed, what
makes conspiracy theories so widely acceptable is that they usually contain
a germ of truth. But there is a great difference between locating conspiracies
in history and saying that history *is,* in effect, a conspiracy, between singling
out those conspiratorial acts that do on occasion occur and weaving a vast
fabric of social explanation out of nothing but skeins of evil plots. . . .

Nevertheless, when these qualifications have been taken into account, it remains true that Populist thought showed an unusually strong
tendency to account for relatively impersonal events in highly personal
terms. An overwhelming sense of grievance does not find satisfactory expression in impersonal explanations, except among those with a well-de-
veloped tradition of intellectualism. It is the city, after all, that is the home
of intellectual complexity. The farmer lived in isolation from the great
world in which his fate was actually decided. He was accused of being unusually suspicious,[17] and certainly his situation, trying as it was, made thinking in impersonal terms difficult. Perhaps the rural middle-class leaders of
Populism (this was a movement of farmers, but it was not led by farmers)
had more to do than the farmer himself with the cast of Populist thinking.
At any rate, Populist thought often carries one into a world in which the
simple virtues and unmitigated villainies of a rural melodrama have been
projected on a national and even an international scale. In Populist thought
the farmer is not a speculating businessman, victimized by the risk economy
of which he is a part, but rather a wounded yeoman, preyed upon by those
who are alien to the life of folkish virtue. A villain was needed, marked
with the unmistakable stigmata of the villains of melodrama, and the more

remote he was from the familiar scene, the more plausibly his villainies could be exaggerated. . . .

One feature of the Populist conspiracy theory that has been generally overlooked is its frequent link with a kind of rhetorical anti-Semitism. The slight current of anti-Semitism that existed in the United States before the 1890's had been associated with problems of money and credit.[18] During the closing years of the century it grew noticeably.[19] While the jocose and rather heavy-handed anti-Semitism that can be found in Henry Adams's letters of the 1890's shows that this prejudice existed outside Populist literature, it was chiefly Populist writers who expressed that identification of the Jew with the usurer and the "international gold ring" which was the central theme of the American anti-Semitism of the age. The omnipresent symbol of Shylock can hardly be taken in itself as evidence of anti-Semitism, but the frequent references to the House of Rothschild make it clear that for many silverites the Jew was an organic part of the conspiracy theory of history. Coin Harvey's Baron Rothe was clearly meant to be Rothschild; his Rogasner (Ernest Seyd?) was a dark figure out of the coarsest anti-Semitic tradition. "You are very wise in your way," Rogasner is told at the climax of the tale, "the commercial way, inbred through generations. The politic, scheming, devious way, inbred through generations also." [20] One of the cartoons in the effectively illustrated *Coin's Financial School* showed a map of the world dominated by the tentacles of an octopus at the site of the British Isles, labeled: "Rothschilds." [21] In Populist demonology, anti-Semitism and Anglophobia went hand in hand. . . .

It would be easy to misstate the character of Populist anti-Semitism or to exaggerate its intensity. For Populist anti-Semitism was entirely verbal. It was a mode of expression, a rhetorical style, not a tactic or a program. It did not lead to exclusion laws, much less to riots or pogroms. There were, after all, relatively few Jews in the United States in the late 1880's and early 1890's, most of them remote from the areas of Populist strength. It is one thing, however, to say that this prejudice did not go beyond a certain symbolic usage, quite another to say that a people's choice of symbols is of no significance. Populist anti-Semitism does have its importance — chiefly as a symptom of a certain ominous credulity in the Populist mind. It is not too much to say that the Greenback-Populist tradition activated most of what we have of modern popular anti-Semitism in the United States.[22] From Thaddeus Stevens and Coin Harvey to Father Coughlin, and from Brooks and Henry Adams to Ezra Pound, there has been a curiously persistent linkage between anti-Semitism and money and credit obsessions. A full history of modern anti-Semitism in the United States would reveal, I believe, its substantial Populist lineage, but it may be sufficient to point out here that neither the informal connection between Bryan and the Klan in the twenties nor Thomas E. Watson's conduct in the Leo Frank case were altogether fortuitous.[23] And Henry Ford's notorious anti-Semitism of the 1920's, along with his hatred of "Wall Street," were the foibles of a Michigan farm boy who had been liberally exposed to Populist notions.[24]. . .

The Populists distinguished between wars for humanity and wars of conquest. The first of these they considered legitimate, but naturally they had difficulty in discriminating between the two, and they were quite ready to be ballyhooed into a righteous war, as the Cuban situation was to show. During the early nineteenth century popular sentiment in the United States, especially within the democratic camp, had been strong for the republican movements in Europe and Latin America. With the coming of the nineties and the great revulsion against the outside world, the emphasis was somewhat changed; where sympathy with oppressed and revolutionary peoples had been the dominant sentiment in the past, the dominant sentiment now seemed rather to be hatred of their governments.

It is no coincidence, then, that Populism and jingoism grew concurrently in the United States during the 1890's. The rising mood of intolerant nationalism was a nationwide thing, certainly not confined to the regions of Populist strength; but among no stratum of the population was it stronger than among the Populist. Moreover it was on jingoist issues that the Populist and Bryanite sections of the country, with the aid of the yellow press and many political leaders, achieved that rapport with the masses of the cities which they never succeeded in getting on economic issues. Even conservative politicians sensed that, whatever other grounds of harmony were lacking between themselves and the populace of the hinterland, grounds for unity could be found in war. . . .

The situation of the oppressed Cubans was one with which the Populist elements in the country could readily identify themselves, and they added their voice to the general cry throughout the country for an active policy of intervention. After the defeat of Bryan, popular frustration in the silver areas, blocked on domestic issues, seemed to find expression in the Cuban question. Here at last was a point at which the goldbugs could be vanquished. Neither the big business and banking community nor the Cleveland and McKinley administrations had much sympathy with the crusading fever that pervaded the country at large, and there were bitter mutual recriminations between conservative and Populist papers. Wall Street was accused of a characteristic indifference to the interests of humanity; the Populists in return were charged with favoring war as a cover under which they could smuggle in an inflationary policy. One thing seems clear: "most of the leading Congressional backers of intervention in Cuba represented southern and western states where Populism and silver were strongest." [25] And it appears that one of the reasons why McKinley was advised by many influential Republicans to yield to the popular demand for war was the common fear, still meaningful in 1898, that the Democrats would go into the next presidential election with the irresistible slogan of Free Silver and Free Cuba as its battle cry.[26] Jingoism was confined to no class, section, or party; but the Populist areas stood in the vanguard, and their pressure went far to bring about a needless war. When the war was over, the economic and emotional climate in which their movement had grown no longer existed, and their forces were scattered and confused. A majority of them, after favoring war, attempted honorably to spurn the fruits of war by taking up the cause of anti-imperialism. Thomas E. Watson, one of the few Populists who had consistently opposed the war, later insisted that "The Spanish War finished us. The blare of the bugle drowned the voice of the reformer." [27] The cause of reform was, in fact, too resilient to be permanently crushed by a short war; but, for the moment, Free Cuba had displaced Free Silver in public interest, and when reform raised its head again, it had a new face.

As we review these aspects of Populist emotion, an odd parallel obtrudes itself. Where else in American thought during this period do we find this militancy and nationalism, these apocalyptic forebodings and drafts of world-political strategies, this hatred of big businessmen, bankers, and trusts, these fears of immigrants and urban workmen, even this occasional toying with anti-Semitic rhetoric? We find them, curiously enough, most conspicuous among a group of men who are in all obvious respects the antithesis of the Populists. During the late 1880's and the '90's there emerged in the eastern United States a small imperialist elite representing, in general, the same type that had once been Mugwumps, whose spokesmen were such solid and respectable gentlemen as Henry and Brooks Adams, Theodore Roosevelt, Henry Cabot Lodge, John Hay, and Albert J. Beveridge. While the silverites were raging openly and earnestly against the bankers and the Jews, Brooks and Henry Adams were expressing in their sardonic and morosely cynical private correspondence the same feelings, and acknowledging with bemused irony their kinship at this point with the mob. While Populist Congressmen and newspapers called for war with England or Spain, Roosevelt and Lodge did the same, and while Mrs. Lease projected her grandiose schemes of world partition and tropical colonization, men like Roosevelt, Lodge, Beveridge, and Mahan projected more realistic plans for the conquest of markets and the annexation of territory. While Populist readers were pondering over Donnelly's apocalyptic fantasies, Brooks and Henry Adams were also bemoaning the approaching end of their type of civilization, and even the characteristically optimistic T. R. could share at moments in "Brooks Adams' gloomiest anticipations of our gold-ridden, capitalist-bestridden, usurer-mastered future." Not long after Mrs. Lease

wrote that "we need a Napoleon in the industrial world who, by agitation
and education, will lead the people to a realizing sense of their condition
and the remedies," [28] Roosevelt and Brooks Adams talked about the threat
of the eight-hour movement and the danger that the country would be "enslaved" by the organizers of the trusts, and played with the idea that Roosevelt might eventually lead "some great outburst of the emotional classes
which should at least temporarily crush the Economic Man." [29]

     Not only were the gentlemen of this imperialist elite better read and
better fed than the Populists, but they despised them. This strange conver-
gence of unlike social elements on similar ideas has its explanation. I believe, in this: both the imperialist elite and the Populists had been bypassed
and humiliated by the advance of industrialism, and both were rebelling
against the domination of the country by industrial and financial capitalists.
The gentlemen wanted the power and status they felt due them, which had
been taken away from their class and type by the *arriviste* manufacturers
and railroaders and the all-too-potent banking houses. The Populists wanted
a restoration of agrarian profits and popular government. Both elements
found themselves impotent and deprived in an industrial culture and
balked by a common enemy. On innumerable matters they disagreed, but
both were strongly nationalistic, and amid the despairs and anxieties of the
nineties both became ready for war if that would unseat or even embarrass
the moneyed powers, or better still if it would topple the established political structure and open new opportunities for the leaders of disinherited
farmers or for ambitious gentlemen. But if there seems to be in this situation any suggestion of a forerunner or analogue of modern authoritarian
movements, it should by no means be exaggerated. The age was more innocent and more fortunate than ours, and by comparison with the grimmer
realities of the twentieth century many of the events of the nineties take on
a comic-opera quality. What came in the end was only a small war and a
quick victory; when the farmers and the gentlemen finally did coalesce in
politics, they produced only the genial reforms of Progressivism; and the
man on the white horse turned out to be just a graduate of the Harvard
boxing squad, equipped with an immense bag of platitudes, and quite willing to play the democratic game.

The Tolerant Populists

WALTER T. K. NUGENT

Choosing the most Populistic of the western states, Walter T. K. Nugent of Indiana University examined the history of Kansas Populism in order to evaluate Hofstadter's carefully qualified charges. Nugent's conclusions portray a narrowly pragmatic political organization, relatively untouched by irrationalities that might have been induced by the frustrating economic circumstances, and operating well within the realities of power in a parliamentary democracy.

Some historians think Nugent's treatment, despite its manifold virtues, makes the Populists more rational and less radical than they actually were. To evaluate Nugent's explication of the Populist mentality one must analyze it rather subtly. One must wonder whether or not Populists were accepting urbanization and industrialization at the conscious level while continuing to resist it at some subconscious level. If so, this might explain the pragmatic electoral behavior and program existing side by side with a conspiratorial rhetoric that indicates other than goal-directed drives.

It is not unlikely that the Populists were responding to real economic grievances with practical political actions and proposals at one level and at the same time on another plane were acting out their feelings about their experience of loss, the loss of the old dependable world of the cooperative rural neighborhood and the local market. These anxieties must have been closely akin to the anxieties a farmer felt when beginning to farm on his own, "becoming his own man," and leaving the comparative security of his parent's farm. Great energy can be summoned up when events in a person's social life parallel and reinforce events in his personal life, though the mobilization need not be regressive. In pursuing this possibility, the historian must take care not to equate intensity of feeling with degree of rationality.

The foregoing chapters have narrated the story of the Populist movement in Kansas, with special reference to the relations between the Populists and non-American ideas, groups, and persons. Although a sizable

From Walter T. K. Nugent, *The Tolerant Populists: Kansas Populism and Nativism* (The University of Chicago Press, 1963), 231–243. © 1963 by The University of Chicago. All rights reserved. Published 1963. Composed and printed by the University of Chicago Press, Illinois, U.S.A.

body of literature appeared during the 1950's that asserted that the Populists were deeply hostile to things non-American, the Kansas story does not support those assertions. In fact, it supports something more like the opposite of each of the outstanding points of criticism.

The Populists have been accused of nativism, both of a personal kind and of an ideological kind; instead, they were friendlier and more receptive to foreign persons and foreign institutions than the average of their contemporary political opponents. They have been accused of "conspiracy-mindedness"; for them, however, tangible fact quite eclipsed neurotic fiction. They have been accused of anti-Semitism, both personal and ideological; instead they consistently got along well with their Jewish neighbors and consistently refrained from extending their dislike of certain financiers, who happened to be Jews, to Jews in general. They have been accused of chauvinism and jingoism, especially with reference to the Spanish-American War; instead, such lukewarm support as they gave collectively to Cuban intervention was based on quite different grounds, and as a group they strongly opposed the imperialism that the war engendered. Finally, they have been accused of selling out their vaunted reform principles by seeking political fusion with the Democratic party, especially in 1896, and thus of revealing a neurotic instability; but instead, fusion was for them a legitimate means to the accomplishment of real, if limited, reform. In the case of Kansas, the largest of the wheatbelt Populist states, the five principal criticisms of Populism voiced by recent writers not only do not square with the facts, but should be replaced with a viewpoint so much in contrast as to be practically the opposite. Briefly put, this viewpoint is as follows.

Populism in Kansas was a political response to economic distress. From the early days of the Farmers' Alliance, the progenitor of the People's party, to about 1892, relief of economic difficulty was virtually the sole reason for the party's existence; after 1892 this purpose was alloyed to some degree with the desire of the party to perpetuate itself as a political organism. In both periods, however, economic difficulties remained the party's chief reason for being, and relief of them its main objective. Populism called for the enactment of a set of legislative reforms by state and federal governments and accepted the extension of governmental power involved in such enactment. In its most complete and ideal form, the Populist program appeared in the national party platform of 1892, the "Omaha Platform," but this platform bore no more nor less relation to the practical operations of the party than platforms usually do. In Kansas the People's party placed its emphasis consistently on the three questions of land, money, and transportation, which were the issues causing greatest distress in that particular state. Since monetary reform seemed to have the broadest political appeal of all the reforms called for in the Populist program, it received more stress than the rest of the program at the time (1894–97) when the party seemed to have its best chance of succeeding.

As Populism followed the ways of practical party politics in the program that it offered and in the issues it chose to stress, it took a practical approach to its sources of support as well. Economic distress cut across lines of religion, of nationality origins, of race, of previous political affiliation, even of occupation and of wealth and status. To so great an extent was this the case that it is not even accurate to say that the Populists accepted or sought the support of third-party men, Republicans, Democrats, immigrants of many kinds, organized labor, city dwellers, and others, to broaden their agriculturalist base. For these groups were in and of Populism from the beginning. The job of the party leaders was therefore not so much to attract new groups but to be sure that the party program appealed to each of those groups already there and to spread the Populist message to further individual members of the existing coalition, of which the lowest common denominator was a desire for one or more specific economic reforms.

As a result, large numbers of every politically consequential foreign-born group then in Kansas, with the exception of the Mennonites, became active Populists. Party leaders received this support warmly and eagerly, except for one or two occasions: the 1894 state convention and probably the one of 1890. At those times, certain influential leaders supported the non-economic issues of women's suffrage and prohibition so vocally that they led the party to take positions unacceptable to many foreign-born groups. Even here, however, the attitude of these leaders to the foreign-born was one of indifference not of hostility. The fact of the matter seems to be, to judge by statements made by the delegates on the floor of the 1894 convention, that many Populists were simply unconcerned with ethnic groups or foreign matters; they were neither favorable nor hostile, except when they thought they might justifiably appeal to ethnic bloc votes or when they cited examples of enlightened foreign institutions to document their own reform program. To the great majority of Populists, in 1894 and at other times, foreignness and certainly Jewishness were simply not affective categories. For practical political reasons, among others, the Populists expressed themselves favorably toward foreign groups, either abroad or close at hand. This was certainly true of the fusionists; it was true of the non-fusionists except when women's suffrage and prohibition got in the way; it was even true, at times, of the Middle-of-the-Road group, which combined an antibanker (including English, Anglo-Jewish, and Wall Street banker) rhetoric with some benevolence toward immigrants as individuals.

Many leading Populists were in fact first or second generation immigrants. In the 1890's the Populists surpassed the Republicans in the proportion of their state legislators who were foreign-born. Foreign-born Populists abounded among county-level officeholders, county committee-men, precinct workers, and delegates to county, district, and state political conventions. Wherever an ethnic group existed, there existed as well its Populist voters and Populist leaders, with the exception of the Mennonites, who were undeviatingly Republican. The Populists, however, had immi-grant blocs of their own, especially on the frequent occasions of county and state-level fusion with the Democrats. The party organization appealed to foreign-language groups with pamphlets, newspapers, and campaign speak-ers. They presented much the same arguments to their polyglot audience as the party was making to the English-speaking voters. The only difference was in window dressing, such as testimonials from Prince Bismarck and from German political economists in support of silver coinage. At their 1894 state convention, and prior and subsequently in their newspapers, the Populists forthrightly condemned the American Protective Association, the most influential and widespread nativist organization since the Know-Nothings.

On three contemporaneous issues relating directly to immigrants, the Populists took positions that might seem at first glance to have been nativistic, but in each case their attitude to the immigrant was neutral or favorable. When they attacked "alien" landholding, they were attacking landlordism, not the immigrant small landholder. When they called for an end to contract or "pauper labor" immigration, they clearly excepted "worthwhile" or "sturdy" immigrants and based their position on labor competition, not on racism. When their congressmen supported the Lodge-McCall literacy test to restrict immigration, they apparently did so as the only practical way to enact the bill's riders, which would have lessened labor competition, and almost never expressed approval of the philosophy of superior and inferior, desirable or undesirable, races put forward by Lodge and the Immigration Restriction League. In each of these three in-stances the Populists based their actions on reasonable economic grounds, if not especially perceptive or laudable ones. Their aim was to attract the political support of organized labor, of tenant farmers, and very likely of Irish-Americans.

The rhetoric of Populism was highly charged with nationalism, but it was a nineteenth-century kind of nationalism that did not include the nativistic or anti-Semitic characteristics of some twentieth-century right-wing nationalists. Only two foreign groups fell under the censure of any considerable number of Populists. This censure was a consequence of two issues firmly rooted in economic realities and in neither case did they grow out of or were they extended to racial or nativistic antagonism. The two groups were English or Anglo-Jewish financiers and English or Anglo-Irish landlords, respectively responsible in part for money stringency and for large landholding. Many Populists feared that the trend toward tighter money and tighter land would continue unchecked unless these two groups, *and their American or Gentile associates,* were stopped. In both cases the antipathy of the Populists clearly extended to all malevolent financiers, monopolists, and land barons, whether English or American, whether Jew or Gentile, whether native or alien. For the Populists, or many of them, to have laid their troubles at the door of a mixed group of English, Anglo-Jewish, and American capitalists may have been naïve and simplistic, but the point is that the common denominator of their hostility was not nativism or anti-Semitism but distrust and dislike of a truly unsympathetic economic class. In some cases their anti-English attitude transcended this economic base, since the economic problem meshed so well with the rather widespread anti-English attitude shared by many nineteenth-century Americans as part of the American Revolutionary tradition. But the English people escaped the censure placed upon certain financially powerful Englishmen, and Jewish financiers escaped any blame whatever as Jews, although a few of them, as investment bankers, shared the criticisms heaped by the Populists, or rather, some of their more outspoken rhetoricians, upon the wickedness of powerful financial interests in general. This was certainly the case with the terms "Shylock" and "Rothschild," which appeared with some frequency in Populist literature but which were cachets not of Jewish conspiracy but of oppressive finance.

So far did Populist expressions of friendliness to Jews as individuals, in Kansas and elsewhere, to Jews as a group, to English immigrants, to English institutions such as co-operatives and public ownership of utilities, outweigh the expressions that might be construed with effort as Anglophobic or anti-Semitic, and so specious are the grounds upon which the Populists have been accused of Anglophobia, anti-Semitism, or nativism, that these accusations must simply fall without support. There is an exception that proves the rule. A handful of Populists sometimes let their antipathies include "racial characteristics" of these two groups, especially the English, and thereby they evidenced irrationality and prejudice. They were atypical. Many, in fact nearly all, of these Populists were attached to the Middle-of-the-Road Populist splinter group in 1894 and 1896. This group attempted to overthrow the recognized state leadership, whose reform credentials were at least as old and respectable as the dissidents'; it was in all probability subsidized by the Republican state organization; and it received the support of less than 1 per cent of the rank and file at the polls in 1896 and of the Populist press.

In what, then, did their nationalism consist? It is difficult to answer such a question, because to accuse such a pragmatic, anti-intellectual people as these agrarians of having possessed "concepts" or "ideas," much more a "system," is itself a distortion. They did, however, possess felt attitudes that were forced into words to form the rhetoric of their speeches and editorials. Needless to say, the scribes and leaders of Populism came closer than anyone else to expressing these views in logical form, subject, of course, to political exigencies. But it can be assumed that their rhetoric must have been congenial to the rank and file — otherwise they would have been unable to attract and to hold that rank and file. Nonetheless, the rhetoric is undoubtedly more radical, more logically organized, and much more explicit than the views of the mass of the party. In their rhetoric, Populist nationalism consisted of a feeling that the United States was a different *kind* of political society from any that had ever existed before and therefore more worth preserving than any previous one. America was not just another nation-state but an embodiment of certain ideals. It was the embodiment of democratic republicanism: a society where the people rule, where the governed consent to their governors, where the rights of life, liberty, and property are protected because this very protection is the object of their own self-government. It was the embodiment, too, of economic democracy: where resources wanted only honest labor to be translated into the reality of abundance, where opportunity was equal, where the distribution of the nation's wealth was equitable. It was the antithesis of Europe and Europe's corruption, decadence, parasitical upper classes, stagnation, and economic and political oppression. It was a place, in short, where the people rule for themselves and for the protection of their natural rights. Or, at least, so it should have been.

Yet who were the people? The answer is already implied. The people were those who believed in the ideals of democratic republicanism, of economic democracy, and of freedom from European conditions of life. The people were those who actively sought the preservation of those ideals. They were those who labored by their own hands, who had equal opportunities to labor and to accumulate, who used the resources of the United States to produce their own and the nation's wealth. They were those who created wealth rather than those who manipulated wealth already produced. Very often this legitimate wealth-producing activity was defined by the Populists as agricultural and laboring activity; those who farmed or labored were by definition the real people. This corresponded conveniently both to what might roughly be called the Jeffersonian-Jacksonian tradition and to the actual political bases of the People's party's support. Translated into the rhetoric of a political campaign, if often meant emphasizing "the producing classes" or the common bonds of "the farming and laboring people."

The conscious derivation for all of this was the American Revolution, and secondarily, the War of 1812. These struggles successfully created a nation embodying this set of ideals. Such conscious roots made it easy, of course, for some Populists to look upon the machinations of English financiers as a third and final attempt by England to subjugate America. It was primarily through the American Revolution that a nation of, by, and for the people was created and through it that all that was wrong with Europe and Britain was left behind.

Consequently, it was up to the people — often implying the farmers and laborers — to see to it that this nation, this unique society, did not perish from the earth. Who threatened its extinction? Certainly not the refugee from European misery, at least so long as he, too, believed in American republicanism and opportunity. In this unique kind of nation the doors were open to those who wished legitimately to share its benefits. The goods of this nation were not to be shut up inside for the exclusive use of those already there but rather to beckon as to a flourishing haven those who wished to escape the oppression of a decadent Europe. The nation was, in Lincoln's words, a last, best hope of earth. The immigrant was to show his good faith in these ideals by becoming a citizen and remaining permanently (as the Populists' alien land law provided) and by not attempting to destroy the opportunity of individuals already possessing it (as Populist demands for an end to "pauper labor" immigration showed). For an immigrant to take away the job of an American laborer was unnecessary anyway, since opportunity and America were virtually synonymous.

The "worthwhile" or "sturdy" immigrant was not, then, the enemy of American nationality. In fact, he seemed to justify the Populist approach to American nationality — certainly he did in the case of immigrant agricultural colonies in Kansas, which had been very successful — and he was therefore quite welcome. But who then *was* the enemy? To most Populists who thought about the matter beyond their immediate economic distress — and by no means all of them thought through their views of American nationalism with anything like the completeness that this sketch might imply — the enemy lay in certain recently emergent opportunities for malevolence. America was shifting from a predominantly rural and agricultural nation to one predominantly urban and industrial. This shift was in no way evil in itself. Populist spokesmen such as Senators Peffer and Harris had expressly denied any hope of turning back the clock, and if they were not absolutely delighted with a process that seemed to be toppling the farmers and their allies from political and economic predominance (if indeed they had ever possessed it), they were determined to live with such a trend. What is more, they were determined to see that these changes should benefit all the people and not just a few; that they should take place in such ways as to guarantee democratic republicanism and economic democracy. The majority of them therefore accepted industrialization but condemned monopoly, accepted banking and finance but condemned usury and financial sleight of hand, welcomed accumulation but condemned economic feudalism, welcomed enterprise but condemned speculation. It was not industry and urbanism that oppressed them, they thought, but their abuse.

For most Populists these considerations identified the enemy well enough. An appealing program, aimed conveniently at the relief of immediate distress as well as at the placing of new trends within the old ideals, could be constructed without further ado. A rhetoric quickly emerged that concerned itself with attacking landlordism, transportation monopoly, and money shortages, and this rhetoric remained the basic vehicle of Populist ideas from start to finish. In a minority of cases, however, it seemed convenient to personalize the enemy, and in doing so, some Populists passed the bounds of precise statement. At times, American financiers and monopolists such as the Belmonts, Morgans, and Vanderbilts, English financiers such as the Rothschilds, American and English land and mortgage loan companies, and prominent American statesmen such as Sherman, McKinley, and Cleveland, together seemed to form a common and inimical class dedicated to the people's overthrow. Ever since the Civil War this group seemed to have conspired to bring about the economic destruction of the farmers and their allies. This minority of Populists thereby dealt with the money question in terms of a "money power." Yet even they nearly all used the term "conspiracy" in a general sense to mean the common attitudes of an entrenched and powerful minority, and only a tiny proportion meant by the term an explicit conspiratorial agreement, as when they referred to Ernest Seyd and the "Hazzard Circular" of the sixties and seventies. But most Populists did not voice this line, a fact more remarkable if one grants that rhetoric tends to be more radical than the general feeling of its political following. This "conspiracy" was, in addition, a financial one and not a Jewish or English one. To look at a close-knit community of interest and to see in the mind's eye a conspiracy is not necessarily great irrationality but rather a lack of factual knowledge about the competitive methods of late nineteenth-century capitalism. If antibanker, antimonopoly, or anticapitalist statements formed fairly frequent themes in Populist rhetoric, Populists of every hue made it clear that it was usury, irresponsible economic power, and minority rule that they were opposing and not the industrial revolution, urbanism, or capitalism and banking as such. The abuse of new trends, not the trends themselves, had driven them, they felt, from their once uncontested eminence. Now they wanted to regain that eminence and accepted the fact that it could never again be theirs alone. If agrarian class predominance was over and done with, plutocratic class predominance should be scuttled before it progressed any further. Then economic democracy would be reborn.

The Populist view of American nationality, with its stress on democratic republicanism and economic democracy, was therefore intended to be at once majoritarian, individualistic, and humanitarian. That it was a nationalism naïvely humanitarian rather than aggressive appeared very clearly in the Populists' approach to the Cuban insurrection and the Spanish-American War. They sympathized deeply with the insurgent Cubans and viewed their uprising as a struggle for freedom and democracy much like the American uprising of the 1770's. In Kansas this sympathy expressed itself in a moral support for the insurrectionists that sprang from a confident view of their own moral righteousness. Nonetheless, the Populist press and Populist congressmen held back from armed intervention, took a cautious attitude to the blowing up of the *Maine,* restrained themselves from anything more vigorous than sympathetic gestures toward the Cubans in spite of the Spanish "despotism" and "Weylerism" they believed the Cubans to be suffering, and in unison with their Democratic neighbors hoped that war could be avoided. This was very close to the Republican position also. When war came, they supported it as everyone else did, but until then their humanitarian sympathy for the Cubans was checked by the fear that a war beginning with Cuban intervention could only benefit large financial interests. The Kansas Republicans' coolness toward Cuban intervention resulted mainly from the caution that McKinley maintained into April, 1898, and the desire of the Kansas Republicans to support their own administration. The Populists avoided the Republicans' scornful references to Cuban or Spanish racial inferiority and far more frequently than the Republicans took a humanitarian view of the matter. In Kansas the Populists were not violent jingoes. Furthermore, unlike the Republicans in their area, and other people elsewhere, the official Populist position on the question of American imperial expansion for commercial or military purposes, which arose after Dewey's victory in Manila Bay, was to join the Democrats in opposing expansion and in demanding that the United States leave the Philippines and other potential colonies alone. They were interested in the spread of American democratic ideals, in the overthrow of Spanish oppression of Cuba, if this could be done without the commitment of American armed forces, but not at all in American conquest or colonization. Populism in Kansas apparently lost many adherents because of this stand, but it remained the official party position nevertheless.

It is worth noting that Populist opposition to imperialism was much more firmly expressed than Populist sympathy to the Cuban insurrection-

ists, because the Democratic party was also much less firm on the latter question than on the former. As a matter of fact, official Populist rhetoric was
tailored to fit the political exigencies involved in getting along with the
Democrats not only on the war and imperialism issues but on most other
questions as well. Political fusion with the Democrats on all levels marked
Kansas Populism very strongly, and to some writers, fusion has meant that
the Populists lacked any real dedication to the principles they so vigorously
espoused. But the Populist movement chose political means to accomplish
its program of economic reform; it was a political party, not a pressure
group or an ideological front; for better or worse it therefore bound itself
to use partisan methods. If one looks no further than the Omaha platform
of 1892 to find out what Populism stood for and then observes that many
planks in that platform were soft-pedaled in 1892 and later for the sake of
fusion and political success, one might assume that Populist devotion to
reform principles was a sham. But this is a superficial view. Fusion was the
only apparent way to achieve any reforms, any accomplishment of any principles at all, and the degree to which the People's party was willing to fuse
with the Democrats in Kansas was the degree to which it possessed political
common sense. The identification of fusion with dedication to principle,
rather than with a sellout, comes into even greater relief as soon as one re-
calls the shabby story of the Middle-of-the-Road Populists, those self-styled
simon-pure reformers who almost certainly connived at the defeat of the
reform party with the local Republican organization. The prevalence of
fusion sentiment indicates as well the willingness of the Populists to seek out
and accept the support of the foreignborn blocs that ordinarily made their
political home in the Democratic party. It also indicates their pragmatic approach to political action, their willingness to use an obvious means at hand
to achieve legitimate political ends, and their flexibility, which stood in such
contrast to the rigidity of the Middle-of-the-Road Populists.

The political horse sense that provided them with their receptivity
to fusion was a natural outgrowth of the immediacy of the distress from
which their movement sprang. It accounted, too, for the apparent anomaly
of a radical program based on conservative ideals. For the Populists of
Kansas were not a collection of rag-tag calamity howlers, ne'er-do-wells, and
third-party malcontents, as William Allen White and others have suggested
but a large body of people of diverse occupational wealth-holding, and
status levels. As a group they were hardly distinguishable from their Republican neighbors, except for a probably higher mortgage indebtedness, and
their greater degree of political and economic awareness. The great majority
could be called "middle class," and they were interested in preserving what
they considered to be their middleclass American ideals and substance.
These were being threatened, they felt, not by the facts of industrialism and

urbanism but by their existing *shape*. To change that shape, they settled upon the device of a political party.

   Their view of the future was one in which many wrongs would have to be righted, many present trends would have to be redirected to conform to old ideals, for that future to become acceptable. Yet they were confident that this would happen. In several ways they were confused, ill-informed, and behind the times. They were unaware of urban problems, for example, and they never understood that money reform was basically a solution only to agricultural problems, if indeed to them, and not a solution for growing monopoly or for inequities of wealth distribution. Yet if this is true, it is true as well to acquit them of nativism, anti-Semitism, conspiracy-mindedness, jingoism, lack of principle, and of living in some neurotic agrarian dream world. They were bound together not by common neuroses but by common indebtedness, common price squeezes, common democratic and humanitarian ideals, and common wrath at the infringement of them. From this wrath rose the Farmers' Alliance, and from the Alliance their ultimate instrument of protest, the People's party. The Populists were far too concerned with land, money, and transportation, and also, later on, with the mechanics of winning and keeping public office, to have much time to worry about whether their ideals were mythical or their anxieties neurotic. Tight money and foreclosure sales were the products of nobody's imagination. Even in their rhetoric they were too busy preaching positive reforms in a depression to be concerned with racism or anti-Semitism or agrarian Arcadias; and in their practical political activities, they took all the help they could get.

   The Populists were liberal nationalists bringing to radical social changes a radical response. By such means they meant to re-assert what they considered to be the fundamental ideals upon which their society had previously depended — in their view of history — and must continue to depend — in their view of political philosophy. They undertook this task in the Kansas of the 1890's, with its particular kind of social structure, its particular distribution of wealth and income, its specific economic conditions, and its peculiar laws and traditions. These particularities form the limits of historical analogy, and they give no grounds for making the Populists the gawky ancestors of Father Coughlin or of Senator Joseph R. McCarthy. They make it very difficult to call the Populists the descendants of the Jeffersonians and Jacksonians or the precursors of Progressivism or the New Deal, although with these movements the Populists shared a considerable body of ideals. They make it unrealistic even to equate the Kansas Populists with Populists of other regions or other states.

   This particular set of facts, however, allows the Populists of Kansas to be judged on their own grounds. The verdict is very simple. They were people who were seeking the solution of concrete economic distress through the instrumentality of a political party. By this means they would not only help themselves but they would redirect, not reverse, the unsatisfactory trends of their time to correspond with the ideals of the past. This involved profoundly the political co-operation of the foreign-born, and it involved a deep respect and receptivity for non-American institutions and ideas.

Populist Influences on American Fascism

VICTOR C. FERKISS

Everyone should take seriously Richard Hofstadter's warning not to exaggerate the extent to which Populism adumbrated modern authoritarian movements. Victor Ferkiss, a political scientist writing in 1957 when anti-Populist sentiment and evidence was at flood tide, takes this warning to heart, yet he is able to draw thought-provoking parallels between Populism and authoritarian movements. One must be careful to notice the author's definition of fascism and to keep in mind, as Ferkiss does, that historical Populism does not satisfy all elements of that definition. The Populists never advocated the destruction of liberal institutions and procedures, though they did propose to make the political system more responsive to majority will. Construing Populism broadly as the movement of middle-class, debtor farmers for a more favorable monetary policy from the federal government, Ferkiss implies either that Populism was saved from fascism only by its early demise or that Populism became fascistic only in the twentieth century after a prolonged experience with failure. Whether because they lacked power or time, the real Populists were not devotees of authoritarianism. Ferkiss asks why not. Any answer to that question must take into account American politics and the fact that when the disgruntled farmers rummaged around in their past for some old revolutionary clothes, they found, and wore, the garb of the American Revolution and its successors in the Jeffersonian-Jacksonian tradition. Ideology counts, as does historical experience.

The doctrinal roots of American fascist thought have long remained obscure for reasons inherent in recent American history itself. Essentially fascist popular movements grew up in America during the period 1929–41 at a time when American publicists and intellectuals were rediscovering America in their reaction to the growth of fascism and nazism abroad. Increased regard for American tradition among hitherto alienated intellectuals made them reluctant to admit that movements such as those led by Huey Long, Father Coughlin, and Gerald L. K. Smith were not the result of temporary psychological aberrations on the part of the masses but were, instead, the culmination of an ideological development stemming from such generally revered movements as Populism and "agrarian democracy." For them fascism was by definition un-American.

The sentimental quasi-Marxism of many influential writers reinforced this refusal to search for the roots of American fascism in American political history. When not dismissed as exotic imports, fascist ideas were held to be hothouse plants carefully nurtured by domestic capitalists bent on cultivating their own financial gardens while Western civilization was at stake in a death struggle waged by the democratic masses against the new barbarism.

American fascism, however, was a basically indigenous growth. When Anne Morrow Lindbergh spoke of a "Wave of the Future" as American as a New England autumn, she was not so much expressing a hope as enunciating a fact.

Any search for the roots of American fascism must necessarily be preceded by a clear understanding of the essential features of the movement. Few definitions of fascism are without their ardent supporters and violent detractors. Because of space limitations, the definition used herein can only be explicated, not defended.

We hold that the essential elements of fascism in the American context are:

(1) An economic program designed to appeal to a middle class composed largely of farmers and small merchants which feels itself being crushed between big business – and especially big finance – on the one hand, and an industrial working class which tends to question the necessity of the wage system and even of private property itself on the other. Such an economic program will include violent attacks against big business and finance – particularly the latter – and will advocate their control by the government in the interest of the farmer and small merchant.

From Victor C. Ferkiss, "Populist Influences on American Fascism," *Western Political Quarterly*, X:2 (June, 1957), 350–57. Reprinted by permission of the University of Utah, Copyright holder. Footnotes omitted.

(2) Nationalism. International co-operation is held to be a device by means of which supranational conspirators are able to destroy the freedom and well-being of the people. A desire to stay aloof from foreign affairs is the American (and English) fascist substitute for imperialism, and any imperialistic venture undertaken by either of these countries will ordinarily be denounced as a conspiracy engineered by selfish economic interests. Areas or groups with extensive foreign contacts are suspect and are feared as beachheads of the antinational conspiracy, and venom which elsewhere is directed against foreign powers is in America directed against such groups as the Jews. Certain conservative social and religious beliefs are identified as essential parts of the national heritage and attacks on them are considered *de facto* evidence of activity on the part of the conspiracy.

(3) A despair of liberal democratic institutions, resulting from the belief that the press and the other communication media have been captured by the enemy, as have the two major political parties. Political power is held to belong to the people as a whole and is considered to be best exercised through some form of plebiscitary democracy. Leaders with a popular mandate will sweep aside any procedural obstacle to the fulfillment of the popular will, and will purge those institutions which stand in the way of the instantaneous attainment of popular desires. The destruction of liberal institutions such as the press and an independent legislature is not a desired end in itself, but is a necessary means for protecting the nation and effectuating those economic reforms which the popular will demands.

(4) An interpretation of history in which the causal factor is the machinations of international financiers. The American Revolution, the fight of Jackson against the bank, and Lincoln's war against the South and its British allies are all considered episodes in the struggle of the people against the "money power." International finance is held responsible for the "crime of '73," entry into World War I, and the 1929 Depression. Communism is the creation of international finance and a system in which the money power strips off the mask of sham democracy and rules nakedly. A Communist state naturally results when the concentration of economic power in the hands of a few members of the international conspiracy reaches its logical terminus.

The congruence of this body of doctrine with that of the various European fascist movements, especially in the period before they came to power, is virtually complete. The only important differences are the fact that in American (and English) fascism there is virtually no pseudo-mystic exaltation of the State as such, and that nationalism takes the form of isolationism rather than imperialism. In American fascism a strong state is held to be a necessary means rather than an end in itself; it is required in order that the will of the sovereign people may prevail over the conspirators and the corrupted. And, as noted above, nationalism takes the form of isolationism since America needs no foreign empire, and intervention in World War II would be at the behest of those wishing to defend "pluto-democracy" against the rising friends of the people, the fascist powers.

How this creed, on which all the segments of the American fascist movement were in basic agreement, arose logically from the Populist creed, and how the American fascist leaders attracted substantially the same social groups and sectional interests as had Populism is the burden of this paper.

Populism is used herein as a generic term to denote not merely the People's party, or Populism properly so-called, but such closely allied movements as the Greenback party, the Bryan free silver crusades, La Follette Progressivism, and similar manifestations of primarily agrarian revolt against domination by Eastern financial and industrial interests.

The Populist economic program was, of course, tailored to the needs of the farmers of the prairies. The class struggle throughout American history has traditionally been waged not by laborers against employers, but by debtors against creditors. Agrarian discontent had a long history prior to the Civil War. Following that conflict the West was opened to settlers under the Homestead Act. These settlers needed money for capital and were dependent upon the railroads to sell their goods. The value of money appreciated so greatly that they had difficulty in paying their debts. The railroads, controlled by Eastern financial interests, were able to exploit them. The local governments and press were to a considerable extent the creatures of Eastern money, as were most of the local banks. A struggle began for a government which would regulate credit and control the railroads so that the settlers might prosper as middle-class landowners. This struggle reached its climax in Bryan's campaign of 1896 and abated thereafter as a result of the increasing amount of gold in circulation.

ECONOMIC PROGRAM. The motives of these Populists were similar to those which produced the rank-and-file twentieth-century American fascist. The Populists' aim was not the destruction of capitalism as they knew it, but was rather its preservation and extension. They were interested in protecting capitalism and the small entrepreneur from abuse at the hands of the monopolist and the banker. Populism was a middle-class movement; the Populists saw in Eastern finance capitalism a force which, unless controlled, would destroy their status and reduce them to proletarians.

The Populist economic program centered about the need for public control of credit. Senator Peffer of Kansas described the Populist economic creed in the following words:

> If there is any part of the Populist's creed which he regards as more important than another, and which, therefore, may be taken as leading,

it is that which demands the issue and circulation of national money, made by authority of the people for their use, money that they will at any and all times be responsible for, money that persons in business can procure on good security at cost, money handled only by public agencies, thus doing away with all back issues of paper to be used as money.

The extent of Bryan's faith in cheap credit as a panacea is reminiscent of the Chartist faith in universal suffrage as the sovereign remedy for social ills: ". . . When we have restored the money of the Constitution all other necessary reforms will be possible; but . . . until this is done there is no other reform that can be accomplished."

This, then, was the most important plank in the Populist economic platform — the restoration to the people of their "sovereign power" to control money; private control is held to be a violation of the Constitution and a usurpation of a governmental function. In addition, the railroads and similar interests must also be controlled by a strong, central government capable of crushing the selfish few in the interests of the nation as a whole.

> Populists believe in the exercise of national authority in any and every case where the general welfare will be promoted thereby. . . .
>
> Populism teaches the doctrine that the rights and interests of the whole body of the people are superior, and, therefore, paramount to those of individuals. The Populist believes in calling in the power of the people in every case where the public interest requires it or will be promoted.

Public power will protect the national interest against the selfish few.

Though the People's party flirted with the labor theory of value their inferences from it resembled those of Locke rather than those of Marx. Populism was no attack on private property or the wage system. It was the attempt of its adherents to retain the former and avoid becoming subject to the latter; hence Populism's lack of sympathy for and appeal to urban labor. Despite some concessions during the 1896 campaign, Bryan's appeal to the voters, even the Eastern workers, was to put their trust in free silver as the basic solution to all of their difficulties.

NATIONALISM AND ANTI-SEMITISM. Nationalism was to be found in Populism principally in the form of a suspicious isolationism which regarded foreign involvements as inimical to the national interest and as existing solely to promote the interests of Eastern capitalists. Economic nationalism was reflected in Peter Cooper's proposal for protective tariffs, and Populists often advocated severe restrictions on immigration.

The protest against financial interests was frequently associated with a hatred of cities as centers of exploitation and of moral as well as political corruption. Nationalistic impulses cloaked themselves in the garb of sectionalism and Bryan referred to the East as "the enemy's country." Dwight MacDonald has noted that because of the varied national origins of its population, its geographic isolation, and its relatively higher standard of living, the venom of American nationalism will ever be directed against New York City, "which is properly and correctly considered an outpost of Europe on this continent." Populist and, later, fascist nationalism confirms this judgment.

The final ingredient of Populist nationalism was the anti-Semitism endemic throughout the rural West. The correlation between hatred of Jews (though in a mild form and wholly without dialectical formulation) with sentiment for Bryan has been noted by Professor Oscar Handlin. The prairie farmer associated the Jew with the merchant, the financier, and the corrupt and domineering Eastern city.

Populist racial hostility was directed against those believed capable of destroying the small farmer's economic status and way of life. To the Midwesterner, the Negro presented no problem since he was not physically present and since he (unlike the Jew) could hardly be pictured as scheming to undermine the position of Midwestern farmers and shopkeepers from afar. In the South, the situation was more complex. At first white and Negro farmers stood together in a common economic struggle against "the interests." However, it was not too long before the xenophobic feelings to which Populist orators appealed in their attempts to arouse the "red-necks'" opposition to the interests endangered this small-farmer solidarity. Hatred of the different could focus on the black skin of the Negro as well as on the uncalloused hands of the white plantation owner, and the enemies of Populism were not tardy about taking advantage of this fact to divide their foes. Before long such ardent Populist leaders as Senator "Pitchfork Ben" Tillman of South Carolina and Senator Tom Watson of Georgia (earlier a friend of the Negro) became standard-bearers of violent racist doctrines. Eventually hatred of the Negro replaced hatred of the interests as the main subject of demagoguery among Southern poor-whites, and, save in Louisiana which had never experienced a fully developed Populism, the American fascist message of later years fell on ears deafened by the loud cries of the white supremacists.

PLEBISCITARY DEMOCRACY. Populism's predisposition to anti-Semitism and to nationalism and its suspicion of the corruption of urban life are all tendencies opposed to those trends which issue in democratic socialism in the humanist tradition; these proclivities more closely coincide with the patterns of conservative or fascist social beliefs. There is a tendency on the part of observers to overlook the true import of these propensities because of the role played by Populist and Progressive movements in the development of American democracy. To these movements America largely owes, for better or for worse, the direct primary, popular election of senators, the initiative, the referendum and recall, and the Wisconsin tradition of clean, efficient government, conducted with the assistance of experts.

Yet some qualifications must be made of the popular conception of Populism as a democratic or liberal force. First, the agrarian trend toward political reform was rarely based upon any broad ideas about human freedom or the fuller human life. Populist-inspired reforms were instrumental. The farmer wanted particular political changes because he felt they were needed to effect the defeat of the "money power" and to gain for farmers certain direct economic benefits. From their support of these measures we can not infer a willingness on the part of the Populists to support egalitarian measures which would conduce to the benefit of others with different substantive aims.

Secondly, all these reforms serve to strengthen not liberalism but direct, plebiscitary democracy. They are designed to make the will of the majority immediately effective and to sweep away intervening institutions such as the legislatures, the older political parties, and the courts, which have all been corrupted by the money power. The Populist condemnation of the older parties is significant:

> We charge that the controlling influences dominating both these parties have permitted the existing dreadful conclusions to develop without serious effort to prevent or restrain them. Neither do they now promise us any substantial reform. They have agreed together to ignore, in the coming campaign, every issue but one. They propose to drown the outcries of a plundered people with the uproar of a sham battle over the tariff, so that capitalists, corporations, national banks, rings, trusts, watered stock, the demonetization of silver, and the oppressions of the usurers may all be lost sight of. They propose to sacrifice our homes, lives and children in order to secure corruption funds from the millionaires.

If the existing parties are controlled by a gigantic conspiracy and the nation is at the mercy of an "international gold trust" then the trust's opponents cannot be expected to treat these conspirators in quite the fashion one would treat honest dissenters. The rhetoric of "Bloody Bridles" Waite and Mary Ellen Lease is strong even for their times. It bespeaks an unwillingness to compromise, a crusading zeal, and an inability to conceive of a sincerely motivated opposition that ill befits any group participating in parliamentary democracy. So, too, the oft-repeated charge that the press is controlled by special interests, whether true or not, leaves the way open for insuring "true" freedom of the press through the enactment of measures which might endanger freedom of speech as it has traditionally been understood in Anglo-Saxon law.

William Jennings Bryan many years later was to shed light on the devotion of the Populist crusade to liberal institutions when he held that the people in prosecuting Scopes were simply asserting their right "to have what they want in government, including the kind of education they want." The people are the rulers and "a man cannot demand a salary for saying what his employers do not want said."

In short, Populist political thought is compatible in spirit with the plebiscitary democracy of a Huey Long or a Hitler. This is not to say that Populists and Progressives universally opposed free speech as such or that Weaver, Lindbergh, Sr., or the elder La Follette would ever have seized power and then denied to the opposition an opportunity to regain power through constitutional means. They did believe that the opposition, including the press, was corrupt and antisocial; but they still believed that an aroused people could regain control of the government from the selfish few who had usurped it. It is only with the passing of time that Populism degenerates into fascism and comes to believe that the power of the enemy and his ability to corrupt the people is so great that constitutional institutions are a useless sham and that the people can only effectuate their will by modifying these institutions in form or spirit in such a manner as to deny their use to the conspiratorial enemy.

Fear of Man

NORMAN POLLACK

In his intellectual history of midwestern Populism, The Populist Response to Industrial America *(Cambridge: Harvard University Press, 1962), Norman Pollack, of Michigan State University, amassed evidence from Populist writings to support his contention that they put forward a coherent, rational, and radical critque of industrializing America. As one of the first counterrevisionists, Pollack found no evidence to support charges of anti-Semitism, xenophobia, or jingoism. He argues that the attempt by scholars such as Hofstadter and Ferkiss to detect in Populism prefascist intolerance, retrogressive longings, and dangerous majoritarian biases arises from a concern for the viability*

*of liberal parliamentary democracy and from a fundamental
"cynicism and disillusionment over man."*

*Evaluating an argument such as the one Pollack mounts is
very difficult, as it consists of an* assemblage *of ideas and sentiments expressed by many different Populists over a long time.
To come properly to terms with Pollack one must juxtapose his
argument with Nugent's as well as with those of the antagonists
to whom Pollack addresses himself. If Pollack is right about
Populist ideology, then the Populists were engaged in something
much broader than interest-group politics: class politics. The
question for the reader is whether the Populist critique transcended its time and place and whether the Populist outlook com-
prises a radical humanism.*

Ann Lane, in a biting review of Pollack's book in Science and
Society, *XXVIII (Summer, 1964), 326–30, disputes Pollack's attempt to portray the Populists as radicals and calls them instead
"left wing petty-bourgeois egalitarians." As a scholar influenced
by Marxist thought, she particularly objects to his simplistic
equation of Marxism with the Populists' democratic humanism.
Her point is that it takes more to make a Marxist than the labor
theory of value, perceptions of injustice and alienation, and
feelings of oppression.*

*One need not look far in Populist literature to find feelings
of insecurity and oppression, the same feelings through which the
instability of bureaucratic society is made manifest. But even if
we follow Pollack and accept this Weberian analysis, we are left
to wonder about the sources of instability in the nonbureacratic
society in which the Populists lived. The Populist response to
their feelings of insecurity and oppression were not fascistic, but
if we try to explain why not we will better understand Populism.*

Populists sought the establishment of a just social order founded on
a democratized industrial system and a transformation of social values, each
reinforcing the other in the direction of greater concern for the welfare of
all. They rejected unbridled individualism and the competitive mentality,
maintaining instead that neither a few nor a class should enjoy the benefits
of civilization. The quality of life of the masses was the index by which to
measure social improvement. There was little of the self-conscious in the

Presented to the Southern Historical Society in Little Rock in
November, 1964, and printed as "Fear of Man: Populism, Authoritarianism, and the Historian," *Agricultural History,* XXXIX (April,
1965), 59–67. Reprinted by permission of the author.

Populist enshrinement of the common man: Society must be attuned to *his* needs, or it ceases to be democratic. Yet in place of a society suffused with an equalitarian spirit, a society which is responsive to the growth of all and oppresses none, Populists pointed to the mortgage-ridden farmer, the unemployed worker, and the so-called "tramp" moving from one town to the next in search of work. In place of the free citizen, deriving benefit from his labor on the farm or in the factory, determining the policies under which he is to be governed, and enjoying a sense of dignity in his daily life, Populists found man to be impoverished, voiceless and degraded. Thus their critique of existing arrangements went beyond economic conditions to embrace the question of the individual's plight, his dehumanization, his loss of autonomy in a society which rapidly reduced him to a dependent state.

Their protest was a consequence of the times, not only of the 1890's but of the preceding two decades, where the rule was all-pervasive hardship: declining crop prices; increased tenantry and share-cropping; an appreciating dollar; the ever-present mortgage in the West, and even more pressing, the crop-lien in the South; business combinations, tariffs and artificially high prices in the manufacturing sector; a railroad system which practiced discrimination against the farmer, gave preferential treatment to favored shippers, dominated state legislatures, blackmailed towns into issuing bonds, held large tracts of land off the market, refused to assume a proper share of the tax burden, and contributed to the creation of a closed system for the distribution of goods. Populists recognized that the industrial worker confronted similar conditions: subsistence wages, company towns, frequent unemployment, and the use of coercion in the form of Pinkertons, militias and imported strikebreakers to prevent him from rectifying the situation by forming unions. Finally, Populists confronted a political framework where grievances were never aired, and if anything, were obscured by the raising of all manner of diversions from the "bloody shirt" to the cry of tariff. Populists addressed themselves to each of these issues, as well as to others of a like character. Theirs was indeed a response to the times, but it was also something more; it was an attempt to transcend those times, and in the act of transcending the existing social context, to pose an alternative conception for the development of America.

Populism was not a retrogressive social force. It did not seek to restore a lost world of yeomen farmers and village artisans. The reverse was true. Of course Populists borrowed from the past, but they borrowed selectively. What they took was not a petrified pre-industrialism but a set of political principles, principles which they believed could be applied at any point, present and future as well as past. From Jefferson and Jackson came the recurring theme of "equal rights to all, and special privileges to none," from these and other sources came the labor theory of value, and from the

Constitution came the commerce clause and other passages sanctioning government regulation in the general interest. Beyond this Populists did not go,
for their gaze was directed to what lay ahead rather than to what lay behind.

In seeking to democratize rather than abolish industrialism, Populism was a progressive social force. Yet its orientation was progressive not
only because it based its remedies on an accommodation to social change,
but also because in pursuing these policies it adopted a highly affirmative
stance. The two are difficult to separate. For to be forward-looking while not
at the same time possessing confidence that men do have the power to re-
make their institutions and values is to be as helpless, as escapist, as the one
who rests content with a restoration of the past. To acquiesce in social
change does not, by itself, insure a progressive outlook. A more positive
frame of mind is required, and this Populists had. Woven into the texture
of their thought was the insistence that men *could* consciously make their
future. Populists contended that there is nothing inevitable about misery
and squalor, nothing irreversible about the tendencies toward the concentration of wealth and the legitimation of corporate power. Not the impersonal
tendency but men themselves are responsible for the contemporary society,
and for this reason men can — according to Populists, must — alter the
course of that society in a humanistic direction. What stands out, then,
about the Populist mind is an affirmation of man, a faith in man's capability
to shape his own history.

This positive aspect of Populist thought is not exhausted by the fact
that numerous concrete proposals were offered to attack existing problems.
More important was the attitude behind their formulation, and ultimately,
the attitude toward the relation between the individual and his government.
In keeping with the emphasis on men as the wielders of power and the
source of legislation, Populists held that there was nothing sacred about the
status quo, or for that matter, about the institutions which safeguarded that
status quo. They did not repudiate the notion of law and order, but they
did assert that *existing* laws was class law, intended to protect the rich at the
expense of the poor, and that order meant in the contemporary context the
imposition of legalized repression to prevent the broadening of that law.
Thus Populist reforms stemmed from an attitude of healthy skepticism concerning the sacrosanct nature of government. Since government was no more
than an instrument to be used for good or ill by the groups which controlled it, then let the farmers and workers organize to secure that control,
and prevent further encroachments on the general welfare.

Yet Populists found even this to be entirely too negative. Government should be more than a neutral observer. It was created to *serve* man,
and must be a dynamic force in bringing about equality. Thus, Populists
contended, government must be a responsive tool, one which can actively

intervene in the economy to regulate matters affecting the public interest, and when necessary own outright monopolies of this character, and can just as actively aid the underprivileged and work for a more equitable distribution of wealth.

From this brief overview of Populist thought, with the emphasis on its rational, humane and affirmative qualities, it is clear the speaker dissents from the recent interpretation of Populism as the source of American anti-Semitism and proto-fascistic behavior. He does not find the movement xenophobic, irrational, opportunistic and in search of a scapegoat, and he does not transform its social protest into status striving, its discontent into the addiction to conspiratorial delusions, its attempts at farmer-labor alliances into retrogressive utopianism. In sum, he does not conceive Populism as an authoritarian social force. . . .

I did not come here today to rehash the controversies of the past, but to look to the future. I submit that the time for bickering is over, and that the following should be conceded by all, so that we can go on to more pressing problems as historians: one, the past decade and a half has witnessed the unwarranted denigration of Populism, and because Populism has served as the type-form for radicalism, we have also seen the unwarranted denigration of the reform tradition in America as well; two, the critics not only have not worked in the primary materials, but have ignored an impressive array of books, monographs and articles which flatly contradict their case; three, that whatever their motives, and I should like to think these centered upon a commendable endeavor, to ascertain the roots of authoritarianism in American life, they have not only failed to explain the rise of proto-fascism — and have so obscured the picture that we know less today than we did at the start of the 1950's — but historians have turned against the very currents of democracy and humanism resisting its rise. Opposed to scapegoating, these historians have nonetheless, and with no evidence, found their own scapegoat, the Populist movement.

I take these three considerations as no longer open to doubt, and will not stop to offer point-by-point refutations of the critical literature, or summarize the writings of Professors Hicks, Woodward, Destler, Arnett, and a host of others to show the humane character of Populism, or the fact that times *were* hard, and hence that Populists did not respond to non-existent grievances. Therefore, the question must now be asked, why — despite overwhelming evidence to the contrary — did historians embark on the denigration of Populism, and why did the recent interpretation gain such widespread acceptance? Given the facts that critics neither refuted earlier scholarly works nor presented new evidence, given the facts that these earlier works saw not irrationality but the concern for human dignity, and not one pointed to anti-Semitism, given the facts that Populism expressed compassion for the underprivileged, both Negro and white, and that historians had agreed in viewing the movement as the summation of a whole century of American radical thought, where Man, written large, was at the center of the political universe, given this and more, much more, I think it can be said that the justification for the reinterpretation lies not in history but in the mind of the historian, and more specifically, the historian who feels compelled to rewrite the past with a vengeance.

When Professor Woodward suggests in "The Populist Heritage and the Intellectual" that critical currents in historical writing were a response to McCarthyism in the early 1950's, I think his explanation for what has happened is too charitable. I submit that there is a world of difference between standing up against McCarthyism and seeking to understand its roots unencumbered by predispositions as to where to look, on one hand; and not only capitulating but then turning on one's own philosophic heritage by identifying with the hated object, McCarthyism, on the other. Yet, the latter is precisely what happened. Since there was no objective basis for singling out Populism, one can only conclude that the ultimate destructive force of McCarthyism was not to keep men silent, but to make them purge the very tradition of humanitarianism and radicalism for which the Populist movement stood as a notable example in the American experience. It is no coincidence that Professor Hofstadter's archetypal radical turns out to be not the man who protests against social injustice or economic inequality, but one who wants only a larger share of the pie, who wants to scramble up the ladder, who is governed in short by the capitalist-on-the-make mentality. The judgment is revealing. I see here not only a preoccupation with present-day values, and the attempt to read them back into the past, but also the rock-bottom of cynicism and disillusionment over man.

Now, I do not deny that the historian is influenced by the present when writing about the past. Whether Professor Carr in *What Is History?* specified the interaction between present and past to everyone's satisfaction is less important than his insight on how the historian must be aware of the dominant trends of his age when exploring the past. Still, by no stretch of the imagination does this reciprocal relation permit one cavalierly to disregard the past and write solely from the present, which I feel the critics of Populism have done.

Clearly, there is nothing wrong with revisionism as such; this is the dynamic force in the writing of history. Nor should historians avoid the questions which the present generation wants to ask of the past. On the contrary, I must state again that the search for the origins of authoritarianism is a significant endeavor. With this said, however, the overall point remains: one cannot use a legitimate topic, a topic in which all of us are interested, as a shield to hide behind while reading current biases into the past.

I have left the original question hanging, of why the denigration of Populism. Let me relate it to a further line of inquiry: say we did not get off to a false start in the early 1950's, is it probable that historians would look automatically to agrarianism as the source of authoritarian behavior? Would they have maintained at the outset that one can speak of an agrarian life-style which is intrinsically proto-fascistic? If their work were infused with a guiding assumption as to where to start, is it clear they would begin with non-urban instead of urban sources of the problem? I think not.

The standard literature on the middle classes provides ample testimony that the strains of modern society are not confined to the agrarian sector. The writings of Max Weber, Hans Speier, Franz Neumann, Robert K. Merton and C. Wright Mills, just to name a few, are too substantial and too familiar to have been overlooked by students of authoritarianism. Likewise, it seems highly unlikely that a post-World War II scholar could be unaware of the historical and sociological trends contributing to the breakdown of Weimar Germany and the rise of Nazism. The point is that in both cases — the corpus of writings on the nature of industrial society; and the principal example where protofascism erupted into its fully matured form — the signs lead directly to the middle and lower middle classes as the most volatile and unstable stratum in modern times.

The next step, it appears to me, one naturally evolving out of the discussion of the topic, would be to follow through these insights. Yet, despite such obvious signs of non-agrarian authoritarianism, historians resolutely refused to investigate these other social forces. I think the gap reflects a blind-spot; a blind-spot made all the more significant because of the simultaneous willingness to place sole responsibility on agrarianism.

That the blind-spot relates to the larger question of why the denigration of Populism occurred in the first place will be noted momentarily. That it is due in part to the sociological backgrounds of historians themselves can however be mentioned at this time. This is by no means the key to the problem, but it is important. If in fact there are distinctly urban and middle class sources of proto-fascism in the United States, as *is* the case in Western European societies, then historians whose roots are urban and middle class would find it difficult, indeed distasteful, to contemplate such a possibility. And it would be equally painful for American society as a whole to question its foundations. The temptation is very great to look elsewhere for an explanation — to the non-urban, non-middle class movements in American history. In a word, the shortcomings lie outside the prevailing patterns in present-day society; they are products, instead, of the very forces which challenged these patterns.

My point, then, is that while there may be rural sources of authoritarianism, one cannot ignore the urban sources as well. I cannot possibly go into a full-scale examination of these urban sources in a paper of this size. Let me merely indicate that of the writers referred to earlier, I find Max Weber's *Theory of Social and Economic Organization* extremely valuable in pointing to the essential instability of bureaucratic society, an instability he located at the very core of modern industrialism. For Weber, the process of rationalization — the drive for predictability, calculability and efficiency permeating all realms of existence — leads to instability because it generates a sense of depersonalization in the individual, and psychological insecurities in the society at large. As will become clear, it is this instability which serves as an ideal breeding ground for protofascism.

Rationalization is a highly dynamic force. Once it begins, no sector of the society can be exempted, whether work processes, distribution procedures, or legal system. It spreads from the assembly line of the factory, to the assembly line of the white collar world, even to the assembly line of the individual's thought processes. In the quest for stabilization and efficiency, society cannot permit uneven or chaotic development. Spontaneity becomes suspect; it upsets calculations.

As Weber pointed out, rational society can be summarized by two overriding factors: bureaucratic organization and the routinization of tasks. The former, with its rigidity and its pecking order in the chain of command, has received widespread commentary, from Kafka and earlier, down to the trivialized accounts of today about the organization man. I say trivialized because what recent writers fail to comprehend, in their desire to obfuscate the stultifying effects of bureaucratic forms, is Weber's point on the built-in schizophrenia in the society geared to these forms.

But why this built-in schizophrenia in the structure of society? For Weber, the concept of "office" (which is the basic unit in the bureaucratic form of social organization) requires a strict separation of one's public and private lives. The occupant of the office becomes, as it were, divided into two compartments. On the job, his functions are severely circumscribed; he has a narrow sphere of competence, and cannot go outside that sphere. Again a premium is placed on calculability. He is bound by generalized rules. Initiative and creativity are discouraged. Indeed, all personal reactions must be eliminated. This means not only that human problems are treated in terms of categories, itself a sign of the objectification of social relationships; but also, that the bureaucrat must stifle hostility and resentment against the bureaucracy itself.

What are the consequences of these bureaucratic traits (and by bureaucracy I mean of course the dominant pattern of rational society, and do not confine the term to such examples as government) for the rise of authoritarianism? First, the repressed feelings, precisely because they have no outlet within the generalized norms of the bureaucratic structure, will break through in some manner. This institutionalized repression, for that indeed is the dominant feature of the structure, is further compounded by the boredom and sterility of the work itself. The result is that a great deal of tension, with no possibility for release, has been built up. Or, if there is release within the structure, it takes the form of even more slavish devotion to the rules, which in turn only intensifies the repression. This is where Weber's insight into the compulsory separation of roles becomes significant. What is pent-up in one realm of existence will then be expressed in another. That this condition has meaning for the development of proto-fascism should be sufficiently clear, but I will expand this point shortly.

The second general consequence of these bureaucratic traits is more readily detectable. Every aspect of bureaucratic organization points to one underlying response: the uncritical and in time mechanical submission to authority. The command structure serves as an impersonal conveyor belt. One obeys orders from above, and transmits them to those below. The orders themselves are not questioned. Further, one arrives at decisions not on the basis of individual discretion but according to stipulated rules, once more reinforcing the submission to authority. Mutual expectations, the cement of bureaucracy, are established through conformity — conformity to commands, conformity to rules, conformity to bureaucratic patterns of thought.

Combining these two results — the high degree of repression with no effective channels of expression and the proneness to submission — one can see why I am led to the conclusion that rational society, however indispensable to modern industrialism, rests on a precarious foundation.

Turning now to the second major feature of rational society, the routinization of the work process, one finds that this too generates psychological insecurities which lead to authoritarian behavior. In the drive to rationalize, to make the productive system more efficient and predictable, it becomes necessary to alter the relationship between man and the machine. As tasks are reduced to a smaller and smaller number of standardized operations, the individual himself no longer holds his job on the basis of skill and insight. Instead he is transformed into one more interchangeable part in the larger machinery. The culmination of rationality is not only to make man subordinate to the machine, but to make him into a machine. Thus, when these simplified procedures have been introduced, it becomes literally possible to bring in anyone off the street, and teach him to perform the tasks.

As in the case of bureaucracy, the consequences of routinization are also significant. First, the individual, far from deriving intrinsic gratification from his work, experiences utter boredom, or more likely, frustration. Performing a minute segment of a vast operation, he does not even see his contribution to the final result. Not only are tasks reduced to simpler operations, but the individual is reduced to a condition of all-pervasive malaise. Productive forces become impersonal; work becomes impersonal; society itself becomes impersonal. Man is a helpless subject, searching for meaning in a world of objects. And in time, he too begins to feel like an object, which merely serves to intensify his helplessness, and makes his search for meaning all the more frantic.

Second, in a situation where work has been so thoroughly simplified, where skill based on accumulated learning counts for nothing, where one individual can readily be substituted for another, men regard themselves as dispensable and replaceable. Self-respect is destroyed, only to be supplanted by fear. One constantly asks, especially during hard times: when will my turn come — when will I be cast out and replaced by someone else?

Regrettably, there is insufficient time to illustrate the foregoing remarks by looking at specific historical situations, but I submit that the case of the German salaried employee would be instructive. Let me simply state that as the white collar sector expanded, its social level went down. This in turn meant that the social distance, so crucial to the psychological security of the middle classes, was also breaking down. And the result was panic.

Thwarted in his public role, the individual will vent his aggression in his private life. Bewildered, helpless, insecure, he will be ripe for all manner of promises to restore meaning to his life. Trapped in the morass of routinized procedures, he will personalize an impersonal world through the search for a scapegoat. Faced with submergence into the working class, and hence with the destruction of his whole way of life, he will turn on bended knee to The Leader for a solution. Predisposed to authoritarianism from the very workings of bureaucracy, he will be vulnerable to anyone who claims to have the answers. The "salariat," as Sigmund Neumann aptly termed this class, was indeed a source of proto-fascism. The story is a familiar one, and since many of the factors relate not merely to Germany but to bureaucratic society itself, not without meaning elsewhere as well.

The phenomenon I have been discussing is distinctly urban and middle class in character; hence, there is reason to conclude that the strains accompaning the industrial transformation are by no means confined to agrarian sources. Yet, can we face up to this, can we drop our guard long enough to consider the possibility that the traits noted here *might* contribute to American authoritarian behavior, or the further possibility that authoritarianism has become incorporated into the social matrix of our times? Intuitively the historian and the society at large draw back from rigorously looking inward. That is understandable, for we live in an age of uncertainty; we seek reassurance, and not self-knowledge.

This brings me to the main point of the paper. Historians currently engaged in rewriting the past, I suggest, are torn within themselves on viewing the post-war world as both distasteful and pleasant, and in this, they mirror a larger ambivalence in the American mind itself. Our society too is torn. As I see it, the essence of the Enlightenment heritage, the affirmation of the rationality of man and the confidence in his ability to make the world over, is being dessicated under the glaring sun of Cold War stresses. Torn between fear on one hand, and self-glorification on the other, the chief casualty in this ambivalent process has been our faith in human potentiality.

Herein lies the meaning of the denigration of Populism. Why have historians been so quick to strike down the Populist movement, and why have the allegations, although without foundation, enjoyed such widespread acceptance? The question can no longer be evaded. Specifically, I submit that Populism represents all that we are not; it stands for the very affirmation we no longer feel; and because we do not find within ourselves the internal sources of strength to face the modern world, we have turned swiftly and relentlessly on the movement for possessing the courage and other qualities which we today lack. Critics of Populism write from a clearer present-day perspective than they realize. For what we project onto Populism is no more than our own times.

At the risk of repeating myself, let me state again that there was no earthly reason, either in the form of new evidence or in the alleged similarities between Populism and McCarthyism, to account for the denigration of the Populist movement. The heritage was, and is today more than ever, rich in meaning. Its philosophic core was so imbedded in American ideals that even opponents in the following half-century could charge no more than that Populists were misguided, in their eyes, for veering so far to the left. But the ideals themselves were not questioned.

Turning to the present, one would have thought it was the ideal creed in opposing McCarthyism. In Populism, intellectuals had ready at hand ample precedent in the American past for standing their ground against allegations that social welfare thinking and regard for human rights was un-American. Likewise, foreign policy considerations cannot explain the decline of the Populist image. In the 1950's America sought to appeal, and still does, to the underdeveloped nations. Here, above all, the image should have been nurtured. As a tradition of agrarian radicalism, it offered a meaningful appeal to these people. Few experiences in the American past could better promote the sense of common ties based on having gone through the experience of rapid industrialization. So, once more I state that the explanation for the denigration of Populism lies deeper.

In taking stock, I think we can dismiss the critics as being of little importance. Just as there would have been McCarthyism (under whatever label) had the junior senator from Wisconsin not been on the scene, there would also have been an attempt to purge the American past of dissident elements had several scholars not made their respective contributions. The ground swell was too overwhelming to be the work of any one man or group of men. To blame a handful provides too simplistic a solution, for the problem touches on the nature of society and not on the activities of a few historians.

The reasons underlying the denigration of Populism are complex, and cannot be more than tentatively blocked out in this paper. My remark a moment ago that historians are purging the past of dissident elements — a point I made four years ago in connection with *The Age of Reform* — can serve as a point of departure. We have witnessed over the last dozen years a trend in historical writing which superimposes a straitjacket of consensus on the American past. By that I meant in 1960, and still mean, that all traces of social protest are being eradicated in favor of a model which characterizes the historical development of the United States as no more than a euphonious assertion of capitalist-on-the-make values. There was no conflict, only harmony; and certainly not the existence of hard times which might give rise to genuine grievances. In sum, our society exhibits a pattern of splendid equilibrium.

Four years ago, I could not see beyond this point. Today, I should like to ask, what are the larger implications of the consensus framework? Is it a temporary response to Cold War conditions? If so, how does one account for our excessive fear over admitting that social protest existed in the past, or our zeal in superimposing a pattern of equilibrium on that past, or finally our alacrity in accepting the charges against Populism? In a word, does not the quest for consensus reflect a deeper anxiety than that stemming from a concern over McCarthyism at home and tensions on the international scene?

Perhaps the clue to the disease lies in its symptoms. Consensus tells us a great deal about the society receptive to its message. First, it is an unmistakable sign of stereotypic thinking. There is not only the tendency rigidly to categorize data, as a substitute for the analysis of specific evidence in a unique historical situation, but also the endeavor to categorize the entire span of our history in the same mold. We now know that stereotypy is a dangerous trait, and not just the mark of intellectual carelessness. Stereotypy signifies that the capacity for individuated experience is absent; facts are not treated in their own right, but only in terms of pre-arranged categories. In a nutshell, the significance of this pattern of thinking is that it represents the desire to eliminate uncertainty from one's existence. Rigid ego-defenses are erected as a barrier against seeing what one does not want to see. Conflict cannot be tolerated. Contrary ideas cannot be admitted, for fear that they will threaten one's very identity.

Second, consensus militates against adopting an introspective outlook. We are afraid to look inward, afraid to confront our past in all of its intricacies — in all of its blemishes as well as strong points. Anti-introspection betrays an attitude which places a premium on process and form, rather than on what is human in history. Fearing what we might find in ourselves, we regard the problems of man as an unsafe subject of discussion. The same barrenness of ego comes through as in the case of stereotypic thinking. All men, the noble and the base alike, are reduced to a common formula, and made over into the image of ourselves. Populists and Jacksonians are capitalists-on-the-make because we are capitalists-on-the-make. For them to be different, to have dreams and aspirations which differ from our own, might serve as a reproach to our own values. Whether this represents self-glorification of present-day America, or self-loathing, or both, is less important than the larger picture which anti-intraception suggests. American society lacks the confidence in itself to take a close hard look at its past, both the best as well as the worst in that past.

Finally, consensus reveals an even more disturbing trait. By characterizing the American past in terms of a homogeneity in values, experiences and goals, we have promoted the myth of national purity. This is different from the chosen-people strain in our history, for the emphasis has shifted. We are no longer John Winthrop's city upon the hill for all to see and take heart in, nor even the turn of the century expansionists who want to civilize the little brown brother to the South and across the Pacific, although no doubt each of these sentiments persists down into our own times. Rather, the stress is upon uniformity for its own sake. The impulse is entirely negative. For it serves to bring cohesion out of chaos, a sense of belonging where that sense is not felt, in sum, a belief in homogeneity which provides the feeling of self-identification with the ingroup as opposed to the other, the stranger, all those who lie outside the national experience.

Hence, consensus contributes directly to ethnocentric patterns of thought. Through the assertion of purity comes the erection of mental walls, with a rigid ingroup-outgroup dichotomy defining who shall be on either side of the barriers. In such a situation, with stereotypic thinking and anti-intraception as derivative responses, further impetus is given to maintaining homogeneity, past as well as present, at all costs. This uniformity of outlook becomes a crutch: our past stands for fundamental agreement, marking the progressive realization of the expectant capitalist. We now have a sense of continuity between present and past, and the added reassurance that present-day institutions and values are the product of universal approval on this side of the wall, that is, among the ingroup. From here it is but a short step to maintaining that social protest upsets the equilibrium, threatens the consensus, denies the homogeneity of the nation, and thus is a form of treasonable conduct.

It is difficult to escape the conclusion that the critics of Populism and the society which finds the charges so congenial to its temperament exhibit the very traits of authoritarianism they impute to others. Not willing to admit the existence of authoritarian currents in ourselves and in our society, we project them on to others — the outgroup, the Populists, indeed the reform tradition in America.

Thus, Populism becomes for the historian and the larger society what the Jew is for the anti-Semite. Both historian and anti-Semite require a scapegoat, and the character of that scapegoat is incidental. For each hates not Populists or Jews but himself. Each cannot affirm man, each has little faith in human potentiality or confidence in man's ability to shape the future and rationally control society, each cannot confront the possibilities of self-fulfillment in humanity — and frightened by these thoughts, each turns blindly to dependence on the homogeneous folk or the static past. In the final analysis, the denigration of Populism signifies the fear of man.

When I suggest that the consensus framework and McCarthyism are, far from being at opposite poles, actually one and the same underlying trend, I am of course not directing these remarks so much to the critics of Populism as to the society they faithfully mirror. Populism stands as the conscience of modern America. It means frank and full discussion over essentials, and not blind submission to the status quo; it means the people, indeed the much maligned common man, can take the future in hand and make a better world, and not elitist despair over human nature and contempt for popular movements as being degenerate mobs; it means taking the earlier democratic values of American society at face value and trying to implement them, and not the cynical, amoral pragmatism of today which finds the very notion of ideological commitment to be a sign of the crackpot. Populism is our conscience, and we cannot face it.

When I point to similarities of response in the critic and the anti-Semite, I do not mean the former (and society at large) is necessarily anti-Semitic. One need not be an overt anti-Semite to reflect the authoritarian thought patterns outlined here. To call the critic an anti-Semite misses the point, for both share in common a deeper negation of man. We have only begun, since World War II, to appreciate fully that anti-Semitism itself is more basically dehumanizing than an attack solely on Jews. Simply put, we know from psychoanalytic studies that ethnocentrism, stereotypy and anti-intraception, found in critic and anti-Semite alike, constitute the core of the authoritarian personality.

In the comparison I am drawing between the critic (and the society he reflects) and the anti-Semite, I know of no more penetrating analysis of this underlying authoritarianism than that presented by Jean-Paul Sartre in "The Portrait of the Anti-Semite." It is this statement of the problem which best explains what is happening in American society, why so much stress is placed on consensus, and why at bottom we have witnessed the denigration of Populism. When Sartre speaks of the anti-Semite, we could just as readily insert the critic of Populism, or better yet, the form such criticism takes.

For both critic and anti-Semite share in the search for uniformity. And both deny the efficacy and wisdom of social protest, not only out of cynicism of man's desire for human betterment and his ability to achieve improvement (utopian is a term of reproach for both), but also out of the fear that protest leads to change and change means the end to stability and certainty in one's life. Thus both cling to present-day values because they cannot plan for the future. They enshrine the status quo as a means of escaping from the responsibilities of living. Sartre describes this defeatist outlook as the product of men "who are attracted by the durability of stone."

What is consensus but this state of mind? The static equilibrium, the ahistorical consensus, these alone provide reassurance. We see an orientation here, to quote Sartre, "in which one never seeks but that which one has already found, in which one never becomes other than what one already was." And to insure this equilibrium, I might add, both must have a scapegoat. Balance is attained by eradicating the evil one. Then all is well again.

Sartre's portrait of the anti-Semite is summed up in these words: "He is a man who is afraid. Not of the Jews of course, but of himself, of his conscience, his freedom, of his instincts, of his responsibilities, of solitude, of change, of society and the world; of everything except the Jews." This too captures the significance of our own attack on the Populist movement as an escape from ourselves and the challenges of our age. Sartre concludes on a note which reaches to the innermost recesses of the authoritarian mind. "Anti-Semitism, in a word, is fear of man's fate. The anti-Semite is the man who wants to be a pitiless stone, furious torrent, devastating lightning: in short, everything but a man."

Indeed if Populism is the conscience of modern America, I submit we should look to that heritage and take pride in what we see. The Cassandras of despair have had their day. The time has come to call a halt to the erosion of human values, and to the denigration not only of Populism but of man himself. Why fear today and tomorrow when we as a nation have had our share of splendid yesterdays? America has in Populism a rich tradition for moving in the direction of the affirmation of man.

Critique of Norman Pollack's "Fear of Man"

Irwin Unger

Irwin Unger, of New York University, responds directly to Norman Pollack's attack on the presentism of the critics of Populism with a loud tu quoque, *and proceeds to engage Pollack on his own ideological ground. "Much of the recent criticism of late nineteenth century agrarianism is valid," Unger insists, and he challenges Pollack's understanding of the radical nature of Marxism, the sources of modern authoritarianism, and the position of "consensus" historians. It should now be clear that past and present are always engaged in a reciprocal relationship, and that perhaps the conflict between rural and urban value systems in the 1890s is being partially replicated by conflict among historians from rural and urban backgrounds. More is involved than rural-urban conflict, however, though Populism's anticity dimension certainly undermines the contention of those who maintain that the Populists accepted urbanization and industrialization. The question is whether Populism's critique of America implied a radical set of values or, as Unger asks, whether the Populist reform program was in any way radical. If the answer to this question is no, then one must still decide whether the Populists were pragmatic and future oriented, or provincial and simplistic, or governed by irrational fears, or merely nostalgic.*

Norman Pollack is the victim of a serious self-deception. He wants desperately to uncover a viable American tradition of the left,[1]* and since he cannot, for various reasons, find it in the Marxism of De Leon, Debs, and Hillquit, Populism will have to do.

Populism, he says in effect, attempted to deal with industrialism as today's new left — readers of *Dissent*, say, or *Studies on the Left* — might

Presented to the Southern Historical Association in Little Rock in November, 1964, and printed as "Critique of Norman Pollack's 'Fear of Man,'" *Agricultural History*, XXXIX (April, 1965), 75–80. Reprinted by permission of the author.
* [See pp. 155–156 for notes to this article. — Ed.]

have done. His very language betrays him. "Dignity," "dehumanization," "loss of autonomy"; these terms were not used in 1892. They are the verbal small change of twentieth century academic radicalism, and they reveal Mr. Pollack's inadmissable present-mindedness. Pollack is trying to do for the Populists what Arthur M. Schlesinger, Jr., attempted for the Jacksonians, with, I think, as little success. Won't we ever give up trying to impose the present on the past?

In justice to Pollack it must be said that several of his opponents have fallen into the same trap — though one differently baited — when they accuse the Populists of proto-Fascist sympathies. Fascism, I would suggest, like neo-radicalism, is the product of special twentieth century circumstances. It has no direct precursors, certainly not in America, though no doubt — like all political movements — it drew on the past for certain useful ideas and even more obviously for its rhetoric.

But by directing the main force of his attack against a small group of social and political scientists who see proto-Hitlers and Mussolinis behind James Weaver, Jerry Simpson, and Mrs. Mary Lease,[2] Pollack is not being fair to his opponents. The most influential re-interpretation of the Populists, Richard Hofstadter's *Age of Reform,* does not fall into this error. Hofstadter has never called the Populists Fascists; nor is he unwilling to acknowledge that they were indeed deeply concerned with the industrial problems of their day.[3] What Hofstadter says, I believe, is that they were agrarian men with a limited understanding of the complexities of their era. They proposed solutions to current problems which often reflected their ignorance, their isolation from the best thought of the day, and their profound sense of frustration at the intractability of their social and economic environment. Clearly, he implies, we today, in a still more complex world, cannot expect inspiration from such a parochial and limited social vision.

If our choice lay between Mr. Pollack and, let us say, Mr. Victor Ferkiss,[4] we would be in a sad state indeed in our attempt to comprehend Populism. But fortunately it need not. There are alternate possibilities — ones, however, which will bring Mr. Pollack little comfort, I fear.

Let us start with the big issue: the Populist response to the whole of late nineteenth century industrialism. No, the Populists were not American Luddites who would destroy the railroads and the factories. But who seriously makes this charge? Surely it is a straw man? Why should the Kansas farmer, 300 miles from the nearest navigable water, want to tear up the railroad tracks? Why should he wish to burn down the McCormick reaper factory? No, for those productive enterprises which he understood — manufacturing and transportation, let us say — the farmer recommended no such primitive or ill-considered action. But when confronted by a more abstruse and complex aspect of the economy, or when faced by the social change

which accompanied industrialization, he did often embrace naive and simplistic answers.

Take the money and banking systems. The Populists were obsessed
with finance. But wasn't this to be expected? Wasn't Populist concern with
banks, greenbacks, and silver perfectly plausible given existing conditions.
Weren't farmers primarily concerned with the practical matter of reversing
the long-term trend of falling commodity prices? Only in part. There were
such men: men who were chiefly concerned with high interest rates and the
steady decline of staple prices, and who saw inflation as the "producers" salvation. There was this pragmatic, bread-and-butter side of Populist financial
attitudes. But there was another side which was peculiarly abstract and ideological. Many Populists viewed the money question as the key to all that was
wrong with American life. Solve the money problem — by abolishing the
national banks and by issuing government money — and you solved the
problems of poverty and social injustice, as well as the question of who ran
the government. To these men, exhortations to destroy the "banks," the
"bondholder," and the "money power" were a substitute not only for serious
thought about the nation's real financial inadequacies, but often for serious
thought about the major social and political issues of the day. Surely with
all his professed immersion in the literature of Populism, Mr. Pollack cannot have missed this strain in Populist thought.

But there is a common error which obscures this obsessive agrarian
interest in finance and which may explain Mr. Pollack's oversight. The
Populists, we have been told, had the money question foisted on them either
by the mining interests or by the Bryan Democracy, and then only late in
their career.[5] The exaggerated attention to silver after 1895 may perhaps be
explained this way. But it was not true of what the Populists referred to,
in capitals, as "The Money Question." "Money," "Transportation," and
"Land" were the three main issues of the Alliances and the People's party
from 1889 to 1892, long before the union with the silver Democracy was
dreamed of [6]; and of the three "Money" was almost always given first place.
Indeed, eliminate the money question from the Populist platform and you
have virtually reduced it to its peripheral issues.

Consider next Populism and the contemporary "labor problem."
Mr. Pollack has attempted to show us elsewhere that the Populists were
sympathetic to the plight of the wage earner and made a serious attempt to
draw organized labor into the People's party.[7] Clearly such a fact must be
demonstrated if he is to establish the Populists' credentials as precursors of
modern radicalism. But the effort, I think, is unsuccessful. With all his
vehemence, Pollack cannot bury such obtrusive facts as Gompers's repudi-
ation of the Populists in 1892, and Bryan's poor showing in the big cities in
1896. The reason for the Populists' failure to win labor and the big cities, he
has told us, is the conservatism of the urban wage earner as compared to the

farmer! The small free-holders, we are expected to believe, were the radicals, while the property-less laborers of the mills and the shops were the conservatives! [8] But what of the truly radical leaders — what about De Leon and the Socialist Labor Party? Well, we are told, they opposed Populism out of fear and jealousy; and besides, they were so ultra-doctrinaire that even Frederick Engels repudiated them! [9]

No, I think it is on this point — in the Populist failure with urban labor — that Pollack's thesis is wrecked. The Populists did seek an alliance with labor, and they did express sympathy for labor's plight. But they could offer little to industrial labor because they were outside it, and could not understand it. Their solution to the labor problem, like their solution to so many others, consisted largely in destroying the money power and manipulating the finances. From the 1860's on, labor had been skeptical of monetary solutions of its problems,[10] and in 1896 McKinley with the tariff, not Bryan with free silver, won the labor vote.

Consider, finally, the Populist response to the city. Perhaps Americans still have not come to terms with the city, but clearly the Populist attitude was peculiarly primitive and retrograde. That the supporters of the People's party did not like the cities is irrefutable. We have all seen the archetypal Populist cartoon of the transcontinental cow grazing on the prairies while being milked in New York. Who does not know those lines from the "Cross of Gold" speech about the grass growing in the streets of the cities if the farms are destroyed? And who is not aware of the disfranchisement, particularly in the South, of the urban areas by Populist dominated legislatures? Is this all circumstantial? Then hear the direct testimony of C. W. McCune's *National Economist:* "It has been shown again and again that the masses of the people in great cities are volatile and unstable, lacking in partriotism and unfit to support a wise and pure government. The city may be the best place to use them; but the finest types of muscle and brain are almost invariably furnished by the country. . . . If the country is drained to populate the cities, decay is sure to set in." [11] Could the message be plainer?

What is responsible for this animus? Several things, I believe. The first is hinted at in McCune's editorial. The farmer disliked the city because his sons and daughters liked it all too much, and they, the young, the vigorous and the talented, were leaving the countryside to go to the towns, depriving rural America of its most vital element. But besides, the "interests," the "money power" — the enemy — dwelt in the city, especially New York. And, finally, the city was alien; it was inhabited by foreigners who knew nothing of our American virtues, or our values, and who fell easy victim to the most violent and dangerous demagogues.

This last attitude suggests one of the most serious charges of all those levelled against Populism: that it was nativistic, and particularly that it contained a deep undercurrent of anti-Semitism. Pollack has denied this,[12] and, of course, he must if he is to make the Populists ancestral to the modern left. But the facts, I fear, are once more against him. Not all Populists were anti-Semites, of course, and neither were all anti-Semites Populists. Nativism and anti-Semitism, it would seem, were pervasive in America in the nineteenth century.[13] But some Populists clearly disliked foreigners and Jews, and for reasons, in the latter case, that were uniquely Populistic. To Populists, the Jew was a "non-producer," a mere manipulator of money, a parasite, and at the same time representative of the sinister and forbidding power of international finance. "In these evil conditions, made by bad laws, the Jews alone thrive," wrote Ignatius Donnelly. "The reason is they deal only in money; they have no belief in farming, manufacturing, or any other industry; they are mere money mongers. As everything else goes down, money rises in value and those who control it become masters of the world." [14]

In these specific matters, then, of labor, the city, the money power, and nativism, the Populist claim to a progressive vision is, at best, ambiguous. But in a still more fundamental sense, was not Populism a conservative force? Mr. Pollack admits that the Populists borrowed heavily from the past. But he asserts that such borrowing is inevitable in all far-ranging systems of social thought, and he denies that it constitutes retrogressive thinking. But doesn't it? Compare the Populist social vision with the truly radical one of Marxism. In his recent book, Pollack professes to be startled by the similarities between Marxist and Populist diagnoses of society, still another proof, he says, of Populist radicalism.[15] But were the Populists truly future-minded — as the Marxists clearly were? The latter would consign the past to a well-deserved grave. The future would be a clean break with the past, in which property relationships, social relations, even the moral code, would be transformed. Did the insurgent farmers have such a vision? Is it not clear, rather, that they wished to preserve the disappearing but "eternally valid" principles of private property, the family farm, the old-fashioned Protestant morality? An accommodation, of course, would have to be made to modern technology, but the Populist had no grievance against the material and spiritual values of his day and his society, except as they had fallen off from the purity of his own and the nation's youth. Pollack says in his recent book that Populism "offered a highly radical critique" of capitalism.[16] Yet surely this is *Hamlet* without the Prince of Denmark. What is radical in Marxism is not its critique, but its program. Marxism is radical because it demands the "expropriation of the expropriators."

In a word, much of the recent criticism of late nineteenth century agrarianism is valid, although often overstated. This being the case — to adopt one of Mr. Pollack's rhetorical styles — we have already explained, without elaborate psychologizing, the origins of the new view of Populism. There is no mystery about it. Populism had a dark side as well as a light one, [17] and the recent critics of Populism have merely detected and described it. And yet Pollack is surely engaged in a legitimate enterprise in seeking to uncover the origins of the new views. The quest may tell us little about Populism substantively but it does, I believe, reveal much about the nature of the historical profession in America in 1964.

Unfortunately, as an historiographic undertaking Pollack's effort suffers from two fatal flaws: it is too limited in scope; and it is wrong. To begin with, what Pollack doesn't see is that his knife cuts two ways. We must not only ask why recent historians have been so critical of Populism; we must also ask why earlier historians were so uncritical of it. The answer, I believe, is very largely that the social origins of American historians have changed. With the exception of Mr. Pollack, who comes to the issue, as I have suggested, with special concerns, the disagreement over Populism among historians today measures the difference between Buffalo and Brooklyn on the one hand and Vanndale, Arkansas, and Pickering, Missouri, on the other.[18]

The new history of Populism is urban history, and to a large extent, if the urban men can detect the dark side of Populism, it is because they — like urban men in 1892 and 1896 — cannot identify with rural, naive, simplistic agrarianism. Pollack, of course, has noted this urban factor, but he says it produced anti-Populism because intellectuals cannot bear to blame themselves for twentieth century Fascism. But since when haven't urban intellectuals been able to indulge in self-hate? Indeed, the advent of McCarthyism permitted them for the first time in years the refreshing alternative of hating someone else! No. I think it is the inadequacy of Populism for the complex urban world the urban historian sees around him, rather than his own failings, that makes him unreceptive to the style and ideology of Populism.

But beyond this urban rejection of rural values there does loom the very real, though perhaps exaggerated, response of intellectuals to the radical right. Who can forget the fact that those very areas that were like tinder before the Populist conflagration have also burned for Barry? Who can ignore the attacks of the extreme right on the eastern, university educated "establishment" the universities themselves and the literate big city press? And when we extend our memories to the thirties, the overlap between Populism and right wing demagoguery becomes still dearer. Who will deny that both Father Coughlin and Huey Long owed an immense debt to Populism for both their rhetoric and their program? [19] The fit between the Irish priest and Ignatius Donnelly is uncanny.

But I am not falling here into the trap of present-mindedness. I do not believe Huey Long, or Father Coughlin, or Barry Goldwater are either Populists or Fascists. But that they share some of the style, stance, support, and suppositions of Populism is clear, and this resemblance (and this is my point) explains in part why twentieth century intellectuals find Populism so badly flawed. Targets for the last decade of a constant barrage from Oklahoma fundamentalists, midwestern rural Congressmen, and small town newspapers, for their supposed left wing sympathies, their Godlessness, their immorality, is it surprising that the Professors should regard with something less than total enthusiasm those groups in our past whose relationship to cosmopolitanism and urbanity was similar?

It is entirely possible that the urban intellectuals are mistaken in all this analogizing. The parallels between Huey Long and Jerry Simpson may not be valid. But if so, the error is an honest one. Pollack will not grant honesty or good will to his opponents. Instead, they lack both courage and basic decency. Pollack says that McCarthy frightened the intellectuals so badly that they fled to safety in the consensus view of the American past. While I am not always impressed with the courage of the intellectuals, I think in this case they performed relatively well, far better than most other Americans. They did counter-attack, if tardily, and not only took on McCarthy, but also what they believed to be the agrarian roots of McCarthyism. They dared, then, to take on two powerful antagonists: the junior Senator from Wisconsin and the Agrarian Myth which had become part of the standard American piety. It did not endear them to the rural right, most assuredly.

A major supposition of Mr. Pollack's attack on his opponents is that the middle-class, urban nature of Fascism is so apparent that the attempt to find a rural base for it in America must be an attempt to escape from an unpleasant, self-implicating truth. Some six pages of Pollack's essay are devoted to Max Weber's typology of authoritarianism to show that Fascism filled its ranks from just those segments of the population to which the intellectuals themselves belong. This is pretentious and irrelevant. As George Mosse has shown, German Nazism is a unique phenomenon; [20] the generic entity called "Fascism" was in reality a set of loosely related moods and attitudes; and certainly what appeared in the United States in the 1930's and 1950's was not Fascism. This latter belief is an illusion that both Pollack and some of his opponents share.

But besides — to meet Pollack on his own ground for the moment — he has mistaken his facts. One recent student of German National Socialism concludes that the small farm proprietors — the very class the Populists in America represented — were an important source of Nazi strength. Seymour Lipset concludes that this last study as well as several other recent ones, "sharply challenge the various interpretations of Nazism as the product of *anomie* and the general rootlessness of modern urban industrial society." [21]

Let us give Mr. Pollack the benefit of the doubt and say that he does not wish to be unfair to his opponents; he merely fails to understand them. Pollack calls those men who have detected a basic consensus in America apologists for the conservative *status quo*. He may be right about some of them being right. But many of them are really left, and if some critics of Populism have detected a basic consensus in American life, it is often with a sense of regret. Their mood is one of disappointment with the Populists for not offering a true alternative to laissez-faire capitalism, or so alloying it with intolerance, ignorance, fanaticism, and bad temper, as to make it impossible to use.

But do those who attack Populism insist on consensus? They don't deny that Populists were angry and disturbed. They *do* question whether they were angry and disturbed in a completely rational way, or at the right things. Was it rational to make the gold standard or the bankers villians? Was the city or the East the real enemy of the farmer? As I understand it, all that has been claimed by those who have asserted the consensual nature of American politics is that the range of American political life as compared with contemporary Europe was limited. We had no royalists; we had few serious socialists. We all accepted private property and private profit; we all favored universal male suffrage. There were no de Maistre's or Marx's in America. Who will deny these facts except those, who like the Populists themselves, must see the world in Manichean terms, as an eternal struggle between God and the Devil?

The Radical Specter

MICHAEL P. ROGIN

Agreeing with Pollack that Populism was something more than an effort at economic self-help, Michael Rogin, a political scientist in the University of California at Berkeley, interprets Populism as a political mass movement that challenged the political and economic power of "respectable" America. Though Populism had many aspects of the crusade about it, it was not authoritarian, he insists, and it can not successfully be understood as either class

*or status politics. It was instead a nonrevolutionary but radical
movement with broad class and political goals. Rogin attempts
to explain some of the supposed anomalies in Populist behavior
by reference to the peculiar psychology and outlook of American
farmers.*

*Rogin's main concern in the book from which the following
selection is taken is to examine the allegation that Senator
Joseph McCarthy's sources of support were Populistic. To accomplish this examination he uses simple quantitative techniques
to show that McCarthy's support did not come from the same
geographic, ethnographic, or econographic sources. Most strikingly, McCarthy enjoyed widespread support among Catholics
and among local elites, while the Populists did not. In the section
omitted from the chapter here, Rogin reviews the evidence on
Populist nativism and anti-Semitism and finds it unconvincing,
though he concedes, as must everyone, that Populists had a
habit of verbal anti-Semitism, which they shared with most other
Americans of the era, and that instances of Populist nativism are
really traceable to Populist opposition to land monopolies and
contract labor rather than to a dislike of foreigners. If Populism
stirred up a revivalist fervor, Rogin implies, it was all the more
remarkable for avoiding so many of the popular prejudices endemic in the general population. Ought Populism therefore to be
seen as an innoculation against the irrational? The historian
must at least ask the question were Populists nativistic and anti-
Semitic because they were Populists or because they were rural
Americans? On the other hand, the reader must ask himself
whether Rogin's understanding of Hofstadter is a fair one.*

Political movements in a crisis period encompass both ideology and
economic demands. Their proposals look to changes in the wider society and
are in this sense broader than the proposals of interest groups. Their constituents, in deprived positions in society, require more large-scale changes. Moreover, in the disrupted position in which people find themselves during a
crisis, they require some general explanation of the relation between narrow
economic demands and their general welfare. Deprived of power, they are
not likely to be motivated to act to change their situation by appeals to
practical self-interest alone. Because the obstacles to surmount are so great,
such appeals seem illusory and in fact often are. Therefore, some emotional

appeals are essential; protest movements have crusade characteristics. The movements of farmers in the 1890's, workers in the 1930's, and Negroes in the 1960's have all been crusades. The emotional appeals of these movements transcend rationality defined in terms of Benthamite narrow self-interest. But narrow groups are specifically irrational in a crisis period because their methods can succeed neither in achieving results nor in attracting adherents.

To treat mass movements in pluralist terms is to make them a priori irrational. When they are viewed as responses to social crises, a different picture emerges. Populism must be understood not as a foolish departure from interest group politics but as the product of the widespread and severe stresses of rapid industrialization and a serious depression.

The economic and cultural dislocation brought by industrialization has produced mass movements all over the world. These movements can take several forms. They can reject industrialization entirely and favor direct action and sabotage. This approach often dominated anarchist movements. They can reject any sort of liberal society, and seek to resolve economic and cultural problems with totalitarian control. This was the approach of fascism. They can seek to utilize industrialization to solve the problems it itself has created. This was the character of Marxism in Western Europe and Populism in America.

Adam Ulam has suggested that Marxism in Europe, in diverting resentment from the industrial process itself and onto the capitalist, socialized the working class to an acceptance of industrialization. Whereas the Luddites and anarchists fought the industrial work process itself, Marxist workers organized to fight the capitalists. In so doing they took the crucial step of accepting the industrial situation and working to improve their situation within it. Placing anti-industrial feeling in the service of industrial logic, revolutionary Marxism led to reformist trade unionism.[1]*

In *The Paradox of Progressive Thought,* David Noble has made a parallel analysis of American progressivism. Hofstadter suggested that the progressives and Populists feared industrialization. But according to Noble, they reinterpreted it as a mechanism for freeing man from the burden of traditions and institutions and for reintroducing agrarian innocence into an advanced civilization.[2] In Ulam's terms, American reformers channeled a potential anti-industrial emotion in the direction of an acceptance of industrialization for the benefits it could bring if properly controlled. The parallel is exact, for the reformers focused their attacks not on the industrial process itself but on the particular bearers of industrialization — in their terms, the plutocrats and the interests.

* [See p. 156 for notes to this article. — Ed.]

Populist rhetoric and the Populist program were anti-industrial capitalist not anti-industrial. In the words of one Populist paper, "The people do not want to tear down the railroads nor pull down the factories . . . They want to build up and make better everything." Another explained that Populists "shall make of this nation an industrial democracy in which each citizen shall have an equal interest." Technology, the Populists argued, could be used to enslave man but also to liberate him.[3]

Many Populists, although not anti-industrial, were loath to admit that basic and irreversible changes in American society had caused the problems the farmer faced. Kansas Senator William Peffer began *The Farmer's Side* with a long, realistic description of the effect of industrialization and technology on the self-sufficient farmer. The farm situation, he wrote, had been produced not by the machinations or conspiracies of a few men but by the general development of the society. This evolution could not be reversed; rather the farmers should seek to benefit from it. But Peffer followed this section with another in which he blamed usury for all the farmers' troubles.[4] Here Peffer drew back from the real problems brought by industrialization. Money panaceas became a substitute for the more radical program implied by the earlier analysis. Clearly the two aspects of Peffer's argument are mutually contradictory. If industrialization is the cause of agrarian unhappiness, there is no possibility of going back to an earlier utopia. If usury and the evil actions of a few men explain everything, there is no need to deal with the basic problems brought by industrialization.

True, the Populists opposed capitalists who were industrializing America. Does this make the capitalists progressive, the Populists reactionary? An analogous approach makes Stalinism in Russia into a progressive force because it, too, industrialized. Such overviews ignore the particular issues upon which conflict was joined. Conflict between Populists and conservatives was not about industrialization in the abstract, but about the control of railroads, the power of monopolies, the falling prices of crops, the benefits and dangers of inflation, big business control of politics, and other issues which could all have been met as the Populists desired without undermining industrialization.

Populists demanded a graduated income tax, government ownership or regulation of the railroads and the telegraph, control over monopoly, a lower tariff, increased education, direct election of senators, the secret ballot, the initiative and the referendum, an eight-hour day on government work, support for the labor movement, the free coinage of silver, a plan for government loans to farmers at low interest rates, and restriction on alien and corporate landholding. If the Populists longed for a "rural utopia," this longing was not operational.

Had Populism attempted to escape from the problems brought by industrialization it would have relied on finding scapegoats, attacking freedom, and appealing to prejudice. Such a politics could rely — as McCarthyism relied — on the support of local elites. The democratic character of Populism flowed from its willingness to seek concrete, economic solutions to farmer grievances and to challenge local elites in the process.

Because they challenged those in power, Populists could appreciate freedom. They came to see the importance of social relationships rather than individual morality in explaining political attitudes. If conservatives could stress the individual corruption and evil conspiracies of a few men, reformers learned to look deeper. They concentrated on specific economic grievances rather than vague, unfocused resentments. The very existence of agrarian radicals increased the alternatives in rural society, thereby promoting diversity.

Certainly there were aspects of Populism which make the modern observer uncomfortable. Populist leaders appealed to rural suspicion of the city and were unable to suppress their belief in rural superiority. The rural fundamentalist Populist rhetoric made it difficult to attract urban allies, without which the movement was doomed. Many in the Populist crusade were cranky and narrow-minded. But a total assessment of Populism cannot be made so easily. Let us evaluate the movement in light of the specific pluralist attacks.

Some of these charges have to do with the general Populist ideology. Hofstadter has criticized the movement for its naïve belief in a natural harmony of society and a two-sided struggle between the people and the interests. These charges need not long detain us. The Populist rhetoric here derives from Lockean liberalism and was shared by conservatives as well as Populists. Conservatives and Populists attacked each other for interfering with the natural harmony of the world; each saw the other as a special interest. That reality is more complex than political slogans should surprise no one.

More serious is the alleged Populist commitment to a conspiracy theory of history. As a rural movement with religious roots, Populism was especially prone to dramatize experience. It existed at a time when politics as a whole was played at this level. Where Populists saw conspiracies of bankers, conservatives feared anarchist conspiracies. There is little question that many Populist writers exhibited a conspiracy mentality. It is harder to come to an assessment of the importance of that mentality in the movement. Hofstadter argues that Populism was preoccupied with conspiracies. On the other hand, a recent study of Kansas Populism concludes that those who went to "international conspiracy" extremes were a small lunatic fringe of Populism.

More than that, the Populists had been left behind by industrialization, left out of politics by the east and by their own local elites. There were, for example, virtually no farmers in local positions of party leadership in

pre-Populist Kansas and Nebraska. But most of the local Populist leaders
were farmers. Their perception of courthouse "rings" making political decisions was close to the truth. Similarly, on the national level agreements
and conspiracies between capitalists were an important part of industrialization. In the legal world, the American Bar Association played an important
role in cementing close ties and informal contacts between judges and conservative lawyers. Perhaps Henry Demarest Lloyd paid insufficient attention
in *Wealth Against Commonwealth* to the general laws of capitalist development in the creation of Standard Oil. Certainly Sumner and Spencer paid
insufficient attention to the illegal acts and conspiracies of particular men.

In part, Hofstadter recognizes this and suggests a distinction between the perception of particular conspiracies and the perception of history
as a conspiracy. This is an intellectually impeccable distinction, but one
should not overestimate the ease of drawing it in the political practice of the
late nineteenth century. . . .

If specific charges of jingoism and anti-Semitism fail, what of the
general view of Populism as a moral crusade, destructive of individual differences and privacy? One should not underestimate the elements of a crusade in Populism.

Populism was a Protestant revival in an already intolerant rural
setting. There was in rural society little attention paid to the freedom of
individuals as individuals. Individual freedom was enforced, if at all, by
group power rather than by neutral societal institutions concerned with the
protection of individual rights. In practice, the individual Hatfield might be
protected by his family against the individual McCoy, the individual Con-
gregationalist by his church against the Anglicans. In theory, there were few
institutionalized protections for minority rights. For John Locke, the theorist
of rural liberalism, homogeneity seemed to obviate the need for minority
safeguards. The major protections entirely altered the relationship between
the individual and the society — the right to leave and the right of revolution. With the growth of an urban society, anonymity and individual
freedom grew too. Bureaucratic structures concerned with restraints on
government arose. Supreme Court interpretations of the Bill of Rights and
the Fourteenth Amendment to guarantee individual liberties are strikingly
a twentieth-century phenomenon, as is the growth of the American Civil
Liberties Union.

Frederic Howe captured the flavor of rural society well when he described his boyhood in Meadville, Pennsylvania:

> One could be sharp in business, possibly corrupt in politics, but one
> should not forget that life was a serious business, that duty should be
> always before one's eyes, that one should be diligent in things distasteful,

and that self-fulfillment meant getting on in the world, being assiduous to church-going, rather exhibitive in attendance on revivals, the holding to one's particular church denomination, and the avoidance of even the appearance of careless morals, drinking or association with men of questionable opinions.

The other important thing was to live as other men lived, do as other men did, avoid any departure from what other men thought. Not to conform was dangerous to one's reputation. Men who had strange ideas, who protested, who thought for themselves, were quietly ostracized.[5]

As Howe recognized, much of the evangelicalism and intolerance of this rural environment went into the reform movements. Indeed, the roots of Populism in a grass roots, evangelical Protestant mentality cannot be exaggerated. The Populist revolt called forth perhaps the most intense and widespread political involvement in American history. As the historian of the Texas People's Party puts it,

> Populism sprang from the soil. It came into being in many sections of the state within the space of a brief period almost as if by pre-arrangement, yet there was no relation between the various local phases of the movement aside from that provided by the common conditions from which all grew. It was, then, in its incipient stages a spontaneous, almost explosive force.[6]

Progressivism was primarily an elite phenomenon. Populism was a mass uprising. Farmers traveled miles with their families to large camp meetings. They read the immense outpouring of the Populist press, passing the pamphlets and newspapers from hand to hand. They filled local schoolhouses in the evenings, and participated in politics in hundreds of counties throughout the Great Plains and the South. The major parties could count on traditional loyalties, and their local organizations were often moribund. The Populists would have been lost without the remarkable activity of their grass roots supporters.

The revivalist character of this mass uprising is striking. Ministers and ex-ministers were active in the movement; the camp meetings resembled nothing so much as religious revivals. Populist gatherings were sober affairs, suspicious of luxury and full of religious paraphernalia. The party was known as the party of righteousness, and such groups as the Germans feared for their Sunday cards and beer.

Surely this supports the perception of the movement as a dangerous, mass fundamentalist crusade, particularly in light of the Scopes trial, the 1920's Ku Klux Klan, and the more recent manifestations of fundamentalist extremism.

The rural, Protestant Populist environment hardly seems fertile soil for a tolerant, democratic, forward-looking politics. But analyzing the Populist crusade as a product of the intolerance of rural respectability misses a fundamental point. To be an agrarian radical was to challenge respectability. The dominant institutions of nineteenth century rural America — church, press, politicians, local business elites — were all opposed to agrarian radicalism. The established elites owed their political power in part to the cultivation of intolerance; to moralistic appeals to patriotism, Americanism and the like; to religious fundamentalism; and to the power of conformity. Agrarian radicalism in part participated in this style of politics but in a more basic sense had to combat these methods of political control.

Certain kinds of crusades under certain circumstances destroy privacy and individual differences. But the circumstances in which Populism found itself are important. Because it was a minority movement against powerful elites, because it was in an American tradition of individualism and freedom, the movement could see many of the advantages of free speech and privacy. Thus Populists pushed for the introduction of a secret ballot. Nor did Populist "Americanism" cause them to persecute the opposition. Like agrarian radicals during World War I, Populists were the victims of superpatriotism rather than its perpetrators.

There are three specific areas in which the Populist crusade is alleged to have interfered with freedom. The first of these is in the university. In the Populist and progressive periods there was considerable interference with academic freedom, for academic tenure was not firmly institutionalized as it is today. Although many writers cite Populist interferences with academic freedom, in point of fact there is only one example. In Kansas, the Populists ignored academic tenure in reorganizing the Kansas State Agricultural College. This was not, it should be pointed out, because they were suspicious of "overeducation"; they rather had a somewhat naïve faith in what education could accomplish. In Kansas, they desired to introduce a liberal arts curriculum into an exclusively agricultural college. In this case the interference with academic freedom resulted not from anti-intellectualism but from enthusiasm for education. This is not the sort of mentality traditionally associated with attacks on academic freedom. Moreover, the view that the populist attitudes of the American masses make them anti-intellectual ignores the crucial question of which particular elites (if any) are going to lead anti-intellectual crusades or give in to them. On the whole, in America these functions have been performed by conservative elites, and radical intellectuals like Thorstein Veblen have been the victims. The Populists were not the fathers of modern witch-hunts.

Populist support for prohibition is also cited as evidence for the dangerous effects of the Populist crusade. It is true that Populist voters tended to support prohibition referenda and that prohibition was one of the progressive reforms associated with the initiative, the referendum, and female suffrage. In part, this was because liquor interests played a corrupt role in state politics. In part, it was because temperance, like economic reform, was seen as a necessary precondition for individual advancement. In part, it was out of simple intolerance for the habits of particular ethnic groups and urban classes. However, a proviso should be entered here. In the early days of the prohibition movement, the Prohibition Party platform was generally radical. In the 1890's Prohibition platforms resembled Populist platforms. However, the real cultivation of rural ignorance and prejudice came not in this period, but with the rise of the practical, single-interest, conservative Anti-Saloon League.

Moreover, our concern is not only with the attitude of Populist constituents toward prohibition but the attitude of the movement itself. At the county level, Populists and Prohibitionists often had close relationships. Some state Populist parties, as in North Dakota, endorsed prohibition. It was more common, however, for the movement to steer away from that controversial issue, as it did in South Dakota, Iowa, Texas, and generally in Kansas.

Another charge leveled against the Populist crusade is that it sought to destroy representative democracy. Here again one must measure Populist practice against the claims of its opponents. While many Populists favored the initiative and the referendum, the political reforms most stressed by the Populists were the secret ballot and the direct election of senators. Certainly the Populists sought to challenge the political and economic power of those who dominated American society at the turn of the twentieth century. Certainly the direct election of senators increased the power of the people vis-à-vis the elites. But it is highly dubious that such a Populist reform was a threat to representative democracy. Finally, the Populist attacks on the courts indicate disregard for law and order not so much by the Populists as by the courts themselves. In 1895 alone, the Supreme Court invalidated the income tax and refused to apply the Sherman Act to the sugar monopoly while upholding Debs' conviction under it. This consistent, narrow partiality in interpreting the laws and the constitution explains Populist attitudes better than deductions concerning "plebiscitory democracy."

That Populism was in significant measure a Protestant crusade is impossible to deny. It is also true that the conditions permitting a movement of this sort to focus on concrete economic reforms were fast disappearing. Nevertheless, charges that the Populists were authoritarian are not supported by the evidence. Particularly in contrast to the politics it opposed, Populism was clearly a democratic phenomenon.

Are we required, then, to call Populism an example of class rather than status politics? In the categories of class and status politics, we meet the issue of moralism and pragmatism in another form. For the Beardians,

Populism was a pragmatic class movement, representing the special interests of farmers as other groups represented the special interests of their constituencies. The pluralists have seen that Beardian analysis cannot describe the Populist movement successfully. However, in their distinction between "class" and "status" politics they have not transcended Beardian categories. Accepting the narrow Beardian definition of an economic movement and finding that Populism was more than this, they have underplayed its economic character. Rather than transcending the Beardian analysis, they have stood it on its head.

Hofstadter, for example, implicitly interprets Populism as an example of status politics. Distinguishing between the hard and the soft side of the agrarian spirit, he writes,

> The farmer's commercial position pointed to the usual strategies of the business world: combination, cooperation, pressure politics, lobbying, piecemeal activity directed toward specific goals. But the bathos of the agrarian rhetoric pointed in a different direction: broad political goals, ideological mass politics, third parties, the conquest of the "money power," the united action of all labor, rural and urban.

Relating this to Populism, Hofstadter explains that in bad times the farmer rejected his role as a capitalist and "withdrew into the role of the injured little yeoman." The Farmers' Alliance and the Populist Party had their hard side (business methods, pressure politics), he says, but as the depression deepened the soft Populist rhetoric triumphed and all issues were dropped for the silver panacea.[7]

In order to make the progressive movement an example of status politics, Hofstadter argues that status politics is born of prosperity. This will not do for the Populists; since they flourished during a depression, they would become a class political phenomenon. But Hofstadter reserves class politics for narrow interest groups. The term would place the Populists in an incorrect and — for him — too favorable light. He therefore first treats the Populist party as an irrational response to crisis; it appears to be an example of status politics. He then turns to the achievements of practical farm organizations with narrow economic goals. According to him these were associated with agricultural prosperity. This was the same period of prosperity that produced progressive status politics.

Hofstadter could overcome the contradiction here explicitly by excepting rural politics from the normal class-status cycle. But this would hardly render his treatment of Populism itself more convincing. For while Populism was certainly more than a narrow pressure group, it was still an economic movement making practical demands. As C. Vann Woodward has pointed out, the Populist demands did not ignore economics but rather were "obsessively economic." [8] The business ventures of the Farmers' Alliance were in part examples of farmer unwillingness to come to terms with industrial capitalism. In shifting to politics, the farmers recognized the insufficiency of purely business methods. The politicizing of the Alliance was not simply the result of self-pity; the depression rendered nonpolitical solutions futile. In fact, Hofstadter himself later attributes a measure of success to the third party. Finally, if "the bathos of agrarian rhetoric" produced the free silver panacea as well as the third party, why did free silver destroy both the third party and the general third-party demands? The answer is that free silver did not dominate third-party Populism. It was rather the panacea of the more conservative (and practical?) Democrats like Bryan who were too conservative to make demands for basic changes in American society; they preferred panaceas. Indeed, free silver did not dominate the Populist movement until, in its practical desire to win power, it sought fusion with the Democrats. Here is the ultimate irony; Hofstadter damns Populism for the practical, opportunistic concern for power at the expense of broad, ideological principles — the very politics that wins his praise when practiced by the major parties.

Hofstadter's treatment makes of Populism an irrational, unnecessary movement. This is also the consequence of other pluralist arguments. In Kornhauser's scheme, mass movements arise when the masses are available for mobilization and the elites are accessible to influence from below. In his analysis, the only societies where the masses are available but the elites inaccessible are totalitarian.[9] Surely some finer distinctions are in order. One would like to know which elites are accessible and which inaccessible. To which constituencies are elites accessible, to which inaccessible? By what methods are elites accessible, and what methods will they resist or ignore?

In a basic sense, the elites in America are accessible to popular influence, but mass movements generally arise because of the inaccessibility of elites to the interests of the members of mass movements and in this sense their inaccessibility to the pressure group politics of pluralism. Thus in Populist states, politics was often controlled from outside and the elites that made political decisions were not accessible to the bulk of people. On the national level, the elites were also inaccessible. Particularly important here was the role of the Supreme Court in rejecting legislation that reformers were able to pass. Because the Supreme Court was not accessible to reform influence, it played the role of radicalizing political discontent.

Other factors besides the inaccessibility of elites obviously contribute to the rise of mass movements and determine their character. But whether the movements are democratic or totalitarian, their appearance is related to the inaccessibility of elites. By basing mass movements on the accessibility of elites, Kornhauser denies them the possibility of being a rational response to social crises. For if the elites are accessible, mass movements are unnecessary.

Similarly, when Kornhauser writes that the "objects" of mass movements are "remote" and do not "directly concern the individual," he again makes mass movements irrational by definition. Interest rates, railroads, corporations, and the money supply certainly concerned the Populist farmers directly. And the Populists were perfectly reasonable in believing that control over railroads, interest rates, corporations, and the money supply was exercised in places remote from the Great Plains. Would they have been more rational to focus their anger on neighboring shopkeepers?

Just as the distinction between moralism and pragmatism cannot contain the Lockean ideology, so the distinctions between proximate and remote concerns, class and status politics, cannot contain agrarian radicalism. As conceived of by the pluralists, class (proximate) politics are concerned with immediate economic group self-interest, status (remote) politics with position in the social structure. Class politics seek gains for the value of the gains themselves (more money, better working conditions, tax benefits, and so forth). Status politics seeks gains because of what they signify (conspicuous consumption, keeping up with the Jones, demonstrating Americanism vis-à-vis the Anglo-Saxons, etc.). Contrary to the pluralist view, periods of prosperity and satisfaction seem to produce both status and class politics in America. As de Tocqueville recognized, in America these are not so different. The group scramble that dominates politics during prosperity involves both "status" concerns and direct, narrow, economic advancement. In a crisis period, however, neither interest-group nor status politics can succeed. In the Populist period, "business methods" were doomed to failure. Similarly, in Wisconsin during the 1930's depression a precursor of McCarthy attempted to win office on the ("status") issue of communism. Ignoring the economic grievances of the people, he was soundly beaten.

Populism, like Marxism, sought to combine a general program for the political control of industrialization with the concrete demands of a significant social force. But the Populist movement was hardly revolutionary. For better or worse, neither the movement nor the farmers it represented wanted to free themselves from the Lockean inheritance.

Marxism was revolutionary; Populism was not. But this was hardly the only difference between them. If agrarian radicalism played a role in America analogous to the role of Marxism in Europe, then in a sense American farmers took the place of European workers. In Europe industrialization uprooted the peasants from the land and brought them to the cities, where they became revolutionary workers. But the uprooted European peasants who settled in American cities remained conservative. In America the farmers who stayed on the land played the role of European workers as the major force challenging industrial capitalism.

How is this to be explained? The absence of feudalism on the one hand hindered the development of working-class consciousness. On the other hand it provided a yeoman farming class instead of a tradition-bound peasantry. The commitment to individual mobility obstructed the rise of socialist consciousness among workers, but it fostered agrarian radicalism. Farmer mobility, farmer experience in self-help, farmer cooperation along the frontier, all enabled farmers to organize politically. They did not require a Napoleonic leader to represent them. Moreover, fascism, feudal in its corporateness and in its attack on individualism, was less likely to appeal to American farmers. And as the class most committed to self-help and individual success, they reacted bitterly against the neofeudal society they saw being created around them.

For three-quarters of a century after the Civil War, there were continual movements of rural protest in the western Middle West. Movements like Populism and 1920's progressivism arose in response to specific agricultural depressions. But depressions alone cannot explain the continual strength of agrarian radicalism in this period. Both farmers and progressives prospered in the decade before World War I. The Non-Partisan League was organized in North Dakota during prosperity and declined during depression. One must look beyond depressions to the long-term structural situation of the American farmer.

The greater exposure of agriculture to international market conditions after the Civil War increased the instability of agricultural life. To compound dependence on the market, newly settled farmers usually produced a single crop; this exposed the farmers not only to market conditions in general but to the widespread fluctuations in the price of a single commodity. Moreover, farming methods had not yet made much impact on the hazards of weather on the Great Plains. Agrarian radicalism has always been stronger in the wheat than in the corn-hog areas. Wheat farming depends more on the weather and on other events over which the farmer has no control. The wheat farmer is traditionally inclined to take the help he can get from outside sources like the government. Corn-hog farming, on the other hand, depends far more on the day-to-day activities of the individual farmer. The conservative, antigovernment commitment to rugged individualism is more meaningful in the corn belt.

The Populist-progressive era was close to the period of settlement. One cannot speak with certainty about the influence of the frontier, but it seems reasonable to suppose that the frontier unsettled tradition and increased the effort to meet problems through political self-help. As the frontier influence declined, these areas became more conservative.

Ethnic traditions also contributed to political protest. The West North Central states plus Wisconsin had far higher percentages of foreign-born in their populations than the states of any other region in the country.

This concentration of the foreign-born was particularly striking compared to other rural areas. Early studies showed a tendency for the foreign-born to support protest movements more than nativestock Americans. The research here provides no similar evidence within the progressive states. But if the foreign-born as a whole did not disproportionately support agrarian radicalism at the same time, different groups of foreign-born perpetuated it at different times. Scandinavians and Germans were concentrated in the western Middle West. The Scandinavians consistently supported Populism and progressivism. The Germans, usually resistent to agrarian radicalism, kept it alive during and after World War I.

One might argue, moreover, that ethnic conflict provided a challenge to the political systems in the West North Central states. In the eastern cities, this challenge was met by the machine. In the countryside such a solution was impractical for several reasons — the different character of the ethnic groups, the contrasts in urban and rural political styles, the visibility of economic targets for resentment, the conditions of agriculture, the strength of a tradition of agrarian revolt, the greater isolation within rural areas. Therefore, ethnic dissatisfaction focused on broader class and political goals.

Political conditions added their weight to economic and cultural factors. Politically, the farmers of the Middle West were isolated from the centers of power in the society. This did not mean that they were ignorant of the problems of the larger society so much as it meant that the larger society did not understand their problems. The midwest rural world lacked the power to make the outside political elites sensitive to agrarian demands and moderate on agrarian issues. Political control in the trans-Mississippi West was more nakedly in the hands of railroads and other businesses than was the case in states with a longer political tradition. In many instances, the western states were controlled by outside railroads and corporations. This elite inaccessibility provoked radical demands and radical movements.

Agrarian society, however, was not static. The changes that had produced agrarian radical movements finally undermined them. Consider for the moment only the decline in farm population. In 1860, 59.7 percent of all workers in the country worked on farms. By 1900, the figure was down to 35.7 percent. Farmers were no longer a majority of the population. The decline in the relative number of farmers continued in the twentieth century. From 1920 to 1944, there was a large net migration from the farms. In the West North Central states, where agrarian radical movements had flourished, this decline was especially pronounced. Between 1920 and 1944, the net migration from farms in the West North Central states averaged about 2 percent for each four-year period. By 1950 less than 15 percent of the total United States population lived on farms. Thus, if farmers in America played the role of workers in Europe, workers were the wave of the industrial future on both continents. A farmer-labor alliance in the 1890's might have altered the course of American development, but labor was turning in a different direction. Workers voted against Bryan in 1896, and Gompers had earlier refused to ally the AFL with the Populist Party. As he interpreted working class mentality, it was through with the middle-class radicalism that had permeated the labor movement since Jacksonian days. Before the rise of the AFL, the aim of working-class organizations had been to keep the class structure fluid, to provide for social mobility. This led to alliance with "the people" (farmers and others of the small middle class) rather than to specific class action and specific job-oriented demands. In joining purely class-oriented craft unions, workers accepted the permanency of the wage-earning status for themselves if not for their children. When European workers organized on a class basis, they recognized their wage-earning status only in order to challenge the permanency of a system which had wage-earning statuses in it. But in America, class action was a substitute for a general challenge to the industrial capitalist system.

The class organizations of American workers, then, tended not to participate in broad movements of social change from the Populist period through the 1920's. (However, at certain times and in selected areas some American workers allied themselves with socialism and progressivism.) After the defeat of Populism, agrarian radicalism continued to flourish to the First World War and beyond. But the New Deal and the rise of the CIO reoriented American politics. Workers came to supply the main base of reform, not in alliance with rural areas but against them. Farmer leadership in American radicalism had come to an end.

Neither Revolution nor Reform

SHELDON HACKNEY

Like Rogin and Pollack, the author of the following selection believes that self-interest is not a powerful enough motive to explain the intensity that pervaded the Populist experience. Yet, because Populists voted against several forward-looking reform measures in the Alabama legislature, he does not consider them to be future oriented enough to be termed radicals nor pragmatic enough to be considered reformers. An ideology of transformation was the missing ingredient. At the end of the selection reprinted here, Hackney suggests that Populism's power orientation might provide a key to interpretation.

Social movements come in many different varieties and can be catalogued according to many different traits, but one of their most interesting differentiating characteristics is their power/ value dimension. Movements in which value drives predominate seek to reform policies, establish new norms, or change the values that govern conduct. Such changes might require new institutional arrangements so that the new rules might apply, but probably no great change in the sort of men who occupy positions of authority. The woman's suffrage movement, the temperence movement, and the birth control movement are all value oriented, as are the various reform components of Progressivism.

Power-oriented movements, on the other hand, focus on power relationships. They are preoccupied with the individuals and groups who wield power rather than with public policy. All revolutionary movements, especially coups d'etat, have strong power orientations, and if the major political parties were movements rather than institutions they would also make prime examples. But a more precise instance of power orientation is the "Share Our Wealth" movement of Huey Long.

One way to distinguish between power-oriented and value-oriented movements is the form taken by the movement if it goes astray, becomes corrupted, or somehow ceases to pursue its legitimate goals. For value-oriented movements, the chief danger is that it will settle for symbolic victories rather than pressing for substantive change. Power-oriented movements, by contrast, sometimes are misled by expressive leaders, demagogues who might call attention to the grievances of the discontented and assert the worth of their life style but who accomplish no real changes in their situation.

Power orientations predominated in Populism. Without grasping this it would be difficult to understand the metaphor of revolution that permeated Populist rhetoric. Henry Demarest Lloyd was appealing to this anticipation of an overturning and a renewal when he wrote in 1894, "Revolutions never go backward. If the People's party goes backward it is not a revolution, and if it is not a revolution it is nothing." The intended revolution, however, may have been largely in the identity of the people in power rather than in their policies or in existing institutions.

While clinging to a platform consisting of planks developed in earlier stages of the agrarian protest movement or borrowed from other reform forces, the Populists were quite willing in practice to trim their program to a single mass-appeal issue on the hope that it would catapult them to power. The polarization implied

by the Populist bifurcation of the world into producers and nonproducers, their insistence that everyone choose sides in this
confrontation, and their emphasis upon throwing the rascals out
all point toward the power end of the value-power continuum.
Populist performance in legislatures was frequently marked by a
greater emphasis on increasing the number of Populist office
holders than on fulfilling platform pledges. To say this may be
only to say that Populists began very early to act as a political
party normally acts, but that explanation leaves unanswered the
important question of why Populists did not follow the agrarian
reform tradition as represented earlier in the Grange and the
Farmers' Alliance or later in the pressure group tactics of the
American Farm Bureau Federation.

Several forces were at work urging disgruntled farmers toward
the power orientations of a third party. It may be a general trait
of movements formed out of downwardly mobile social elements
that, because of their insecurity, power orientations predominate.
This characteristic would be particularly valid if the movement
has drawn into its vortex people who are normally politically
apathetic or socially disorganized. The deepening farm crisis
produced in the men who became Populists a sense of desperation. The absence of a sympathetic response from those holding
formal positions of responsibility, in conjunction with the ridicule
of the farmer's movement by the polite press, must have convinced the sufferers that relief would only come when the power
structure was remanned with men who were much closer to the
soil — or at least closer to the tillers of the soil, and who thus
would understand the plight of the farmers. In addition to these
factors, the Populist leadership depended heavily upon men who
had previous experience in unsuccessful third parties. Ignatius
Donnelly from Minnesota, the author of the preamble to the
1892 Populist platform, was in turn Republican, Liberal Republican, Granger, Greenbacker, Allianceman, and Populist. Gene
Clanton, in Kansas Populism, Ideas and Men (Lawrence: The
University Press of Kansas, 1969), calculates that 59 per cent of
the Populist leadership there had passed through other third
parties. Even if those men were not "outsider" personalities to
begin with, their experience with political failure, and probably
with ridicule, would give them a very jaundiced view of those
who worked within the two-party system. Replacing the in-
cumbents would then become for the "outsider" leaders a primary
aim.

The relative mixture of power and value orientations would
not matter if real differences in behavior did not result. How
might the power/value distinction help us to understand the
tactical decision favoring fusion, the intransigence of the opposi-

tion to Populism, and the slow speed with which Populist ideas filtered into public policy? Those who remain unsatisfied by the ambivalent stance of the following selection or by the power/ value distinction will have to offer an alternative framework that will explain the apparent anomalies in Populist behavior and elevate our understanding.

The Populists in Alabama faced a very frustrating situation. According to their own view, they had been twice cheated out of control of the Democratic Party and now twice defrauded in the regular elections of 1892 and 1894. The irritations of their position were exacerbated by the fact that Alabama still had no legal provision for contesting elections. The way in which the Populists adapted to this increasing frustration yields another clue to the nature of the movement.

Their growing unwillingness to submit meekly to fraud is best measured by the anticipations of violence that abounded during and after the campaign of 1894. Frustration was beginning to tell. One Populist editor, I. L. Brock, in 1893 advised the Populists to "MEET FRAUD WITH FORCE." [1]* This was the counterpart of the Tillmanite battle cry from South Carolina which the Troy *Jeffersonian* echoed a year later, "Ballots or Bullets." [2] Such slogans could be dismissed if they were not accompanied by many other rumors and portents of violence. A Birmingham man warned the *Jeffersonian* that "the Jonesite faction must be kicked out of power, or we may have a sample of the times in bleeding Kansas in 1855." [3] Two months later the *Jeffersonian* observed that the "demagogues in congress do the will of the plutogogues in Wall Street." The paper added ominously that "if relief for the masses does not come through equitable law it will come through revolution." [4] . . .

The congressional elections held on November 6 cast some light on the psychological condition of Alabama voters. The results showed that a candidate's ideological position mattered much less than his orientation toward the groups contesting for power. Milford W. Howard, the Populist candidate in the 7th District, won a resounding victory over a free-silver Democrat, W. H. Denson. In three other districts Democratic candidates were apparently elected, only to be unseated later by Congress. A. T. Goodwyn, a Populist, successfully contested the election of James E. Cobb, a free-

From Sheldon Hackney, *Populism to Progressivism in Alabama* (Princeton: Princeton University Press, 1969), 63–88. Reprinted by permission of Princeton University Press. Footnotes selectively omitted.
* [See pp. 156–157 for notes to this article. — Ed.]

silver Democrat. Gaston A. Robbins and Oscar W. Underwood, Democrats, had both courted the Alliance and had sought the support of the silver advocates. They were unseated by W. F. and T. H. Aldrich, Republican brothers endorsed by the Populists, who were coal operators and consistent advocates of high protective tariffs and sound money.

Shortly after the election, on November 12, the joint Jeffersonian and People's Party convention met in the Montgomery Theater. Fearing that they would never give up the Capitol once inside, Governor Thomas G. Jones had denied them the usual courtesy of the use of the building. Dr. Grattan B. Crow wanted to seize the Capitol by force and had raised an armed force to help in the venture. The gathering was enthusiastic but took no drastic step. It did vote finally to drop the fictitious dual organization and merge into the People's Party. The delegates also voted not to take any extralegal action until the legislature had had a chance to redress the party's grievances.

In the absence of a contest law, the legislature made short work of the Populist petition which claimed that the Populists had evidence of massive frauds and asked the legislature to disallow the returns from certain counties until the evidence could be heard. On November 17 the General Assembly in joint session ignored the Populist petition and quickly proclaimed Oates the winner of the August election.

Two days later Reuben F. Kolb published a manifesto dated November 17 in his new paper in Birmingham, *The People's Weekly Tribune* — "You, fellow citizens, have twice elected me governor of this state," and declared ominously, "and this time, by the grace of God and the help of the good people of Alabama, I will be governor. December 1 is the day fixed by the law for the inauguration of the governor. On that date I shall be in Montgomery for the purpose of taking the oath of office and my seat as governor." [5] The headlines of a hostile paper screamed: "KOLB TO BE SEATED IF IT IS TO BE DONE BY SLAUGHTERING THE STATE MILITIA." [6] The newspaper reported that the state militia had been given orders to shoot to kill if necessary. The Anniston *Hot Blast* unleashed its doggerel.

> Reuben! Reuben! I've been thinking,
> And I tell you for your health:
> When you start this bad blood spilling,
> Be sure and spill it from yourself.[7]

December 1, 1894 was a good day for a revolution in Montgomery. The sun shone brightly and the temperature was quite warm at noon when William C. Oates took his place at the spot on the Capitol steps where Jefferson Davis had stood to take the oath as President of the Confederate States of America. Chief Justice Brickell was waiting with the Bible Davis

had used in the ceremony 33 years before. These symbols of Southern legitimacy were necessary in view of Oates' cloudy moral claim to the office.

While the inaugural parade passed through the crowded streets on
the way to the ceremony during the hour before noon, Reuben F. Kolb took
the oath of office downtown before a Justice of the Peace. Only a few wit-
nesses and fellow insurgents were present in the drab office on South Court
Street. Then the little party of defiant men marched up the hill to the
Capitol for Kolb to deliver his address from the traditional spot.

Arriving at the Capitol grounds, they found every entrance blocked
by one of the 20 companies of state troops. The troops allegedly were in
town for ceremonial purposes and parade duty, but they carried live ammunition. The little group of Populists made its way through the ranks of the
troops toward the right side of the big stone steps leading down from the
Capitol. A detachment of troops quickly moved between the interlopers and
the strategic steps. Governor Jones was on the steps and told Kolb and Warren S. Reese that they could not speak there. Probably at this point a crowd
urged Kolb to speak anyway. Kolb turned to the firebrand, Joseph C. Manning, and asked his advice. "Go ahead, Captain," Manning replied, "they
may kill you, but you will go down in history as a martyr to the Populist
cause." [8]

Kolb refused this invitation to immortality. The small knot of Populists left the Capital grounds and found an empty wagon nearby on Bain-
bridge Street. Standing in this wagon and speaking to only two or three
hundred people, Kolb made his inaugural address. He insisted he was the
lawful governor and demanded that a contest law be passed, but he urged
that there be no violence. The crowd dispersed quietly. It was distinctly
anticlimactic.

Governor Jones thought his threat of force had kept the Populists
from trying stronger measures. "They planned to kidnap Oates and myself
the day before the inauguration, and to take possession of the Capitol and
inaugurate Capt. Kolb," Jones said years later. But the plan failed because
"they feared that it would have cost them their lives." [9] The failure was
worse than Jones imagined. Few Populists even showed up in Montgomery
on inauguration day despite Kolb's plea. Had thousands of angry Populists
been in the city on December 1, things might have happened differently, regardless of the troops. But the 83,000 men who voted Populist in August did
not feel in December that Populism was worth a revolution or even a show
of force.

The Populists backed away from their revolutionary posture soon
after the inauguration day fiasco. A few evenings later the Populist legislators met in a quiet caucus and agreed to continue to act within the law until
the end of the session. If a contest law were passed, they would abide by its

decision. If the legislature did not pass such an act, or if any other oppressive laws were enacted, the Populists would call another convention to decide a course of action.[10] In January, when Kolb sent to the legislature a request for a contest law, he signed it "Governor of Alabama." The General Assembly passed the contest law in February. Because the bill applied only to future elections and not to the election of 1894, three Populists in the House voted against it. Otherwise they did nothing. When the Populist state Executive Committee met in March it condemned the Democrats for stealing the election, but at the same time it announced that Kolb was abandoning his pretense of being the legitimate governor for the sake of peace, law, and order.

If the Populists were not revolutionaries, neither did they behave like reformers. They repeatedly showed a willingness to vote against reforms to which they were pledged. Populists performed in this bizarre fashion in the biennial legislative session that convened on November 16, 1894. The size of their minority delegation in this legislature was large enough to command consideration from the majority. 35 Populists and 65 Democrats sat in the House of Representatives while 8 Populists and 27 Democrats composed the Senate.

Populists performed variously on minor legislation. They were most consistent in fulfilling their pledges to labor by voting for bills to require the prompt payment of wages and the honest weighing of coal. The same allegiance appeared in their votes against appropriations for the state militia, and against funds to provide a state exhibit at the Cotton States International Exhibition in Atlanta. On a bill to give an enforceable lien to the ginners of cotton, the Populists split. The only votes in the House in favor of yeomen and tenant farmers were Populist votes, but half of the Populists voted with the majority for the ginners. This was an important indication of the internal division which in large part gave rise to Populist inability to define objectives for the party. Spot checks of special bills reveal that Populists were inconsistent and divided in their votes on local prohibition and on authorizations for urban bond issues.

The most important issues to face the 1894 legislature concerned taxation, child labor, and the convict lease system. These were issues which remained of fundamental concern to reform-minded Alabamians for the next 15 years or longer; they were the question that helped to define Alabama Progressivism. When challenged on the grounds of real and immediate need, Populists proved that they were not reformers.

Taxation was always a basic issue. It was on tax policy that Progressives showed their most decisive break with the past and affirmation of the future. The Populists acted differently. In 1894 the state was in debt and running a deficit. One reason was that while the assessed value of property had been climbing since 1876, the legislature had constantly decreased the tax rate from 7 mills in 1876 to 4 mills in the period 1890 to 1894. Early in the 1894–95 session the House passed a bill raising the tax rate to 5½ mills. The Populists voted as a bloc against the tax increase. The constant emphasis on low taxes and inexpensive government in Populist papers leaves little doubt that they were still wedded to the idea of minimum government, despite frequent infidelities of thought. Their fear of debt casts doubt on their grasp of the future needs and direction of society. The Populist vote could have been a demand for a change in the tax structure, for the tax structure discriminated against the owners of real property devoted to agriculture. But as their performance on the revenue bill showed, Populist motivation lay elsewhere.

Sponsored by Sam Will John, an important Progressive who in 1907 was [B. B.] Comer's floor leader in the House of Representatives, the revenue bill was designed to shift the burden of taxation to the broad shoulders of railroads and other corporations. It provided for an excise tax on bank deposits and intangible assets, and more stringent machinery to make assessments more truthful and less easy to escape.

The John bill faced tough opposition from the friends of railroads and corporations. With the help of the Populists, John staved off attempts to amend or kill the bill. However, when the clerk was reading the bill for the third time just prior to passage, Populists leaders circulated the word among their followers to vote against the bill for "tactical reasons." The House then defeated it 32 to 49. No Populist voted for the bill.

The following day a special committee worked out a compromise, and the House passed it the same day. The compromise omitted the excise tax on corporations and weakened the machinery for assessing property. The legislature passed the compromise bill with the Populists still solidly in opposition.

Populist legislators performed unpredictably on another reform measure sponsored by Sam Will John — one aimed at the convict lease system. The *Register* pointed out that the death rate at Coalburg, operated by the Sloss Company, was more than twice the mortality rate among convicts in Mississippi and 10 times that of Ohio convicts. Unhealthful conditions and a 66-hour workweek undoubtedly contributed to these figures. There were also nonhumanitarian reasons for abolishing the system. Miners opposed the lease system because convict labor had the effect of setting a ceiling on the wages of free miners and depressed what were already unsafe working conditions. In 1893 Julia Tutwiler, Alabama's great lady reformer, said the system was "one that combines all the evils of slavery without one of its ameliorating features."[11] Governor Jones was proud of the small beginning the legislature had made during his administration toward changing the purpose of the system from profit to self-sufficiency with decent conditions — which was all destroyed under Oates.

Sam Will John felt "that the whole system is a shame to any Christian state, and cannot be too soon blotted out forever." [12] He introduced an amendment which aimed at doing just that. Unfortunately the House tabled his measure by a vote of 34 to 30. In their platform the Populists promised to abolish the convict lease system, yet some of them were distinctly unenthusiastic about fulfilling that pledge; 11 voted against John's reform and 10 voted for it.

The Populists performed with no greater consistency with regard to child labor. Alabama law prohibited employers from compelling women to work more than eight hours per day, and forbade children under 14 years of age to work more than eight hours per day. Governor Oates recommended that the legislature repeal this restriction in order to lure outside capital into the state. The legislature complied. On December 4 the repeal bill passed, 53 to 7. Perhaps it is significant that of the 7 opposing votes, 6 were Populists, but 17 Populists voted with the majority to repeal the female and child labor law.

The antireform votes of the Populists pose a problem, particularly because their performance in subsequent legislatures and in the Constitutional Convention of 1901 continued to follow the same pattern. The most likely explanation is that the Populists wanted to demonstrate their potential as a balance-of-power voting bloc. Even if this were so, it demonstrates at the least that, unlike the Progressives, the Populists were not primarily issue-oriented. They were, patently, not reformers.

It may be that revolution was not a real possibility in 1894 either, or that there was any danger the Populists would use force or take any extralegal steps. Historians can never be certain. The psychology of rumor, however, indicates that there is danger of violence when rumors begin to assume a specifically threatening form. Before mobs erupt, there is usually a period of unstructured milling about during which the common feelings of members of the mob are frequently mentioned and reinforced by supportive attitudes from other members. This previolence condition evidently was closely approximated in Alabama in the fall of 1894 among the Populists. The element possibly missing was the clash between hostile belief systems. Conflicts over ideologies are less easily resolved than conflict over power. When the Alabama revolution of 1894 did not happen, it was most likely because there was no great ideological division between the opposing forces.

What sort of social movement was Populism? Was it reformist or revolutionary? Was it concerned with the here, the now, and the possible, or was it devoted to an outmoded past or perhaps to a chiliastic future? Was the

Populist mind rooted in reality or disoriented by anxiety? Much of the evidence needed to answer these questions has been presented above. The missing information has to do with the Populist state-of-mind, an imprecise area of investigation at best, and made more so by the great distances in time and environment between the investigator and the "typical" Populist.

Nevertheless, a good starting point in assessing Populist self-image is a revealing description of the composition of the movement written by an ordinary Populist. This letter to the editor declared that Populism was composed of "that class that makes a country rich, great, powerful, honorable and respectable, the people called the middle class, the people that pay the taxes to support government, produce the country's exports, fight its battles when need be to defend its honor. For you know that neither plutocrats or paupers will expose their lives and their blood in defense of the principles that advance civilization and tend to the uplifting of humanity." [13] Hardworking but poor, Populists had good reason to feel angry and defensive. Yet this particular Populist and those he resembled did not think of themselves as members of a persecuted minority, but rather as a victimized majority. Outsiders struggling for entry usually do not question the central norms and values of the class or society to which they aspire; they frequently adopt its standards long before they are actually members, and may zealously overconform to the group's ways after they achieve membership. On the other hand, loyal members who observe the rules and are denied the rewards may begin to wonder what is wrong with the system — the Populists belong in this category. In the 1890s one important rule was that work was morally good and success was supposed to accrue to those having moral worth. It was therefore natural for the hardworking poor to resent those who seemed to work less yet were materially more successful.

Milford W. Howard made a career of expressing the antagonistic feelings of persecuted failures toward "immoral" successes. He himself had played the game of speculator and promoter in the 1880s and lost, so he undoubtedly found the theme congenial. In Congress, where he served for two terms, Howard preached against the concentration of wealth in the United States. "How will you remedy this concentration?" he asked the Congress; "How can you reconcile a nation of paupers to toil in the shadow of splendor and magnificence to support the idle, worthless few?" [14]

And there was to be no mistake about who the idle, worthless few were. Howard wrote a book about them: *If Christ Came to Congress*. It was patterned very closely after W. T. Stead's popular exposé, *If Christ Came to Chicago;* Howard even included a map of the red-light district of Washington, as Stead had of Chicago. To leave absolutely no doubt as to where his sympathies lay, he dedicated his book to Grover Cleveland, "President of the United States, and his drunken, licentious cabinet and certain members of Congress." . . .

Such a striking example as Howard's is a reminder that the South in the 1890s was the sort of society that has frequently spawned millennial movements. Rapid economic changes were threatening the way of life of the small independent farmer and undermining the cohesion and stability of the social structure. In such a situation there may be a paranoiac response among those who feel impotent, exposed, and cast out. The Populists fit this pattern to a considerable extent; certainly their response was aggressive.

Basic to Howard's book, and fundamental to Populism, was the reaction of the people against their traditional leaders. Warren Reese perceived this growing alienation in his important speech at Brundidge, Alabama in August 1891 when he said the people no longer believed that wealth was distributed by society in a just way, "and the people in their sovereign might have determined that there shall be a radical change in our form of government." [15] . . . Another Populist editor commented that "the politicians have been promising the people relief for the last ten years, but they have never attempted to keep their promises. The people will depend on them no longer." [16] In short, the Populist movement was based on the belief that the people had lost control of their government.

Just as deeply imbedded in Populist psychology was the feeling that a conspiracy was afoot to deprive them of what should be rightfully theirs under the existing system with the existing concepts of justice and equity. The right of the laborer to the fruits of his labor, a maxim derived from the Protestant work ethic and not from Marx, was perhaps the most persistently invoked doctrine. "This much talked of labor struggle is not only between employer and employed, boss and wage worker," said a Populist paper, "but between the doers and the do-nothings, those who give an equivalent for what they receive and those supported by rent, interest and monopoly." [17] "Labor produces all wealth," another Populist paper stated. "Labor should enjoy what it produces." [18]

The bounties of nature were provided by God to be turned into wealth by labor. Therefore idle land was sinful — particularly when there were farmers willing to work who needed land. "See that, Mr. Landlord," the Populists asked in tones familiar to traditional rural classes complaining about land monopoly, "God says the land is His. How come you with more than you can use yourself to the exclusion of others who want and need it?" [19] In all Alliance and Populist platforms there was a demand for the government to reclaim unused land from railroads and alien landholders. These land speculators were good examples of the nonworkers who were trying to subject labor to unjust conditions. "Labor should be king," rang the battle cry, "instead of abject slave." [20]

Populist literature was also saturated with more general conspiracy theories. For instance, the *Alliance Herald* declared that "the Rothschilds are the head and front of the greatest financial conspiracy ever attempted in the history of the world." [21] "The Rothschilds are the kings of the earth, with their faithful allies and watchful coadjutors in every land," echoed the *Choctaw Alliance*.[22] The Troy *Jeffersonian* confirmed that "the money oligarchy is running the country." [23] Years later Joseph C. Manning still thought that capitalism meant "Invisible Government" and that the people could not trust it. Populists looked out upon the world with hostility and suspicion. They obviously felt oppressed, outcast, and powerless. "Oh wretched people that we are," cried the *Jeffersonian,* "who will deliver us from the oppression of heartless corporations?" [24]

The Populists were in a receptive mood to new doctrines in the early 1890s, as substantiated by their approval of reforms so at odds with traditional Jeffersonian dogma as federally financed rural credit plans, government ownership of railroads, a managed currency, and a protective tariff. But they retained major segments of the old set of values, never breaking completely away. The same platforms and pronouncements that demonstrated Populist willingness to break with the past in search of solutions for their real problems also gave voice to the continued desire for minimum government in the Jeffersonian mold. It is significant that their voting record was more consistent with negative government theory than with a new view of the possibilities of positive action by government.

Populists sometimes ridiculed the dominant overproduction theory of the depression, in favor of an underconsumption theory, and occasionally envisioned a new order of society that would not depend on unbridled competition. Such an order, they thought, would come closer to institutionalizing the brotherhood of man and would provide for the dignity of each individual. Their reforms suggested the use of government to protect weak portions of society against the stronger segments.

The ambivalence of Populists concerning the competitive system indicates that they had not completely liberated themselves from it despite their leanings in that direction. Milford Howard, invoking the image of Christ the Provider, wrote that "if He were here now would He not go among these, His starving children, and feed them, even though He had to convert every stone in the Capitol into a loaf of bread?" [25] But elsewhere in his novel Howard wrote that if Christ came to Congress, "He would, if it were in His power, make it possible for them to earn their bread." [26] This inconsistency was more than an inability to choose between work relief and the dole. When Hilary Herbert, the Alabamian who was Cleveland's secretary of the navy, said that it was the duty of the rich to give liberally to charity in order to allay discontent, the Troy *Jeffersonian* argued in reply that "what the involuntarily idle want is an equal chance in the struggle for existence." [27] Not a change of rules, but the equitable enforcement of the existing rules was what most Populists desired.

Populism did not offer the exciting new vista of the future that would have motivated an uneducated, insecure, but obviously susceptible electorate. Recent studies of modern revolutions and primitive rebelliousness emphasize the need for ideology.[28] Basic emotions such as hatred or resentment cannot sustain a protest movement for the long term, especially in a political system which continuously accommodates itself to popular pressures. The Populists lacked an ideology that would connect their sad economic plight — which motivated them in the first place — with a train of causation leading back to the political process. All they had were conspiracy theories, and conspiracy theories implied that the situation could be cured by quashing the conspiracy and thereby reestablishing a traditionally just system. Consequently there was little attempt to analyze the system, and solace was gained by heaping a great deal of bad feeling on the supposed corrupters. Populists needed an ideology that would have given cohesion and direction to their unformed yearnings for change.

If anomie is defined as the condition of anxiety resulting from a deterioration in the old belief system when society possesses no common values or morals which effectively govern conduct, then clearly the Populists do not qualify. If anomie is the personal bind arising from a discontinuity between culturally induced aspirations and the social structure's limitation on opportunity, then the Populists were definitely eligible. That they perceived the disjunction in their situation is without question, but they did not react by rebelling. Populists were not willing to launch a physical revolution, and they were not rebels in the sociological sense of rejecting the existing cultural goals and the institutional ways of attaining them and substituting a new ideology giving legitimacy to fresh values pertaining to ends and means. To be true rebels, Populists needed to transcend the given nature of their society, and they failed to do so.

This is not to say that the Populists did not have occasional glimpses of the problem which had to be solved. "In this country of undeveloped resources, rich in the endowments of nature," they frequently said in various ways, "no man should go idle who wants work. Under a proper distributive system no man who works should be poor." [29] This is a noble sentiment, but it depends on existing values pertaining to the ends and means of society and the substitution of new values. The Populists never went that far, nor did they have a clear conception of how the transition to the ill-defined new order was to take place. Milford Howard, for instance, was not specific as to how the Christian ethic was to be translated into institutions in order to usher in the millennium. He went only so far as to say that the existing situation would be changed by electing pure men. In a similar vein the Populists called "for the masses of the people to stand together in their omnipotence and take control of the law-making power of the government." [30] Power, not a new system, was what the people required.

All social movements contain a mixture of value and power orientations. Even revolutionary movements will cling to cherished values at the cost of losing popular appeal. When power comes to be the dominant consideration in any movement, the group will soften its demands and deemphasize its distinctiveness from the rest of society. This is precisely what happened to the Populists. In their campaign propaganda they did not stress nationalization of transportation and communications, nor the subtreasury scheme, nor the income tax, nor their other advanced proposals. In an effort to appeal to more people they ignored their formal program and resorted to bland slogans. Carrying this tendency to an absurd extreme, the *Choctaw Advocate* in its last issue before the election of 1894 attempted to stir the masses by writing that a vote for Kolb was a vote for "freedom and good government." In their campaigns for state office, the Populists relied heavily on the demand for "a free vote and a fair count." This pointed to a legitimate issue, and it was couched in terms that should have evoked a sympathetic response, but it is significant that it also was concerned with access to office and power. All the indications are that the Populists were a power-oriented protest movement.

NOTES

The Silver Panacea, C. VANN WOODWARD

1 Interview with Marion Butler, Washington, August 7, 1934; Florence Smith, "The Populist Movement and Its Influence in North Carolina," Ph.D. dissertation, University of Chicago, *passim.*

2 John D. Hicks, *The Populist Revolt* (Minneapolis: University of Minnesota Press, 1931), 344–348.

3 For an explanation of the origin of the term see *Ibid.,* 346.

4 *People's Party Paper,* July 26, 1896, quoted in Alex M. Arnett, *The Populist Movement in Georgia* (New York: Columbia University Press, 1922), 190.

5 *People's Party Paper,* June 19, 1896.

6 Correspondence in Watson MSS.; letters in *People's Party Paper,* 1895–1896.

7 Quoted in *Progressive Farmer,* June 30, 1896.

8 Editorial in *Ibid.*

9 From a letter written by Lloyd, July 10, 1896, in Caro Lloyd, *Henry Demarest Lloyd* (New York: G. P. Putnam's Sons, 1912), I, 259.

10 Henry D. Lloyd, "The Populists at St. Louis," *Review of Reviews,* XIV (September 1896), 300; Hicks, *The Populist Revolt,* 350.

11 Editorial in the *Progressive Farmer,* June 30, 1896; Hicks, *The Populist Revolt,* 352–354.

12 Jesse E. Boell, "William Jennings Bryan before 1896," master's thesis, University of Nebraska, *passim.*

13 St. Louis *Globe-Democrat,* July 20, 1896; Frederick E. Haynes, *James Baird Weaver* (Iowa City, Iowa: The State Historical Society of Iowa, 1919), 374.

14 *People's Party Paper,* June 26, December 13, 1896.

15 *Ibid.,* June 19, 1896.

16 Arnett, *The Populist Movement in Georgia,* 197.

17 St. Louis *Globe-Democrat,* July 21–27, 1896; H. D. Lloyd, "The Populists at St. Louis," 293.

18 *Ibid.,* 300.

19 St. Louis *Globe-Democrat,* July 20–23, 1896; Hicks, *The Populist Revolt,* 359–62.

20 St. Louis *Globe-Democrat,* July 22, 1896.

21 *Ibid.,* July 20 and 21, 1896.

22 *Ibid.,* July 22 and 23, 1896; Hicks, *The Populist Revolt,* 359–362.

23 St. Louis *Globe-Democrat,* July 24, 1896.

24 Carl Snyder, "Senator Marion Butler," *Review of Reviews,* XIV (October 1896), 429.

25 New York *World,* July 25, 1896.

26 Interview with J. L. Cartledge of Augusta, who wired Watson from St. Louis; New York *World,* July 26 and 27, 1896; editorial in the *People's Party Paper,* July 21, 1896; Watson's letter of acceptance in the *People's Party Paper,* December 13, 1896; Atlanta *Journal,* July 25, 1896.

27 Release of the National Reform Press, in the *People's Party Paper,* November 12, 1891; H. L. Young to T. E. Watson in the *People's Party Paper,* June 24, 1892; Augusta *Chronicle,* October 26, 1894.

28 St. Louis *Globe-Democrat,* July 25 and 26, 1896; New York *World,* July 25, 1896; *People's Party Paper,* July 31, 1896.

29 Published in New York, 1895.

30 St. Louis *Globe-Democrat*, July 25 and 26, 1896; *People's Party Paper*, July 31 and December 13, 1896; Atlanta *Constitution*, July 25, 1896.

31 St. Louis *Globe-Democrat*, July 25, 1896; New York *World*, July 25, 1896; Caro Lloyd, *Henry Demarest Lloyd*, I, 261.

32 St. Louis *Globe-Democrat*, July 26, 1896; *People's Party Paper*, November 13, 1896; Hicks, *The Populist Revolt*, 366.

33 St. Louis *Globe-Democrat*, July 26, 1896; Caro Lloyd, *Henry Demarest Lloyd*, I, 262.

The St. Louis Convention, ROBERT DURDEN

1 Photostat of Marion Butler to William M. Stewart, July 13, 1896, Stewart MSS, Nevada State Historical Society. Also the Raleigh *Caucasian*, July 16, 1896.

2 Henry M. Teller to William Jennings Bryan, July 18, 1896, Bryan MSS, Library of Congress.

3 Stewart to Butler, July 14, 1896, as cited in Effie M. Mack, "Life and Letters of William Morris Stewart, 1827–1909," unpublished dissertation, University of California, 1930, 272–273.

4 New York *Times*, July 25, 1896.

5 St. Louis *Globe-Democrat*, July 21, 1896, has the quotations and identifies the Texan delegate as Judge Lee M. Callaway of Corsicana; Woodward, *Watson*, 293.

6 St. Louis *Globe-Democrat*, July 21, 1896. Hicks, *Populist Revolt*, 357, describes and quotes Simpson's views and adds this sentence: "So also thought Weaver and Allen and a host of minor lights, some of whom had an eye on the loaves and fishes." This impugning of the motives of the Populists who supported Bryan is hardly fair. The argument could also be made, though it should not be, that southern midroaders feared fusion with Democrats because their local offices would be jeopardized by such a program. The correspondent for the Democratic Atlanta *Constitution*, for example, charged on July 23, 1896, that the "whole fight of every 'middle of the road' man is for the possession of office, to get some one in a snug berth."

7 Lloyd to A. B. Adair, October 10, 1896, Lloyd MSS, State Historical Society of Wisconsin. Lloyd's important article, "The Populists at St. Louis," *Review of Reviews*, XIV (September 1896), 298–303, is more sympathetic toward the action of the convention than his private comments at the time, although the article too is misleading.

8 For evidence that Butler had a North Carolinian in mind for the Populist vice-presidential nomination, possibly Walter Clark, an associate justice of the North Carolina Supreme Court, see W. J. Peele to Butler, July 18, 20, 1896, Butler MSS, Southern Historical Collection, University of North Carolina Library.

9 St. Louis *Globe-Democrat*, July 20, 1896; St. Louis *Republic*, July 20, 1896. Since no official record of the Populist convention was ever published, the historian must rely largely on contemporary accounts in the newspapers — and be accordingly alert for the difference between fact and rumor.

10 St. Louis *Globe-Democrat*, July 20, 1896.

11 For Butler's initial hostility to Sewall, see Raleigh *Caucasian*, July 16, 1896; for the same sentiment among a larger group of Populist editors in the Reform Press Association which met in St. Louis on the eve of the Populist convention, see St. Louis *Globe-Democrat*, July 20, 1896.

12 St. Louis *Globe-Democrat*, July 21, 1896.

13 *Ibid.* Jones also attempted to block the movement to ignore Sewall by promising that Populist endorsement of the Democratic ticket would be followed by his naming two or three Populists to the executive committee that would manage Bryan's campaign. New York *Herald*, July 21, and St. Louis *Globe-Democrat*, July 22, 1896. The *Herald* reporter mixed all sorts of rumors designed to discredit Jones and the Democrats in his detailed stories.

14 St. Louis *Republic,* July 20, 1896; Raleigh *News and Observer,* July 22, 1896.

15 New York *Herald,* July 19, 1896.

16 William Jennings Bryan, *The First Battle: A Story of the Campaign of 1896* (Chicago: W. B. Conkey Company, 1896), 259–264, reprints the text. The New York *Herald,* July 23, 1896, reported that Butler's "adroit" speech made such a strong impression that many delegates were mentioning him for the vice-presidential nomination. His age, however, would have made that constitutionally impossible, since he was only thirty-three.

17 Raleigh *Caucasian,* July 30, 1896, has many of these details in a firsthand account that was probably written by the editor, Hal Ayer, who was also a delegate to the convention; see also St. Louis *Globe-Democrat,* July 23, 1896, and Raleigh *News and Observer,* July 24, 1896.

18 Raleigh *Caucasian,* July 30, 1896; St. Louis *Globe-Democrat,* July 23, 1896.

19 St. Louis *Globe-Democrat,* July 23, 1896; Raleigh *News and Observer,* July 23, 1896. The correspondent of the Atlanta *Constitution,* July 23, 1896, referred to a "terrific cyclone" that hit the city as night fell. After quoting the editor of the *Southern Mercury* about the "fusion gang's" plunging the hall into darkness to confound the midroaders, Hicks, *Populist Revolt,* 361, states: "Whatever the situation might have been had the lights not gone out, next morning the fusionists were clearly in the majority." For later and continuing charges by Texans about a pro-Bryan plot in connection with the episode, see Roscoe Martin, *The People's Party in Texas* (Austin: The University of Texas Press, 1933), 241.

20 The platform is reprinted in Bryan, *First Battle,* 271–276; the New York *Herald,* July 25, 1896, reports its adoption. The Populist platform also denounced "the wholesale system of disfranchisement" that Mississippi and South Carolina had already adopted.

21 The National Silver party also began its convention in St. Louis on July 22 but had little influence on the Populists. After nominating Bryan and Sewall on Friday, July 24, the Silver party adjourned without waiting for the Populist nominations.

22 Raleigh *Caucasian,* July 30, 1896, has the most detailed account of this but see also St. Louis *Globe-Democrat,* July 25, 1896, St. Louis *Republic,* July 25, 1896, and Raleigh *News and Observer,* July 25, 1896. Some accounts give the final vote as 738 to 637, but in any case the point is clear that North Carolina's votes were necessary for the minority report on the order of business to win.

23 Raleigh *Caucasian,* July 30, 1896. See also the comment in the St. Louis *Globe-Democrat,* July 24, 1896, that the "middle-of-the-road men have acted more like a disorganized mob than anything else since they've been in St. Louis."

24 Raleigh *Caucasian,* July 30, 1896; New York *Herald,* July 25, 1896; Hicks, *Populist Revolt,* 365; and Bryan, *First Battle,* 270–71. Mann Page of Virginia was also nominated.

25 Atlanta *Constitution,* July 26, 1896; telegram from Watson to New York *Herald,* July 28, 1896.

26 Alex M. Arnett, *The Populist Movement in Georgia,* 199, names two of the Georgia delegates who made this claim in 1896 and then told it to him years later. Arnett adds: "Mr. Watson declared to the writer in a recent interview that Jones never denied making such a promise. Jones seems to have ignored the charge." Both Watson and Arnett were wrong. Newspapers before, during, and after the Populist convention carried Jones's emphatic denial of precisely this charge. One example: "I have never stated to any one that there is any likelihood of Mr. Sewall withdrawing from the ticket." Jones to T. M. Patterson, July 24, 1896, in St. Louis *Globe-Democrat,* July 26, 1896. William W. Brewton, *The Life of Thomas E. Watson* (Atlanta: the author, 1926), 268–69, tells virtually the same thing as Arnett. Brewton, an ardent admirer of Watson who had access to his papers after his death, adds that Watson was really not surprised that Sewall would not resign and that "it was only" to prevent the split in the party that he had "wired his consent to fusion." Hicks, *Populist Revolt,* 365, states that "most of the compromisers at St. Louis" believed that the Democrats would withdraw Sewall and cites Arnett and Brewton. Woodward, *Watson,* 298, writes that Watson "was given to understand" that the Democrats would withdraw Sewall and cites an interview with one J. L. Cartledge of Augusta, Georgia, "who wired Watson from St. Louis."

27 New York *Herald*, July 25, 1896. Despite the late hour, the argument might be made that Weaver, Allen, and others were afraid to proceed to the nomination of the presidential candidate when Populist partisanship ran high in the wake of Watson's nomination. On the other hand, Bryan's position was still ambiguous as far as most delegates knew at 1 A.M. It would be much less so, and more embarrassing for his Populist supporters, after the morning newspapers appeared.

28 Jones to Bryan, telegram, July 21, 1896, Bryan MSS. An example of what Jones meant: the Georgia delegation wired Bryan on July 24 asking if he would accept the Populist nomination on the Populist platform, and the penciled notation on the telegram in the Bryan MSS is "not answered."

29 St. Louis *Globe-Democrat*, St. Louis *Republic*, New York *Herald*, Augusta, Georgia, *Chronicle* (cited by Arnett, *Populist Movement in Georgia*, 200), and Atlanta *Constitution*, all July 25, 1896.

30 Text of Weaver's speech is in Bryan, *First Battle*, 276–79. Hicks, *Populist Revolt*, 366, Woodward, *Watson*, 300, and other accounts mention Chairman Allen's refusal to read to the convention another telegram from Bryan or to allow Democratic Governor Stone of Missouri to read it during the roll call of the states for nominations. Although this episode has been made a part of the "conspiracy" interpretation, Allen argued that a Democratic governor had no right to the floor of the Populist convention and that he, Allen, was not going to tell the delegates again what they already knew. It should be noted also that in none of his various telegrams did Bryan say categorically that he would not accept a Populist nomination, if it were proffered, even in the face of his published request that he not be nominated without Sewall. Ignatius Donnelly raised this question without getting an answer in the convention's last session. See Martin Ridge, *Ignatius Donnelly: The Portrait of a Politician* (Chicago: The University of Chicago Press, 1962), 356.

31 New York *Harold*, July 26, 1896; Raleigh *Caucasian*, July 30, 1896. Some accounts give fewer votes for Norton, but 340 seems to be correct. Eleven or twelve votes were scattered among Ignatius Donnelly, Eugene Debs, and Jacob S. Coxey.

32 Lloyd, "The Populists at St. Louis," 303; Caro Lloyd, *Henry Demarest Lloyd*, I, 262. Norman Pollack, *The Populist Response to Industrial America: Midwestern Populist Thought* (Cambridge: Harvard University Press, 1962), 103–105, is an intellectual history which persuasively argues that fusion meant "the last chance to advance radicalism" and was "a long-term groping toward effective radical action."

The Negro in the Populist Movement, JACK ABRAMOWITZ

1 Nelson A. Dunning (ed.), *The Farmers' Alliance History and Agricultural Digest* (Washington, D.C.: Alliance Publishing Co., 1891), 153.

2 For two lesser known examples of alliance attempts to win over the Democratic party see Homer Clavenger, "The Farmers' Alliance in Missouri," *Missouri Historical Review*, XXXIX (October 1944), 24–44; and J. A. Sharp, "The Entrance of the Farmers' Alliance Into Tennessee Politics," *The East Tennessee Society's Publications*, No. 9 (1937), 72–92.

3 *Atlanta Constitution*, September 1, 1890.

4 *Atlanta Constitution*, December 4, 5, 1890.

5 *Ibid.*, December 8, 1890.

6 The intricate story of the successive conventions is best told in John Hicks, *The Populist Revolt* (Minneapolis: University of Minnesota Press, 1931). All students of Populism are indebted to Professor Hicks for this pioneering work. Unfortunately only minor attention was given to the role of the Negro. The Warwick election episode is taken from the minutes of the convention contained in the *National Economist*, March 5, 1892.

7 Elizabeth N. Barr, "The Populist Uprising," *History of Kansas*, ed. William E. Con-

nelley (5 vol.; New York: American Historical Society Inc., 1928), II, 1164. *Indianapolis Freeman,* September 6, 1890.

8 *Indianapolis Freeman,* September 13, November 8, 1890.

9 Quoted from Polk's paper, *Progressive Farmer,* October 28, 1890, in Stuart Noblin, *Leonidas LaFayette Polk: Agrarian Crusader* (Chapel Hill: University of North Carolina Press, 1949), 224.

10 Wynne P. Harrington, "The Populist Party in Kansas," *Collections of the Kansas State Historical Society,* XVI, 425. The Topeka *American Citizen,* August 26, 1892 contains the fusion slate running in Kansas City. *Topeka Call,* August 9, 1891. The *Citizen* and *Call* were both Negro papers. See also the *Times-Observer,* November 7, 21, 1891.

11 Topeka *Weekly Call,* November 21, 1892; *Parsons Weekly Blade,* November 12, 1892.

12 *Indianapolis Freeman,* October 4, 1890; Helen M. Blackburn, "The Populist Party in the South, 1890–1898," unpublished Master's thesis, Howard University, 1941, 44.

13 *Southern Mercury,* June 30, 1892. This was the official weekly of the Texas Alliance. The "war horse" referred to was General Henry E. McCulloch, nominated for Governor by the convention. He later stepped aside. See also the *Mercury,* July 7, 1892.

14 *Southern Mercury,* August 11, 1892.

15 Ernest W. Winkler, *Platforms of Political Parties in Texas* (Austin: The University of Texas, 1916), 332. Roscoe C. Martin, *The People's Party in Texas* (Austin: The University of Texas, 1933), 127, 133.

16 *Southern Mercury,* April 9, 16, June 26, 1896.

17 Winkler, *Platforms of Political Parties in Texas,* 383.

18 C. Vann Woodward, *Tom Watson, Agrarian Rebel* (New York: The Macmillan Co., 1938), 175–177.

19 *Atlanta Constitution,* September 2, 1892.

20 *National Economist,* September 10, 1892; C. Vann Woodward, "Tom Watson and the Negro in Agrarian Politics," *The Journal of Southern History,* IV (1938), 14; Helen M. Blackburn, "The Populist Party in the South, 1890–1898," Unpublished master's thesis, Howard University, 46.

21 *National Economist,* September 24, 1892.

22 *Atlanta Constitution,* September 8, 1892.

23 Woodward, "Tom Watson and the Negro in Agrarian Politics," 21–22.

24 *Atlanta Constitution,* October 4, 5, 1894.

25 Woodward, "Tom Watson and the Negro in Agrarian Politics," 21.

26 *Southern Mercury,* July 28, 1892.

27 Quoted in Simon Delap, *The Populist Party in North Carolina* (Durham: Trinity College Historical Society, 1922), 51.

28 Stuart Noblin, *Leonidas LaFayette Polk* (Chapel Hill: University of North Carolina Press, 1949), 253.

29 *National Economist,* October 8, 1892.

30 J. Fred Rippy (ed.), *F. M. Simmons: Statesman of the New South, Memoirs and Addresses* (Durham: Duke University Press, 1936), 535. Rebecca Cameron to Alfred M. Waddell, quoted in William Alexander Mabry, *The Negro in North Carolina Politics Since Reconstruction* (Durham: Duke University Press, 1940), 48.

31 First printed in the Chicago *Record* and reproduced in the Toledo *Journal* on December 11, 1898, this poem by Paul Laurence Dunbar was never published in his works. See Virginia Cunningham, *Paul L. Dunbar and His Song* (New York: Dodd, Mead and Co., 1947), 185.

Southern Populists and the Negro, ROBERT SAUNDERS

1 Richmond *Planet,* November 11, 25, 1893. This was Mitchell's explanation for the comparatively low Negro turnout. In the absence of a Republican candidate, however, the Negroes furnished a high percentage of the Populist votes.

2 *Virginia Sun,* July 6, 20, 1892.

3 *Southern Mercury,* July 26, 1894.

4 *Augusta Chronicle,* September 18, 1894. The *Chronicle* claimed also that Georgia Populists forced Negroes to sign pledges to vote Populist. *Ibid.,* October 23, 1894.

5 *Dallas Morning News,* October 20, 1894.

6 *Ibid.,* October 28, 1894. This writer was unable to determine if any of the Negroes actually served on the jury.

7 *People's Party Paper,* November 2, 1894.

8 *Ibid.*

9 Quoted in *Augusta Chronicle,* November 22, 1894.

10 Richmond *Dispatch,* September 22, 1893.

11 Roanoke followed the classic southern pattern in bringing the legal structure to bear against the participants in the lynching. A grand jury severely condemned the mob and indicted some twenty men on various charges. About a month later the harshest penalty meted out to the defendants was a $100.00 fine and thirty days in jail for one man. Two other men were fined $1.00 and sentenced to one hour in jail. Richmond *Dispatch,* October 22, 24, November 23, 1893.

12 *Dallas Morning News,* February 17, 1893. For a nearly identical account of what was probably the same interview in which Nugent labeled Hogg's recommendations "essentially unwise and unjust," see Catharine Nugent (ed.), *Life Work of Thomas L. Nugent* (Chicago: Laird and Lee, 1896), 249.

13 *People's Party Paper,* September 28, 1894. The law would have done away with the distinction between first class and second class accommodations. Ironically, the Johnson proposal, if enforced, would have upgraded facilities for Negroes, most of whom rode in the 2nd class compartments.

14 Raleigh *Caucasian,* January 10, 1895.

15 *People's Party Paper,* September 27, 1895. Early in 1896 Watson sketched Booker T. Washington's life and career and detailed the Tuskegee philosophy of industry, thrift, and staying on the land. Watson concluded that this was "mighty sound doctrine!" Watson rather defensively justified printing the story on the grounds that Washington was involved in a worthy task and perhaps the "benevolence" of some *People's Party Paper* readers would lead them to extending a Christian hand. *People's Party Paper,* April 3, 1896. Watson's views on Washington's philosophy paralleled that of the *Augusta Chronicle's* just after the Atlanta Exposition speech. *Augusta Chronicle,* September 21, 1895. In fact, the *Chronicle* in early 1895, before Washington's speech, argued that Negroes were better off in the South and contended that whites and Negroes worked together harmoniously, although there was no social mingling. The *Chronicle* pointed out that this was better than in the northern cities where white carpenters and bricklayers would not even work with Negroes. *Augusta Chronicle,* February 25, 1895.

16 Signed editorial by T. E. W., *People's Party Paper,* March 22, 1895. Governor O'Ferrall's denial of foreknowledge of a Negro's presence in the Massachusetts delegation does not have the ring of truth. A Richmond Negro, identified only as Mitchell (probably John E. Mitchell, Jr., editor of the Richmond *Planet*), was also invited. Mitchell's presence suggests he was invited to provide a social companion to the Massachusetts Negro. Apparently Mitchell came with the mayor of Richmond.

17 *People's Party Paper,* March 29, 1895.

18 Raleigh *Caucasian,* March 28, 1895.

19 *People's Party Paper,* September 21, 1894.

20 *People's Party Paper,* November 2, 1894.

21 *Ibid.*

22 *Ibid.*

23 *Augusta Chronicle,* September 26, 1895.

24 *Ibid.* This is one of the few direct appeals to the Negro for his vote, but it is in keeping with the *Chronicle's* moderate racial editorial policy in 1894 and 1895.

25 Birmingham *News,* July 20, 29, 30, 1894.

The Folklore of Populism, RICHARD HOFSTADTER

1 James C. Malin, "Mobility and History," *Agricultural History,* XVII (October 1943), 182.

2 Quoted by C. Vann Woodward: *Origins of the New South* (Baton Rouge: Louisiana State University Press, 1951), 194. During the late 1880s, when farm discontent was not yet at its peak, such farm organizations as the Farmers' Alliances developed limited programs based upon economic self-interest; in the 1890s, when discontent became most acute, it produced a national third-party movement.

3 Thomas E. Watson, *The Life and Times of Andrew Jackson* (Thomson, Georgia: Press of the Jeffersonian Publishing Co., 1912), 325: "All the histories and all the statesmen agree that during the first half-century of our national existence, we had no poor. A pauper class was unthought of: a beggar, or a tramp never seen." Cf. Mrs. S. E. V. Emery, *Seven Financial Conspiracies Which Have Enslaved the American People* (Lansing: L. Thompson, 1896), 10–11.

4 Note for instance the affectionate treatment of Jacksonian ideas in Watson, *The Life and Times of Andrew Jackson,* 343–344.

5 James B. Weaver, *A Call to Action* (Des Moines: Iowa Printing Company, 1892), 377–388.

6 B. S. Heath, *Labor and Finance Revolution* (Chicago: Ottaway and Company, 1892), 5.

7 For this strain in Jacksonian thought, see Richard Hofstadter, "William Leggett, Spokesman of Jacksonian Democracy," *Political Science Quarterly,* XLVIII (December 1943), 581–594. Also see Richard Hofstadter, *The American Political Tradition* (New York: Alfred A. Knopf, 1948), 60–61.

8 Elizabeth N. Barr, "The Populist Uprising," *A Standard History of Kansas and Kansans* (ed.), William E. Connelley (5 vols.; Chicago: American Historical Society, Inc., 1928), II, 1170.

9 Ray Allen Billington, *Westward Expansion* (New York: The Macmillan Co., 1938), 741.

10 Allan Nevins, *Grover Cleveland* (New York: Dodd, Mead & Co., 1934), 540. Heath, *Labor and Finance Revolution,* 27: "The world has always contained two classes of people, one that lived by honest labor and the other that lived *off* of honest labor." Cf. Governor Lewelling of Kansas: "Two great forces are forming in battle line: the same under different form and guise that have long been in deadly antagonism, represented in master and slave, lord and vassal, king and peasant, despot and serf, landlord and tenant, lender and borrower, organized avarice and the necessities of the divided and helpless poor." James A. Barnes, *John G. Carlisle* (New York: Dodd, Mead & Co., 1931), 254–255.

11 George H. Knoles, *The Presidential Campaign and Election of 1892* (Stanford: Stanford University Press, 1942), 179.

12 William A. Peffer, *The Farmer's Side* (New York: D. Appleton & Co., 1891), 273.

13 *Ibid.,* 148–150.

14 Weaver, *A Call to Action,* 5.

15 In this respect it is worth pointing out that in later years, when facilities for realistic exposure became more adequate, popular attacks on "the money power" showed fewer elements of fantasy and more of reality.

16 See, for instance, the remarks about a mysterious series of international assassinations with which Mary E. Lease opens her book, *The Problem of Civilization Solved* (Chicago: Laird and Lee, 1895).

17 Frederick L. Paxson, "The Agricultural Surplus: A Problem in History," *Agricultural History,* VI (April 1932), 58; cf. the observations of Lord Bryce in *The American Commonwealth* (New York: The Macmillan Co., 1897), II, 294–295.

18 Anti-Semitism as a kind of rhetorical flourish seems to have had a long underground history in the United States. During the panic of 1837, when many states defaulted on their obligations, many of which were held by foreigners, we find Governor McNutt of Mississippi defending the practice by baiting Baron Rothschild: "The blood

of Judas and Shylock flows in his veins and he unites the qualities of both his country-men. . . ." Quoted by George W. Edwards, *The Evolution of Finance Capitalism* (New York: Longmans, Green and Co., 1938), 149. Similarly we find Thaddeus Stevens assailing "the Rothschilds, Goldsmiths, and other large money dealers" during his early appeals for greenbacks. See James A. Woodburn, *The Life of Thaddeus Stevens* (Indianapolis: Bobbs-Merrill, Co., 1913), 576, 579.

19 See Oscar Handlin, "American Views of the Jew at the Opening of the Twentieth Century," *Publications of the American Jewish Historical Society*, no. 40 (June 1951), 323–344.

20 William Hope Harvey, *A Tale of Two Nations* (Chicago: Coin Publishing Co., 1894), 289. Cf. also p. 265: "Did not our ancestors . . . take whatever women of whatever race most pleased their fancy?"

21 William Hope Harvey, *Coin's Financial School* (Chicago: Coin Publishing Co., 1894), 124. For a notable polemic against the Jews, see James B. Goods, *The Modern Banker* (Chicago: C. H. Kerr and Co., 1896), chapter xii.

22 I distinguish here between popular anti-Semitism, which is linked with political issues, and upper-class anti-Semitism, which is a variety of snobbery. It is characteristic of the indulgence which Populism has received on this count that Carey McWilliams in his *A Mask for Privilege: Anti-Semitism in America* (Boston: Little, Brown & Co., 1948) deals with early American anti-Semitism simply as an upper-class phenomenon. In his historical account of the rise of anti-Semitism he does not mention the Greenback-Populist tradition. Daniel Bell, "The Grass Roots of American Jew Hatred," *Jewish Frontier*, XI (June 1944), 15–20, is one of the few writers who has perceived that there is any relation between latter-day anti-Semites and the earlier Populist tradition. See also Handlin, "American Views of the Jew." Arnold Rose has pointed out that much of American anti-Semitism is intimately linked to the agrarian myth and to resentment of the ascendancy of the city. The Jew is made a symbol of both capitalism and urbanism, which are themselves too abstract to be satisfactory objects of animosity. *Commentary*, VI (October 1948), 374–378.

23 For the latter, see C. Vann Woodward, *Tom Watson* (New York: The Macmillan Co., 1938), chapter xxiii.

24 Keith Sward, *The Legend of Henry Ford* (New York: Rinehart, 1948), 83–84, 113–114, 119–120, 132, 143–160. Cf. especially 145–146: "Ford could fuse the theory of Populism and the practice of capitalism easily enough for the reason that what he carried forward from the old platforms of agrarian revolt, in the main, were the planks that were the most innocent and least radical. Like many a greenbacker of an earlier day, the publisher of the Dearborn *Independent* was haunted by the will-o'-the-wisp of 'money' and the bogey of 'race.' It was these superstitions that lay at the very marrow of his political thinking." For further illustration of the effects of the Populist tradition on a Mountain State Senator, see Oscar Handlin's astute remarks on Senator Pat McCarran in "The Immigration Fight Has Only Begun," *Commentary*, XIV (July 1952), 3–4.

25 J. E. Wisan, *The Cuban Crisis as Reflected in the New York Press* (New York: Columbia University Press, 1934), 455; for the relation of this crisis to the public temper of the nineties, see Richard Hofstadter, "Manifest Destiny and the Philippines," in Daniel Aaron, ed., *America in Crisis* (New York: Alfred A. Knopf, 1952).

26 Alfred Vagts, *Deutschland und die Vereinigten Staaten in der Weltpolitik* (2 vols.; New York: The Macmillan Co., 1935), II, 1308.

27 Woodward, *Tom Watson*, 334.

28 Lease, *The Problem of Civilization Solved*, 7. Thomas E. Watson wrote in 1902 a lengthy biography, *Napoleon, A Sketch of His Life, Character, Struggles, and Achievements*, in which Napoleon, "the moneyless lad from despised Corsica, who stormed the high places of the world, and by his own colossal strength of character, genius, and industry took them," is calmly described as "the great Democratic despot." Elsewhere Watson wrote: "There is not a railway king of the present day, not a single self-made man who has risen from the ranks to become chief in the vast movement of capital and labor, who will not recognize in Napoleon traits of his own character; the same unflag-

ging purpose, tireless persistence, silent plotting, pitiless rush to victory . . ." — which caused Watson's biographer to ask what a Populist was doing celebrating the virtues of railroad kings and erecting an image of capitalist acquisitiveness for his people to worship. "Could it be that the Israelites worshipped the same gods as the Philistines? Could it be that the only quarrel between the two camps was over a singular disparity in the favors won?" Woodward, *Tom Watson,* 340–342.

29 Matthew Josephson, *The President Makers* (New York: Harcourt, Brace and Co., 1940), 98. See the first three chapters of Josephson's volume for a penetrating account of the imperialist elite. Daniel Aaron has an illuminating analysis of Brooks Adams in his *Men of Good Hope* (New York: Oxford University Press, 1951).

Critique of Norman Pollack's "Fear of Man," IRWIN UNGER

1 Actually the attempt dates at least from Chester M. Destler's essay of 1944, "Western Radicalism, 1865–1901: Concepts and Origins," reprinted in *American Radicalism, 1865–1901: Essays and Documents* (New York: Octagon Books, 1963).

2 Most notably Peter Viereck, Edward A. Shils, and Victor Ferkiss in, respectively, the following works: "The Revolt Against the Elite," in Daniel Bell (ed.), *The Radical Right* (Garden City: Doubleday and Co., 1963); *The Torment of Secrecy: The Background and Consequences of American Security Policies* (Glencoe: Free Press, 1956); "Populist Influences on American Fascism," *Western Political Quarterly,* X (June 1957).

3 At one point he writes that "Populism was the first modern political movement of practical importance in the United States to insist that the federal government has some responsibility for the common weal; indeed, it was the first such movement to attack seriously the problems created by industrialism." See *The Age of Reform: From Bryan to F.D.R.* (New York: Alfred A. Knopf, 1956), p. 61.

4 The reference is particularly to Ferkiss' essay cited in note 2 above.

5 See, for example, John D. Hicks, *The Populist Revolt: A History of the Farmers' Alliance and the People's Party* (Minneapolis: The University of Minnesota Press, 1931), Chap. XIII. For a contrary view of the late arrival of free silver among the Populists see Robert F. Durden, "The 'Cow-bird' Grounded: The Populist Nomination of Bryan and Tom Watson in 1896," *Mississippi Valley Historical Review,* L (December 1963), pp. 397 ff.

6 See the series of Alliance and Populist platforms included as appendices in Hicks, *op. cit.,* pp. 427–444.

7 Norman Pollack, *The Populist Response to Industrial America: Midwestern Populist Thought* (Cambridge: Harvard University Press, 1962), Chap. II.

8 *Ibid.,* pp. 61 ff.

9 *Ibid.,* Chap. IV.

10 See, for example, I. Unger, *The Greenback Era: A Social and Political History of American Finance, 1865–1879* (Princeton: Princeton University Press, 1964), pp. 94–114, 181–190.

11 *National Economist,* March 14, 1891. See also *ibid.,* February 14, 1891; April 25, 1891.

12 Pollack, "The Myth of Populist Anti-Semitism," *American Historical Review,* LXVIII (October 1962).

13 See John Higham, "Anti-Semitism in the Gilded Age: A Reinterpretation," *Mississippi Valley Historical Review,* XLIII (March 1957).

14 *Representative,* September 5, 1894. In the succeeding issue of his paper Donnelly, admittedly, apologized for this extended anti-Jewish diatribe, but clearly anti-Semitism was an inescapable part of his make-up. For other examples of Populist anti-Semitism see *National Economist,* February 21, 1891; January 3, 1891; and January 31, 1891. A similar phenomenon may be observed earlier among Greenbackers who in their hates as well as their likes contributed so much to Populism. For Greenback anti-Semitism see Unger, *op. cit.,* pp. 210 ff., 340.

15 Pollack, *The Populist Response,* Chap. IV.

16 *Ibid.,* p. 82.

17 Richard Hofstadter distinguishes a "soft side" and a "hard side" to the farmers' movement in America, the first ideological and broadly humane, the other pragmatic and self-seeking. My distinction here is somewhat different, referring to two different sides, morally speaking, of the ideological aspect of American agrarianism. For Hofstadter's definitions see *Age of Reform,* pp. 47–48.

18 I am, of course, referring to Richard Hofstadter, Oscar Handlin, C. Vann Woodward, and John Hicks respectively.

19 On Coughlin, see S. M. Lipset, "Three Decades of the Radical Right: Coughlinites, McCarthyites, and Birchers — 1962," in Bell, *op. cit.,* pp. 314–326; and Ferkiss, *op. cit.,* 360 ff. On Huey Long see T. Harry Williams, "The Gentleman from Louisiana: Demagogue or Democrat?" *Journal of Southern History,* XXVI (February 1960), p. 7.

20 See his *The Crisis of German Ideology: Intellectual Origins of the Third Reich* (New York: Grosset and Dunlap, 1964), especially Chap. XVIII.

21 Seymour M. Lipset, *Political Man: The Social Basis of Politics* (New York: Doubleday and Company, 1959), pp. 146, 147 f.

The Radical Specter, MICHAEL P. ROGIN

1 Adam B. Ulam, *The Unfinished Revolution* (New York: Random House, 1960), 28–57 and *passim.*

2 David W. Noble, *The Paradox of Progressive Thought* (Minneapolis: University of Minnesota Press, 1958), vi–viii and *passim.*

3 Quoted in Norman Pollack, *The Populist Response to Industrial America* (Cambridge: Harvard University Press, 1962), 15–16 and 22–25.

4 William A. Peffer, *The Farmer's Side: His Troubles and Their Remedy* (New York: Appleton, 1891), 3–64 and 75–123.

5 Frederick C. Howe, *Confessions of a Reformer* (New York: Scribner's, 1925), 17–18.

6 Roscoe C. Martin, *The People's Party in Texas* (Austin: The University of Texas, 1933), 44.

7 Richard Hofstadter, *The Age of Reform* (New York: Alfred A. Knopf, 1955), 46–47.

8 C. Vann Woodward, "The Populist Heritage and the Intellectual," *American Scholar,* XXIX (Winter 1959), 63.

9 William Kornhauser, *The Politics of Mass Society* (Glencoe: The Free Press, 1959), 39–40.

Neither Revolutions nor Reform, SHELDON HACKNEY

1 *The Alliance Herald,* May 4, 1893.

2 Troy *Jeffersonian,* July 27, 1894.

3 *Ibid.,* March 2, 1894.

4 *Ibid.,* May 4, 1894.

5 Reprinted in the Mobile *Register,* November 20, 1894.

6 *Ibid.,* November 13, 1894.

7 Quoted in *ibid.*

8 Warren S. Reese to Joseph C. Manning, December 2, 1927, in Manning, *The Fadeout of Populism* (New York: T. A. Hebbons, 1928), 142–144.

9 Jones to John W. DuBose, September 21, 1911, DuBose Papers, Alabama Department of Archives and History.

10 Albert Burton Moore, *History of Alabama* (Tuscaloosa: The University of Alabama, 1951), 979.

11 *Ibid.,* 979.
12 Alabama, *House Journal, 1894,* 1,098–1,099.
13 *The Piedmont Inquirer,* July 14, 1894.
14 Quoted in *The People's Weekly Tribune,* June 4, 1896.
15 *People's Reflector,* November 10, 1892.
16 *The Alliance Herald,* July 7, 1893.
17 *Choctaw Alliance,* September 12, 1894.
18 Troy *Jeffersonian,* September 21, 1894.
19 *Ibid.,* October 12, 1894.
20 Tuscaloosa *Journal,* October 10, 1894.
21 May 4, 1893.
22 September 12, 1894.
23 May 4, 1894.
24 Troy *Jeffersonian,* August 3, 1894.
25 Howard, *If Christ Came to Congress,* 292.
26 *Ibid.,* 5.
27 Troy *Jeffersonian,* May 18, 1894.
28 E. J. Hobsbawn, *Primitive Rebels: Studies in Archaic Forms of Social Movement in the 19th and 20th Centuries,* Manchester, England, 1959; and Frantz Fanon, *The Wretched of the Earth,* preface by Jean-Paul Sartre, translated by Constance Farrington, New York, 1965, particularly 111–115.
29 Troy *Jeffersonian,* September 14, 1894.
30 *Ozark Banner,* July 28, 1898.

SUGGESTIONS FOR FURTHER READING

The starting point for all students of Populism is John D. Hicks, *The Populist Revolt* * (Minneapolis: University of Minnesota Press, 1931), which enshrined the Populists heroically in the democratic tradition. Four decades of scholarship have added facts, amended emphases, and challenged some interpretations, but no comprehensive history has replaced it. An earlier, slighter, but still significant treatment is Solon Buck, *The Agrarian Crusade* * (New Haven: Yale University Press, 1920). The failure of these two standard works to pay appropriate attention to the South is corrected in the magnificent history of the South by C. Vann Woodward, *Origins of the New South, 1877–1913* * (Baton Rouge: Louisiana State University Press, 1951), and in *Farmer Movements in the South, 1865–1933* * (Berkeley: University of California Press, 1960), by Theodore Saloutos. An old-fashioned and not very sophisticated Marxist account is provided by Anna Rochester in *The Populist Movement in the United States* (New York: International Publishers, 1943). Going against the grain of prevailing scholarship, Chester MacArthur Destler in his fruitful study, *American Radicalism, 1865–1901* * (New London: Connecticut College, 1946), stresses the radical potential of Populism in the Midwest and the strength of the farmer-labor bond. The most recent narrative survey of Populism is H. Wayne Morgan, "Populism and the Decline of Agriculture," in H. Wayne Morgan (ed.), *The Gilded Age* * (rev. and enl.; Syracuse: Syracuse University Press, 1970). The long view is provided by Carl C. Taylor, *The Farmers' Movement, 1620–1920* (New York: American Book Company, 1953). For the first genuine attempt to understand the Populists through cross-national comparison, see the essay by Kenneth Barkin in Herbert J. Bass (ed.), *The State of American History* (Chicago: Quadrangle Books, 1970).

Another important aspect of Populism that was inadequately treated in the early histories is race relations within the movement and the effect of the movement on race relations in general. An influential statement of the claim that Populists tended toward racial equalitarianism is found in C. Vann Woodward, "Tom Watson and the Negro," *Journal of Southern History*, IV (February, 1938), 14–33 and in a more carefully qualified form in the *Strange Career of Jim Crow* * (New York: Oxford University Press, 1955), an unsurpassed essay on the history of race relations. The issue is given balanced treatment with conclusions similar to Woodward's in two articles by Jack Abramowitz, "The Negro in the Agrarian Revolt," *Agricultural History*, XXIV (April, 1950), 89–95 and "The Negro in the Populist Movement," *Journal of Negro History*, XXXVIII (July, 1953), 257–289. Slightly different conclusions are reached by Herbert Shapiro in his similarly

---

* An asterisk following a title indicates that it is available in paperback.

judicious essay, "The Populist and the Negro: A Reconsideration," in August Meier and Elliott Rudwick (eds.), *The Making of Black America* (New York: Atheneum, 1969), II, 27–36. Robert Saunders maintains the tradition of urbanity but argues more strenuously against the equalitarian implications of the evidence in his articles, "Southern Populists and the Negro, 1893–1895," *Journal of Negro History*, LIV (July, 1969), 240–261 and "The Transformation of Tom Watson, 1894–1895," *Georgia Historical Quarterly*, LIV (Fall, 1970), 339–356. The same point of view, without the urbanity or subtlety, is expressed by Charles Crowe, "Tom Watson, Populists, and Blacks Reconsidered," *The Journal of Negro History*, LV (April, 1970), 99–116, in which the author argues that "Watson and his movement had little to do with radicalism or with the fate and aspirations of Black people." The possibility that blacks may have been reluctant to vote Populist because they did not perceive it to be in their own interest to do so is argued by William H. Chafe, "The Negro and Populism: A Kansas Case Study," *Journal of Southern History*, XXXIV (August, 1968), 402–419. Rayford Logan, *The Negro in American Life and Thought: The Nadir, 1877–1901* * (New York: The Macmillan Company, 1954), provides a justifiably gloomy narrative of black history, including a cynical view of the chance for improvement through Populism. The brief section on Populism in Hanes Walton, Jr., *The Negro in Third Party Politics* (Philadelphia: Dorrance and Company, 1969), is not very helpful. The intellectual history of Negroes, with some attention to Populism, is perceptively covered by August Meier in *Negro Thought in America, 1880–1915: Racial Ideologies in the Age of Booker T. Washington* * (Ann Arbor: University of Michigan Press, 1963). Vincent P. DeSantis, in *Republicans Face the Southern Question: The New Departure Years, 1877–1897* (Baltimore: The Johns Hopkins Press, 1959), deals with the relationship of the national Republican party to the southern question, another instance of black rights being sacrificed for white opportunism. Stanley Hirshson covers the same ground in *Farewell to the Bloody Shirt: Northern Republicans and the Southern Negro, 1877–1893* (Bloomington: Indiana University Press, 1962). One of the immediate results of the Republican retreat from commitment can be studied in Paul Lewinson, *Race, Class and Party: A History of Negro Suffrage and White Politics in the South* * (New York: Russell and Russell, Inc., 1965). Lewinson's story of disfranchisement, first published in 1932, must be brought up to date by consulting more recently published monographs on particular states. Among the best of those not mentioned elsewhere in this bibliography are the following: Charles Wynes, *Race Relations in Virginia, 1870–1902* (Charlottesville: University of Virginia Press, 1961); George B. Tindall, *South Carolina Negroes, 1877–1900* (Columbia: University of South Carolina Press, 1952); William A. Mabry, *The Negro in North Carolina Politics Since Reconstruction* (Durham: Duke University Press, 1940); Vernon Lane Wharton, *The Negro in Mississippi, 1865–1890* * (Chapel Hill: University of North Carolina Press, 1947); Frenise A. Logan, *The Negro in North Carolina, 1876–1894* (Chapel Hill: University of North Carolina Press, 1964).

The election of 1896 was a sharp and durable realignment of national political loyalties, a turning point that has been incorporated by V. O. Key, Jr., into his model of political stability and fluctuation found in "A Theory of Critical

Elections," *The Journal of Politics,* XVII (February, 1955), 3–18. An interesting quantitative confirmation of this theory is the article by Michael Rogin, "California Populism and the 'System of 1896,'" *Western Political Quarterly,* XXII (March, 1969), 179–196, also found in Michael Rogin and John Shover, *Political Change in California: Critical Elections and Social Movements, 1890–1966* (Westport, Conn.: Greenwood Publishing Corporation, 1970). Rogin argues that ethnic cleavage rather than economic interest was the key to party realignment and that in the long run the Democratic party was weakened by the Populist movement, but that one can not be too confident about the results of a country level analysis of aggregate data when the Populist vote comprised less than 20 per cent of the total. Carl Degler, in his article, "American Political Parties and the Rise of the City," *Journal of American History,* LI (June, 1964), 41–59, reinforces the critical election perspective on 1896 by finding the shift in city votes crucial. The short term adverse effect on Populism of urban votes is highlighted by William Diamond in "Urban and Rural Voting in 1896," *American Historical Review,* XLVI (January, 1941), 281–305. Alan F. Westin contributes a very interesting and well-informed examination of the Supreme Court as an issue on the election of 1896 in his article, "The Supreme Court, the Populist Movement, and the Campaign of 1896," *Journal of Politics,* XV (February, 1953), 3–41. The comprehensive study of the election by Stanley L. Jones, *The Presidential Election of 1896* (Madison: University of Wisconsin Press, 1964), is useful and thorough but leaves much analysis yet to be done. Robert Durden's revisionist rendering of Populist politics at the national level in 1896 is fruitfully meticulous in *The Climax of Populism* * (Lexington: University of Kentucky Press, 1965). Gilbert C. Fite analyzes the relative success the Republicans achieved among farmers when they argued that farmers would benefit more from the tariff than from silver, in "Republican Strategy and the Farm Vote in the Presidential Campaign of 1896," *Mississippi Valley Historical Review,* LIV (July, 1959), 787–806.

Some interesting sidelights on Populism are available in the extensive journal literature on the subject. David Trask has suggested perhaps Populism was precipitated when town merchants became so dissatisfied and economically damaged that they joined the agrarian protest movement. This idea, contained in his article, "A Note on the Politics of Populism," *Nebraska History,* XLVI (June, 1965), 157–161, unfortunately does not fit the facts outside Nebraska. The radical strains in Populism receive emphasis from numerous interesting articles: George H. Knoles, "Populism and Socialism with Special Reference to the Election of 1892," *Pacific Historical Review,* XII (September, 1943), 295–304; Leon W. Fuller, "Colorado's Revolt Against Capitalism," *Mississippi Valley Historical Review,* XXI (December, 1934), 343–360; Donald K. Pickens, "Oklahoma, Populism and Historical Interpretation," *Chronicles of Oklahoma,* XLIII (Autumn, 1965), 275–283; Martin J. Klotsche, "The 'United Front' Populists," *Wisconsin Magazine of History,* XX (June, 1937), 375–389; Grady McWhiney, "Louisiana Socialists in the Early Twentieth Century: A Study in Rustic Radicalism," *Journal of Southern History,* XX (August, 1954), 315–336.

McWhiney, in the article just cited, demonstrates that the aftermath of Populism in Louisiana took a radical turn. Other historians have looked in the opposite direction to discover in Populism the seeds for later reform thrusts. Such is the concern of Wayne Fuller, "The Rural Roots of the Progressive Leaders," *Agricultural History*, XLII (January, 1968), 1–14. The problem with Fuller's argument is that the rural roots of Progressivism that he can document are not Populist roots, nor does a rural background distinguish Progressives from conservatives. The same caveat applies to Arthur Link's important article, "The South and the 'New Freedom': An Interpretation," *The American Scholar*, XX (Summer, 1951), though it is not easy to dismiss his contention that the philosophy underlying the agrarian crusade furnished the theoretical spirit of Wilsonian Progressivism in power. David P. Thelan in his article, "Social Tensions and the Origins of Progressivism," *The Journal of American History*, LVI (September, 1969), 323–341, treats Populism as a learning experience for men who, even when they opposed Populism, thereby became convinced that reform was necessary and set about to create Progressivism. Writing about the same state, which had a very weak and atypically urban Populist movement, Herbert Margulies in his book, *The Decline of the Progressive Movement in Wisconsin, 1890–1920* (Madison: State Historical Society of Wisconsin, 1968), finds ex-Populists supporting Robert La-Follette. This is congruent with the position stated by John D. Hicks in the last chapter of *The Populist Revolt* that the spirit of Populism has been beneficially at work throughout twentieth-century American history, a position from which he has never retreated and which is reiterated among other places in "The Legacy of Populism in the Middle West," *Agricultural History*, XXIII (October, 1949), 225–236; "Some Parallels with Populism in the Twentieth Century," *Social Education*, VIII (November, 1944), 297–301; and with Theodore Saloutos, *Agricultural Discontent in the Middle West, 1900–1939* (Madison: University of Wisconsin Press, 1951). James C. Malin, "The Farmers' Alliance Subtreasury Plan and European Precedents," *Mississippi Valley Historical Review*, XXXI (September, 1944), 255–260, uses another technique to confer legitimacy upon, and raise doubts about the originality of, one of Populism's central proposals.

Some of the most important new insights into Populism in general have been developed in articles and books on Populism in particular states. Our most secure knowledge of the identity of the Populists, for instance, is probably contained in an article by Walter T. K. Nugent, "Some Parameters of Populism," *Agricultural History*, XL (October, 1966), 255–270, and one by Stanley B. Parsons, "Who Were the Nebraska Populists?" *Nebraska History*, XLIV (June, 1963), 83–99. The southern state most richly endowed with scholarship is Alabama. James F. Doster has traced the powerful effect of railroads on politics and persuasively argues that the Populists were not particularly antagonistic toward railroads, despite the importance of railroads to the conservative political machine, in two places, *Railroads in Alabama Politics, 1875–1914* (Tuscaloosa: University of Alabama Press, 1951), and "Were Populists Against Railroad Corporations? The Case of Alabama," *Journal of Southern History*, XX (August, 1954), 395–399. William Warren Rogers in *The One-Gallused Rebellion: Agrarianism in Alabama, 1865–1896* (Baton Rouge: Louisiana State University Press, 1970) sympathetically tells the story of the farmer revolt with major attention paid to the Populist party. *Populism to Progressivism in Alabama* (Princeton: Princeton University Press,

1969) by Sheldon Hackney brings quantitative techniques and social science concepts to a close analysis of Populism, Progressivism, and the connections between them. The books by Rogers and Hackney largely supersede the older work by John B. Clark, *Populism in Alabama* (Auburn, Ala.: Auburn Printing Company, 1927).

In addition to Clark's study of Alabama, the pioneer scholarship on southern Populism was surprisingly good. The best of the group is Roscoe C. Martin, *The People's Party in Texas* (Austin: University of Texas, 1933), closely followed by Alex M. Arnett, *The Populist Movement in Georgia* (New York: Columbia University Press, 1922), neither of which has been surpassed or outdated. *Populism in the Old Dominion* (Princeton: Princeton University Press, 1935), by William DuBose Sheldon, was an undergraduate essay that justifiably found its way into print and has not been replaced for Virginia. The first complete study of Populism in North Carolina, *The Populist Party in North Carolina* (Durham: Trinity College Historical Society, 1922) by Simeon Delap, is still useful but one must also refer to Helen G. Edmonds, *The Negro and Fusion Politics in North Carolina, 1894–1901* (Chapel Hill: University of North Carolina Press, 1951), which makes the Populists seem less than racial equalitarians, and Joseph Steelman, "The Progressive Era in North Carolina, 1844–1917," unpublished Ph.D. dissertation, University of North Carolina, 1955, which is a bit unwieldy but very solid. An interesting sidelight on Populist-Progressive continuity in North Carolina is provided by H. Larry Ingle, "A Southern Democrat at Large: William Hodge Kitchin and the Populist Party," *The North Carolina Historical Review,* XLV (April, 1968), 178–194. A well-informed narrative of campaign politics in Mississippi is provided by Albert D. Kirwan, *Revolt of the Rednecks: Mississippi Politics, 1896–1925* * (Lexington: University of Kentucky Press, 1951), which may be supplemented by James Ferguson, "Agrarianism in Mississippi, 1871–1900: A Study in Nonconformity," unpublished Ph.D. dissertation, University of North Carolina, 1952. *Bourbonism and Agrarian Protest: Louisiana Politics, 1877–1900* (Baton Rouge: Louisiana State University Press, 1969), by William I. Hair, is an excellent study, which places emphasis upon social history as well as politics. The issue of the lottery, unique to Louisiana, is covered by Henry C. Dethloff, "The Alliance and the Lottery: Farmers Try for the Sweepstakes," *Louisiana History,* VI (Spring, 1965), 141–159, who contends that the antilottery battles of 1892 restructured Louisiana politics and paved the way for Progressive reforms. Mark T. Carlton in "The Politics of the Convict Lease System in Louisiana, 1868–1901," *Louisiana History,* VIII (Winter, 1967), 5–25, follows the convolutions of a more universal issue on which southern Populists were virtually ineffective. A more general treatment of this issue can be found in Jane Zimmerman, "The Penal Reform Movement in the South During the Progressive Era, 1890–1917," *Journal of Southern History,* XVII (November, 1951), 462–492.

Fortunately, the most important Populist state in the Midwest has also been the one to receive the most scholarly attention, ranging from the old but important article by Raymond C. Miller, "The Background of Populism in Kansas," *Mississippi Valley Historical Review,* XI (March, 1925), 469–489, to the eccentric but insightful work of James C. Malin, *A Concern About Humanity: Notes on Reform, 1872–1912, at the National and Kansas Levels of Thought* (Lawrence, Kan.: by the author, 1964). The entire issue of the *Kansas Quarterly*, I (Fall, 1969) is devoted to Populism, and Walter T. K. Nugent used Kansas as his laboratory to test Populism for scapegoating and other irrational fevers. He gives Populism a clean bill of health in *The Tolerant Populists: Kansas Populism and Nativism* (Chicago: The University of Chicago Press, 1963). Similarly, an extensive but simple analysis of the ages of office holders in Kansas by James C. Malin demonstrates that age was not a differentiating trait of reformers, "At What Age Did Men Become Reformers?" *Kansas Historical Quarterly*, XXIX (Autumn, 1963), 250–261. O. Gene Clanton in his book, *Kansas Populism, Ideas and Men* (Lawrence, Kan.: The University Press of Kansas, 1969) provides a general history that sharply focuses on intellectual and social analyses of the leaders and achieves some significant findings through prosopography. Some of the background of Kansas Populism can be learned from Paul W. Gates, *Fifty Million Acres: Conflicts Over Kansas Land Policy, 1854–1890* (Ithaca: Cornell University Press, 1954).

After Kansas, the literature on Populism at the state level in the West thins out rapidly. Frederick E. Haynes, *Third Party Movements Since the Civil War, With Special Reference to Iowa* (Iowa City: State Historical Society, 1916), is therefore still useful. Good examples of a first-rate scholar making a sound job look simple in the early years of Populist studies are "The Economic Basis of the Populist Movement in Iowa," *Iowa Journal of History and Politics*, XXI (July, 1923), 373–396 and "The Populist Movement in Iowa," *Iowa Journal of History and Politics*, XXIV (January, 1926), 3–107, by Herman C. Nixon. Roy Vernon Scott, *The Agrarian Movement in Illinois, 1880–1896* (Urbana: University of Illinois Press, 1962) is an important study of a not so important state that demonstrates again Populism's lack of appeal to diversified farmers. A more appropriate quantity of effort is found in Ernest D. Stewart, "The Populist Party in Indiana," *Indiana Magazine of History*, XIV (December, 1918), 332–367 and XV (March, 1919), 53–74. The further fringes, beyond the heartland of Populism, receive brief but interesting comments in an excellent state study, Lewis Gould, *Wyoming, A Political History, 1868–1896* (New Haven: Yale University Press, 1968). Terry Paul Wilson, "The Demise of Populism in Oklahoma Territory," *Chronicles of Oklahoma*, XLIII (Autumn, 1965), 265–274, finds that free silver and fusion wrecked the party in Oklahoma.

The demise of Populism is better understood than its origins, which are generally sought among the economic conditions affecting farmers in the late nineteenth century. The best place to begin to understand the crucial issue of monetary supply and the secular drop in farm prices is Milton Friedman and Anna J. Schwartz, *Monetary History of the United States, 1867–1960* (Princeton: Princeton University Press, 1963). Some of the other economic factors can be studied in Richard A. Easterlin, *Trends in the American Economy in the Nineteenth Century* (Princeton: Princeton University Press, 1960). Charles Hoffman, in his article, "The Depression of the Nineties," *Journal of Economic History*, XVI (June, 1956), 137–164, provides a tentative multivariate analysis of the economic collapse and concludes that government policy was not responsible for the depression. This treatment should be supplemented with Hoffman's book, *The Depression of the Nineties: An Economic History* (Westport, Conn.: Greenwood Publishing Corporation, 1970). To understand the origins of the money question, one should refer to Irwin Unger, *The Greenback Era: A Social and Political History of American Finance, 1865–1879* (Princeton: Princeton University Press, 1964).

Farmers reacted to their situation over a long period of time. The precursors of Populism are chronicled by Solon Buck in *The Granger Movement* (Cambridge: Harvard University Press, 1913), a book that is generally recognized as a classic. Paul H. Johnstone's essay, "Old Ideals Versus New Ideas in Farm Life," in U.S. Department of Agriculture, *Farmers in a Changing World, Yearbook of Agriculture, 1940* (Washington: Government Printing Office, 1940) is an unacknowledged classic. Two excellent general histories of agriculture exist for this period: Fred A. Shannon, *The Farmers' Last Frontier: Agriculture, 1860–1897* * (New York: Farrar and Rinehart, 1945) and Gilbert C. Fite, *The Farmer's Frontier, 1865–1900* (New York: Holt, Rinehart and Winston, 1966). Douglass C. North in *Growth and Welfare in the American Past: A New Economic History* (Englewood Cliffs, N.J.: Prentice-Hall, Inc., 1966) calls into question the traditional assumption of the farmers' economic rationality. Much of his ammunition comes from two books by Allan Bogue, *From Prairie to Corn Belt* (Chicago: The University of Chicago Press, 1963) and *Money at Interest: The Farm Mortgage on the Middle Border* (Ithaca: Cornell University Press, 1955). John Bowman's study, "An Economic Analysis of Midwestern Farm Land Values and Farm Land Income, 1860 to 1900," *Yale Economic Essays*, V (Fall, 1965), lends weight to the opinion that farmers had little legitimate complaint against the gold standard and the alleged monopolists. Robert Higgs argues unconvincingly that the Populist complaint about high railroad rates was justified: "Railroad Rates and the Populist Uprising," *Agricultural History*, XLIV (July, 1970), 291–297. The picture that existed previously was first stated, somewhat condescendingly, by Frank L. McVey, "The Populist Movement," *Economic Studies*, I (1896), 135–209, and it was later developed by a number of articles in the 1920s. The most important of these are: Benjamin B. Kendrick, "Agrarian Discontent in the South, 1880–1900," *American Historical Association Report, 1920* (Washington: Government Printing Office, 1925), 265–272; Herman C. Nixon, "The Cleavage Within the Farmers' Alliance Movement," *Mississippi Valley Historical Review*, XV (June, 1928), 22–33; Hallie Farmer, "The Economic Background of Frontier Populism," *Mississippi Valley Historical Review*, X (March, 1924), 406–427; Hallie Farmer, "The Economic Background of Southern Populism," *South Atlantic Quarterly*, XXIX (January, 1930), 77–91; John D. Barnhart, "Rainfall and the Populist Party in Nebraska," *American Political Science Review*, XIX (August, 1925), 527–40. In his article, "An Historical Definition of Northwestern Radicalism," *Mississippi Valley Historical Review*, XXVI (December, 1939), 377–394, which discusses the West North Central states, Benton Wilcox demonstrates again the imperviousness to Populism of dairy and corn-hog farmers. An essential element in the understanding of discontent in the South is explained by Thomas D. Clark in "The Furnishing and Supply System in Southern Agriculture Since 1865," *Journal of Southern History*, XII (February, 1946), 24–44. The context in which Populism grew in the Dakota's is brilliantly examined with a sympathetic afterword about Populism itself by Howard Lamar in *Dakota Territory, 1861–1889: A Study in Frontier Politics*

(New Haven: Yale University Press, 1956). Ralph Smith describes the efforts of
organized farmers in Texas in two useful articles: "The Grange Movement in
Texas, 1873–1900," *Southwestern Historical Quarterly*, XIII (1938–1939), 297–
315, and " 'Macuneism' or the Farmers of Texas in Business," *Journal of Southern
History*, XIII (May, 1947), 220–244. Fred A. Shannon, a great agricultural historian, takes a brief look at one of the great agricultural activists in his piece,
"C. W. Macune and the Farmers' Alliance," *Current History*, XXVIII (June,
1955), 330–335.

No one, unfortunately, has written a full length biography of C. W.
Macune because the materials for such a study do not exist, a limitation that
pertains for obvious reasons to most of the Populist party's leadership as well. The
Populist candidate in 1892, an old third-party war horse, is the subject of a
biography by Frederick E. Haynes, *James Baird Weaver* (Iowa City: State Historical Society of Iowa, 1919). The two most important Populist theoreticians,
both from the Midwest, have received superior treatment from sympathetic historians: Chester M. Destler, *Henry Demarest Llyod and the Empire of Reform*
(Philadelphia University of Pennsylvania Press, 1963) and Martin Ridge, *Ignatius
Donnelly: The Portrait of a Politician* (Chicago: The University of Chicago Press,
1962). "Bloody Bridles" Waite, the Populist governor of Colorado, turns out to be
less interesting in print than in the flesh, but his biography by John R. Morris,
"Davis Hanson Waite: The Ideology of a Western Populist," unpublished Ph.D.
dissertation, University of Colorado, 1965, does illuminate the evolution of Populist thinking. Michael J. Brodhead, *Persevering Populist: The Life of Frank
Doster* (Reno: University of Nevada Press, 1969), concludes that the sometimes
inconsistent Kansas judge was nevertheless truly devoted to reform, but the author
is interested mainly in Doster's public life and thought, not in broader problems
concerning Populism.

Stuart Noblin has provided us with a very careful study of the most im-
portant southern Populist, whose early death crippled the movement: *Leonidas
LaFayette Polk: Agrarian Crusader* (Chapel Hill: University of North Carolina
Press, 1949). By far the best biography of any of the agrarian figures is the one by
C. Vann Woodward, *Tom Watson, Agrarian Rebel* * (New York: The Macmillan
Company, 1938), which also teaches a lot about the South and about Populism.
One must guard against the tendency, however, to view Populism as Tom Watson
writ large, and that is sometimes difficult when faced with such a powerful and
involving biography. For the South after Polk and Watson, one must turn to
pseudo-Populists for biographies that will yield an understanding of the era as
Populists experienced it. The best of these is by Francis Butler Simkins, *Pitchfork
Ben Tillman, South Carolinian* * (Baton Rouge: Louisiana State University Press,
1944), a sympathetically revisionist study of an important figure who now needs a
new assessment. Dan M. Robison, *Bob Taylor and the Agrarian Revolt in Tennessee* (Chapel Hill: University of North Carolina Press, 1935), is an interesting,
though sometimes wrong, study of the charismatic leader who supposedly kept
angry farmers in the Democratic party. It should be supplemented by Roger Hart,
"Bourbonism and Populism in Tennessee, 1875–1896," unpublished Ph.D. dissertation, Princeton University, 1970. The notion that Populist leaders were fre-

quently devoted to something other than the reform principles they loudly espoused is given a boost by Karel Denis Bicha in the article, "Jerry Simpson: Populist Without Principle," *The Journal of American History*, LIV (September, 1967), 291–306. The most important quasi-Populist, of course, was Bryan, of whom the most extensive modern study is very sympathetic: Paola E. Coletta, *William Jennings Bryan* (3 vols.; Lincoln: University of Nebraska Press, 1964–69). Perhaps the most influential treatment of Bryan, however, is the urban-biased hatchet job executed by Richard Hofstadter in *The American Political Tradition and the Men Who Made It* * (New York: Alfred A. Knopf, 1948). Some balance is restored by Lawrence Levine, *Defender of the Faith: William Jennings Bryan, the Last Decade, 1915–1925* (New York: Oxford University Press, 1965).

The most informed and insightful criticism of the Populist tradition is in the interpretive history by Richard Hofstadter, *The Age of Reform: From Bryan to F.D.R.* * (New York: Alfred A. Knopf, 1955). Various other shades and degrees of fault finding are represented in the following list: the essays by Daniel Bell, Peter Viereck, Talcott Parsons, Seymour Martin Lipset, and Richard Hofstadter in Daniel Bell (ed.), *The New American Right* * (New York: Criterion Books, 1955); Peter Viereck, *The Unadjusted Man* (Boston: Beacon Press, 1956); Oscar Handlin, "American Views of the Jew at the Opening of the Twentieth Century," *Publications of the American Jewish Historical Society*, XL (June, 1951), 323–344, *Race and Nationality in American Life* * (Boston: Little, Brown & Company, 1957), and "Reconsidering the Populists," *Agricultural History*, XXXIX (April, 1965), 68–74; Victor C. Ferkiss, "Ezra Pound and American Fascism," *Journal of Politics*, XVII (May, 1955), 173–197; Edward A. Shils, *The Torment of Secrecy* (Glencoe, Ill.: The Free Press, 1956), and "The Intellectuals and the Powers: Some Perspectives for Comparative Analysis," *Comparative Studies in Society and History*, I (October, 1958), 5–22. More recently, Karel D. Bicha has concluded that Populism was a "genuinely mixed bag," championing sectional reconciliation but also state rights and fiscal conservatism. See "A Further Reconsideration of American Populism," *Mid-America*, LIII (January, 1971), 3–11.

The counterattack has been extremely vigorous, as the following list indicates: C. Vann Woodward, "The Populist Heritage and the Intellectual," *The Burden of Southern History* (rev. and enl.; Baton Rouge: Louisiana State University Press, 1968); Walter T. K. Nugent, *The Tolerant Populists: Kansas Populism and Nativism* (Chicago: The University of Chicago Press, 1963); Michael Paul Rogin, *The Intellectuals and McCarthy: The Radical Specter* (Cambridge: The M.I.T. Press, 1967); John Higham, "Anti-Semitism in the Gilded Age: A Reinterpretation," *Mississippi Valley Historical Review*, XLIII (March, 1957), 559–578; William P. Tucker, "Ezra Pound, Fascism and Populism," *Journal of Politics*, XVIII (February, 1956), 105–107; Paul S. Holbo, "Wheat or What? Populism and American Fascism," *Western Political Quarterly*, XIV (September, 1961), 727–736. The most sustained and most fundamental defense of the faith has been mounted by Norman Pollack in a long series of articles and books: *The Populist Response to Industrial America: Midwestern Populist Thought* (Cambridge: Harvard University Press, 1962); *The Populist Mind* * (Indianapolis: The Bobbs-Merrill Company, Inc., 1967); "Hofstadter on Populism: A Critique of 'The Age of Reform,'"

Journal of Southern History, XXVI (November, 1960), 478–500; "The Myth of Populist Anti-Semitism," *American Historical Review,* XLVIII (October, 1962), 76–80; "Handlin on Anti-Semitism: A Critique of 'American Views of the Jew,'" *Journal of American History,* LI (December, 1964); "Ignatius Donnelly on Human Rights: A Study of Two Novels," *Mid-America,* XLVII (April, 1965), 99–112; "Fear of Man: Populism, Authoritarianism and the Historian," *Agricultural History,* XXXIX (April, 1965), 59–67. Though he disagrees with Pollack's radical view of Populism, Theodore Saloutos insists that the traditional, Progressive interpretation of Populism has emerged virtually unscathed from the reinterpretive efforts of the 1950s and 1960s in "The Professors and the Populists," *Agricultural History,* XL (October, 1966), 235–254.

Those students interested in knowing more of the political context in which Populism operated have several general political histories to consult. Harold U. Faulkner provides a standard survey in *Politics, Reform and Expansion, 1890–1900* * (New York: Harper and Row, Publishers, 1959). A sprightly treatment of the period, connecting Populism with an ongoing liberal movement and emphasizing the role of changing popular ideas, is Eric F. Goldman's *Rendezvous With Destiny: A History of Modern American Reform* * (New York: Alfred A. Knopf, 1953). Samuel P. Hays, in an overly schematic but stimulating interpretation, *The Response to Industrialism, 1885–1914* * (Chicago: The University of Chicago Press, 1957), casts Populism into the role of romantic reaction against, rather than rational adaptation to, the forces set loose by industrialization. A much more sophisticated social analysis stressing the changing bases of social cohesion can be found in the excellent book by Robert Wiebe, *The Search for Order, 1877–1920* * (New York: Hill and Wang, 1967). A more diffuse cultural interpretation is Ray Ginger, *Age of Excess: The United States from 1877–1914* * (New York: The Macmillan Company, 1965). Matthew Josephson, *The Politicos 1865–1896* * (New York: Harcourt Brace Jovanovich, 1938), set a cynical but high standard for political historians of the late nineteenth century. H. Wayne Morgan has produced the first subsequent comprehensive political history, *From Hayes to McKinley: National Party Politics, 1877–1896* (Syracuse: Syracuse University Press, 1969). The Democrats have been more appealing to scholars than have Republicans, witness the work of J. Rogers Hollingsworth, *The Whirligig of Politics: The Democracy of Cleveland and Bryan* (Chicago: The University of Chicago Press, 1963) and Paul Glad, *The Trumpet Soundeth: William Jennings Bryan and His Democracy, 1896–1912* (Lincoln: University of Nebraska Press, 1961). *McKinley, Bryan and the People* * (Philadelphia: J. B. Lippincott Company, 1964), also by Paul Glad, is a pro-Bryan essay dealing with the symbolic meaning of the "battle of the standards" and is designed for classroom use. An introduction to the Republican party can be found in George H. Mayer, *The Republican Party, 1854–1966* (2nd ed.; New York: Oxford University Press, 1967), but for equal treatment, students of Republicanism must turn to the excellent essay by Lewis Gould, "The Republican Search for a National Majority," in H. Wayne Morgan (ed.), *The Gilded Age* (rev. and enl.; Syracuse: Syracuse University Press, 1970). The same collection contains solid essays on all the major aspects of the age, including a good treatment of the Democratic party by R. Hal Williams. Horace Merrill, a biographer of Grover

Cleveland, has also studied the Democratic party in a single region, *Bourbon Democracy of the Middle West, 1865–1896* (Baton Rouge: Louisiana State University Press, 1953), and Russell B. Nye gives a sweeping rendition of the history of the same region in *Midwestern Progressive Politics: A Historical Study of Its Origins and Development, 1870–1950* (Lansing: Michigan State University Press, 1951). Dewey Grantham underlines the importance of factional conflict within the Democratic party in his interpretive essay on postbellum southern politics, *The Democratic South* * (Athens: University of Georgia Press, 1963). Paul Kleppner, with new techniques and fresh insights, points the way to the future for political historians in *The Cross of Culture: A Social Analysis of Midwestern Politics, 1850–1900* (New York: The Free Press, 1970). The best general introduction to Populism in the trans-Mississippi West can be extracted from Ray Allen Billington, *Westward Expansion, A History of the American Frontier* (2nd ed.; New York: The Macmillan Company, 1960).

Those who, for whatever reason, wish to refer to other collections of essays or documents regarding Populism may consult the following: Irwin Unger (ed.), *Populism: Nostalgic or Progressive?* * (Chicago: Rand McNally, 1964); George B. Tindall (ed.), *A Populist Reader: Selections from the Works of American Populist Leaders* * (New York: Harper and Row, Publishers, 1966); Norman Pollack (ed.), *The Populist Mind* (Indianapolis: Bobbs-Merrill Company, 1967); Theodore Saloutos (ed.), *Populism: Reaction or Reform?* * (New York: Holt, Rinehart and Winston, 1968); and Raymond J. Cunningham (ed.), *The Populists in Historical Perspective* * (Boston: D. C. Heath and Company, 1968).